RlJ Publications
Atlanta, GA USA

Improvisation, Inc.

Revised Edition
2017

Improvisation, Inc.

Revised Edition
2017

An
Applied Improvisation
Handbook

Robert Lowe

Improvisation, Inc. is dedicated
to my son, Jonathan Michael Mawle Lowe;
to all people who build and grow things
with communication and cooperation;
to you dear reader, and to God in
all her love, wisdom, and mercy.

CONTENTS

Preface to the Revised Edition

The Real Reason to Write about Improvisation is for the Love of the Art!

"Isn't Improvisation best learned as an activity?"
"Of course it is."
"Isn't that enough?"
"Yes, and there is even more."
"Like what?"

Along with playing, and never to replace playing, we must read, read,

read,[1] and attend shows and conferences, festivals and workshops; and talk, and philosophize, and study, and think about it, and read some more. There is a wonderful history and extraordinary insight to be gained from the growing number of long term veterans, and wise adults who have been able to maintain their childlike nature without becoming childish.

Anything else?

Yes, and if you wish to become a Professional, please first teach as a volunteer wherever you can: at your children's schools, for senior centers, for not-for profit events, and on street corners if you must. Our most powerful source of wisdom comes from our students at first, and our clients later. This will help you find your voice.

Well? What else?

Write about this amazing and wonderful art yourself. Write because you love it. Write because we love you. We all need to hear your stories and about your experiences.

Is that enough?

Yes, and there will always be more. Much more to learn and experience. Because you love it enough to write about it, even if only in a personal journal, you may be ready to advance to the level of a Professional Applied Improviser.

As you are working on these things, even before you are on top of it, when you are asked to teach about our fine art and science, then say, "Yes, . . . and", then go forward to do it as a "Improviser", playfully, in the spirit of creating a safe atmosphere, and in the pursuit of joyous learning.

Joseph Chilton Pearce tells us that "Intelligence grows by moving from the known-predictable into the unknown-unpredictable." This is a primary foundation of Improvisation in all its forms.

An Early Path

My experience began with Improvisational Dance in San Diego. One of the dancers told me about an improvisational comedy show in which she played. At the time all I knew about such work were the names of "The Second City", and SCTV. The players turned out to be wonderfully quick and funny people, and I laughed more than at any other comedy experience in my life. I had been brought up as a fan of the classic comedians, and comedies of the first half of the 20th century, mostly before Improv was rebirthed in 1955.

It happened that something cancelled on me two weeks later and I decided to stop by to see the Improv again.

I was transfixed. The players had only been through a workshop, a

---

1 The bibliography offers a guided tour of a delicious and growing body of literature.

show, and another workshop, and yet the ensemble, and every individual, including the director, was visibly better than before. They had grown more than I had ever seen in any setting over such a short a time.

Following the show I almost ran to the stage to ask the Director, Don Victor, how I could become involved. He said, "Our free, and open workshops are on Wednesdays". There was nothing I could do other than show up the next week and my life path was set for the next 37 years.

After about two and a half years of workshops and shows, and continuing my membership of the Improv Dance Troupe, "Motion", In 1983 I arrived in Atlanta for a job. I had assumed that there would be people to play with in this large and growing city. To my surprise there was no practicing Improvisation troupe anywhere in the Southeast.

Any Gathering, any Purpose, any Exercise

This revision is offered as a premise for encouraging the use of Applied Improvisation for the professional, the consultant, or for the organization, individual, family, or community of interest seeking more Improvisational Thinking in life.

Years of conversations, in person, on the AIN web site[2], on Face Book, at conferences, in workshops, and after shows it has been common for a particular question to surface in the following form.

"I will be working with a group of (business leaders, accountants, resistant people, older people, teenagers, couples, etc.) and I am seeking suggestions for games that will work best with such a group."

My first answer is to let the Improv, and the nature of the gathering, determine what is to be used. Otherwise you may find yourself being only a consultant, or coach, or trainer using some Improvisation tools. There is nothing wrong with that, however it is simply not Professional, Applied Improvisation.

The reason for this answer is that when essential AI ideas are understood, I am certain all the basic structures, can be used successfully in ANY setting, with ANY gathering, and with ANY outcome desired.

Being present as a successful Improviser includes: **_insuring the safety of the setting. and the participants_**, having fun, making connections among everyone, and yourself, AND taking small, successful, incremental steps, will open the doors to amazing experiences. The "games" have the power to guide and direct us if we will become fully engaged in the process. It may also be that you will need to invent a brand new form, then and

---

2 The Applied Improvisation Network. http://appliedimprovisation.network/

there, as required by the realities of the moment, and the fact that there is no such thing as "all the structures", and there may never be, for such is the nature of creativity.

This is not to be confused with lack of preparation as you will note below in the section entitled "Fundamental Preparation for the use of Applied Improvisation."

The suggested order in which these first Improvisation forms are presented here have proved to be very effective in working with gatherings that have little or no familiarity with Improvisation. It is fortunate that they can also be used in complex, complicated situations with people who are just as informed about creativity and Improvisation as are you. A major use is using them for assessing the openness of the group, their willingness to accept change, and the speed at which you will be able work.

When I was young a wize teacher gave me invaluable advice about reading new, challenging, and high level information. She said that if I did not understand what was being said, I should never continue reading past a word when I did not know, or have a good idea of the meaning of the word. She said getting its definition would slow me down some to begin with, yet the time savings in comprehension as I progressed would more than compensate.

This idea works for Applied Improvisation as well. If you move on to the next without the gathering having successfully completed the game you are working on, you will create greater problems in the long run.

In some circumstances you may need to "cut bait" and go back to the beginning, or to a simpler structure, maybe even one you have already used. If you must do this it is best to tell the group what you are doing, and take full responsibility for the need.

Success will come if you *take small, successful, incremental steps toward the goal.*

Why a Revised Edition?

This edition of *Improvisation, Inc.* is required as an update to the vast expansion of the power and range of our great art and science; the development is showing that it can encompass all aspects of human endeavor. The second purpose is to re-introduce to a whole new generation, the ideas that hold true today, 20 years after the inception of the original book.

When the first edition was being written Improvisational Comedy theatre was known primarily in the major enclaves of Chicago, Toronto, New York, Los Angeles, Atlanta, London, and Calgary. Second City TV (SCTV), ending in 1984, had been a sketch comedy show from Toronto that somewhat expanded familiarity with the idea of Improvisation, though the shows were actually scripted. At the same time there were bud ding troupes and organizations in smaller cities and towns, and colleges.

In South America Improvisation had beginnings with the work of Augusto Boal and his "Theatre of the Oppressed" in the early 1970s, published under that title in 1985. Improvisation was beginning to show up in some theatre and drama classes, and a few movie and television industry people were beginning to ask for some demonstration of Improvisation skills in auditions.

The Great Improvisation Proliferation

Today in the U.S. there are Improvisation Troupes, theatres, classes, and schools in each of the 50 largest cities, as well as in Washington D.C., Puerto Rico, Guam, and the U.S. Virgin Islands. There are hundreds more Improv organizations appearing in smaller cities and towns across the country.

American Colleges and universities are sponsoring Improvisational Comedy Troupes with such a compelling general appeal that students having multiple choices are said to be making decisions based on whether there is Improvisation on the campus. Improv is also appearing in growing numbers of high schools and middle schools. One of my brilliant early students, Deb Calabria, is producing full Improv shows at her school with Kindergarten to sixth grade elementary students. At last count, and it is difficult to keep up, there are more than 50 Improvisational Comedy festivals scheduled in the U.S. in 2017, and another 20 between Europe, Asia, and Australia.

In Canada, Improv Comedy is to be found in all 13 provinces, and "Canadian Improv Games" are being played in more than 400 high schools across the country with an annual competition event now in its 39th year.

Beside all this, Improvisational Theatre and applications of Improvisation are sweeping across the globe with innovative organizations and movements all over Europe and Asia, and with new Improvisation birth taking place in India, Turkey, Saudi Arabia, Brazil, Mexico City, Honduras, Viet Nam, and South Africa. The first Improvisational Comedy Troupe in Kathmandu was formed early in 2016 with the support of J Star, the founder and Director of Atlanta's "Basement Theatre". It is called "8,848 Improv Nepal", reflecting the height of Mount Everest in meters. Our fine art and science has literally been taken to the top of the world.

A *short list* of fields in which practitioners are successfully using the ideas of Applied Improvisation includes work with people in the Autism Spectrum, with Alzheimer's patients and their families, with negotiation teams in medical and hospital settings, with students of all ages and learning abilities, in language education, among drug abusers, among prisoners, in psychotherapy, community building, in the work of disaster prepared-ness and relief in the Philippines, with the global work of Pablo Suarez and the Red Cross/Red Crescent Climate Center, and with Central American refugee children coming across the border into the United States. The list grows as the movement spreads like dandelion seeds upon the wind.

Some History and Something about the Literature

Neva Leona Boyd[3] must be honored as the great grandmother of the modern Improvisation movement. She was using Improvisation and Appl-ied Improvisation at the Chicago School for Playground Workers and at Hull House as early as 1914, and working with American War Veterans in later years. Her student, Viola Spolin, is the mother of modern American Improvisation as well as the mother of Paul Sills, co-founder of both "The Compass Players", the first Improv Troupe in America in 1955, and "The Second City", the first Improvisational Theatre in 1959.

Keith Johnstone first extended the theory of Improvisation into teach-ing theory with *Impro, Improvisation and the Theatre*, in 1975. Stephen Nachma-novitch published *Free Play: Improvisation in Life and Art*, in 1990 as the first book to delve deeply into Improvisation as a philosophy of life.

I began writing *Improvisation, Inc.: Harnessing Spontaneity to Engage People and Groups* in 1997. It was published in 2000. By then the use of Improvisa-tional Philosophy outside the theatre was still in its infancy. In England in 1998, Paul Z. Jackson had published *Impro Learning: How to make your training creative, flexible, and spontaneous*. Paul would become a co-founder of The Ap-plied Improvisation Network, along with Michael Rosenberg, and Alain Rostain, in 2002. Kat Koppett gave us *Training to Imagine: Practical Improvisa-tional Theatre Techniques for Trainers and Managers to Enhance Creativity, Team-work, Leadership, and Learning* in 2001. In 2005 Patricia Ryan-Madson gave us *Improv Wisdom: Don't Prepare, Just Show Up*, taking the concept to another level of the spirit.

Though a number of books and papers had touched on many aspects of the expanded use of Improvisational Technology and Theory, *Improvisa-tion, Inc.* was the first in North America to specifically name and detail the use of the Improvisation as a human communication, business, and organ-izational development tool. The first edition of this book was presented in an illustrated workbook format, designed to attract the interest of busi-ness managers and trainers who were completely unfamiliar with the art.

This information and exploration is of value to the novice who may not

---

3 Neva Boyd - http://www.socialwelfarehistory.com/people/boyd-neva-leona

even have Improv Theatre experience, as well as to the veteran Improviser, and Applied Improviser.

Capitalizing the Words Improvisation and Improvisational

Improvisation has become a term of art that describes an important growing field of exploration, research, and human endeavor. It is my belief that this expansion is the foundation of a revolution in communication and community development that will influence all of the next millennium, and should therefore be considered a "proper" word. You will also note the tendency to capitalize the words being modified for the same reason, as in: Improvisational Theory, Improvisational Practice, Improvisation Troupe, Improv Technique, Improvisational Philosophy, Improvisational Thinking, and the like.

You may also note that the British rules of grammar, and computer programming rules of logic, and whims of the author are used to govern the positions of quotation marks, commas, and periods.

Throughout the book you will find words that are becoming *terms of art*, with important distinctions to be considered.

*Impro*visation. The concept of using this particular set of tools for generating creativity, and communication. There are applications to learning, growing, exploring, coaching, guiding, and teaching people to think quickly and with delight. Improvisation occurs in theatre, in comedy, in most music forms; especially in Jazz, in dance, fine art, presentation art, poetry, creative writing, Zen pottery, parenting, and in simply being a human being. Today business, industry, and academia are introducing Improvisation and Improvisational thinking in curriculum and training.

Improv is an abbreviation for the entire field of *Impro*visation, or any part of it, or its use in the world.

"The *Improv*" or "Improv" is the franchise business name of a large number of Stand-up comedy clubs from New York to Los Angeles. Stand-up is as different from Improv as throwing pottery is different from oil painting

Impro is a word coined by Keith Johnstone to describe the altered state of consciousness which is active when a person or group, or whole theater are engaged at the highest levels of possibility.

Theater is the building or venue where a theatrical event takes place.

Theatre is anything having to do with the concept and development of forms that are typically performed in a theater.

Improvisation, Inc, Revised Edition - 2017: An Applied Improvisation Handbook goes beyond an introduction to alternative applications of

Improvisational Comedy Theater Techniques. It also delves into underling theories that are usable in all human endeavors, from personal enrichment to every aspect of organizational development and co-operation. It includes ideas, theory, structures, methodology, stories, notes, references, and practices, as well as exercises that can be used in any setting where learning and change are desired.

This revised edition is also about tapping sources of creativity, in your gatherings and in your life. The material is intended to be used by individuals, within families, community development organizations, in government, in the military, in not-for-profit systems, religious gatherings, among business owners, executives, and companies, by corporate career-track leaders, trainers, educators, teachers, motivational presenters, and all others who understand how important it is to communicate effectively and easily, and to work cooperatively as we trudge our way through this ever increasingly complex, urgent, delicate, and small world.

It is my wish that you will think your time well spent exploring this fine art and science of Improvisation. My further wish is that you will use this material to develop your own Applied Improvisational skills, theories, and guidance methods, and that you will pass them on to the people with whom you live, love, work, and play. Use the information to build creative, laughter-filled environments in all realms of your life. You will experience an increase in the creativity and spontaneity in your existence, and in our world.

It has been my privilege to have worked with a great number of people who are still making real and valuable changes in their lives and in our world by exploring and developing Improvisation as a revolutionary human evolutionary tool. Working with these powerful ideas and practices will allow you to discover benefits neither of us have considered or expected.

Come with me now and follow through a set of thoughts, and ideas and considerations and stories and delights and experiences. Let me introduce experiences, applications, guidelines, parameters, philosophies, and a very few rules that will open new portals to working, learning, and teaching. Follow me into an "Impro", where we may discover unique doorways leading to your own personal best-possible practices.

Forward

The majority of people who come to the philosophy of Improvisation arrive through an interest in Improvisational Performance Comedy. The desire to apply the skills and lessons elsewhere usually arise naturally. People grow older and become involved in family, community, and professions, and the time available for practicing and performing with a group often becomes limited, and becoming only an audience member does not satisfy the deep wonder that has been activated. The discovery that Improv can still be part of their lives creates a force I call *the next iteration* of the art, and science of Improvisation.

Today, however, more and more people are coming directly to us from such fields as training and development, coaching, human resources, community activism, hospitality, the art of hosting, government, and general business. They are looking to Improvisation beyond its value as an inter-personal communication tool. Most who come to the discipline today say they are looking to learn how to think more quickly on their feet, to be more at ease in front of a group, and to teach these skills.

Applied Improvisation is a source of knowledge and skill far beyond this. In 1999 it was reported that the revenues of The Second City Comedy Club, in Chicago, which is the longest running Improvisation organization in the U.S. were expected to be surpassed by revenues from classes in Im-provisation, taught to business professionals hoping to loosen up and lighten up to keep ahead of the game.[4]

As you may know, the professional use of Applied Improvisation is growing right along with the general proliferation of the movement around the world.

The Applied Improvisational Professional

Your interest may be centered in becoming a professional Applied Im-proviser, or in using the skills in a general consulting business, in any of the many fields mentioned here, or in the exploration of laughter, humor, playfulness, joyous celebration, and delight in living. Whatever it is, you will gain these things from exploring *Improvisation, Inc.*

Over the years, time and again, people with whom I have worked and played have said the same thing, using almost the same words.

"I don't want to do this for a living. I mean, I am not a performer, really. But it seems that I am using this stuff all the time in my work, in my daily life, even with my family".

Often the speaker's eyes are lightly glazed over as he or she shares this experience.

Since teaching my first classes, and conducting my first professional workshops, I have watched as thousands of people have come to the sud-den realization of the power and the wonder of working cooperatively, in the current moment, in an atmosphere of safety, acceptance, and mutual support.

The theories, practices, structures, techniques, games, and systems that you learn to use here, along with the methods you have and will de-velop with your own experience, will serve you in your practice. Ulti-mately, however, it will the sharing, and watching the force of these reve-lations that will become your basic foundation if you are to become a sen-sational Applied Improvisation Professional.

These sorts of responses are what made me a professional in the field, and continue to be the reasons for *Improvisation, Inc.* Revised.

---

4 "Corporate drones head to improv (sic) class.", The Wall Street Journal, June 15, 1999.

Some of the Wonderful People with whom I Have Worked

I have been blessed by working with an extraordinary range of people and organizations. My good fortune has brought me into contact with community developers, business executives, construction workers, IT people, sales folk, moms and dads, clerks, lawyers, teachers, military leaders, nurses, physicians, educators, professors, administrators, social workers, farmers, actors and comedians, radio artists, painters, dancers, potters, and writers. Among them have been some of the most bold and some of the more shy people imaginable.

The information in this edition now comes from 37 years of real-time experience exploring human communication, adult playfulness, organizational development, and creativity through Improvisation. My work has been developed and presented for sole practitioners and Fortune 100 companies, for service industries, volunteer organizations, medical institutions, prisons, not-for-profit corporations; in academic circles for teachers, professors, school administrators, school counsellors, and social workers; in public and private schools, from kindergarten through university, and in a wide range of open public workshops. I mention these thoughts to prompt your thinking about where this great philosophy can be applied.

Applied Improvisation is always a work in progress, and you are the primary actor.

About Creativity

Access to the wealth of your own creativity can give you answers to you most pressing questions, and solutions to your most serious problems. To generate and release creativity in all aspects of your life and work is a really nice life skill. Exploration and play with Improvisation techniques can develop and strengthen your ability to communicate, to think, to act, to behave creatively, and to create creativity.

Involvement of key players, decision makers, directors, executives, managers, supervisors, and informal leaders can lead to the greatest possible long-term benefits. With Improvisation we may address problems associated with resistance to change, such as adherence to tradition, misconceptions about purpose, "goal denial", un-attractiveness of possibilities, and fear of results.

Among a long list of uses Improvisation tools can be used to facilitate and enhance personal development, conflict resolution, problem solving, strategic planning, long term goal setting and management, meeting and change management, team building, stress management, and program presentation. Most of the tools presented here can be used with little training or practice. The full development of the use of these tools is also a lifetime exploration and practice.

Communication Begins with Playfulness

Mammals learn to communicate mostly through play and playful exploration (finding toes, fingers, tails, and belly buttons), and by taking action (wiggling toes, and sticking fingers into ears and belly buttons). Among humans these magical events are the foundation of the basic functions of communication and learning, from walking and talking, on to our most complex patterns of existence.

We know that children learn, grow, develop, and can communicate more readily when they are completely engaged by their activities in a safe environment. Training and teaching systems use all manner of games and diversions, toys, and graphics to encourage this. Today, in a world in which education competes with so many forms of media, educators must also use attractive, pleasant, playful, or at least acceptable methods to frame information as interesting enough to be noticed and integrated into the learners' memory and behavior.

We Learn Seriously Organized Games

Eventually we give up "hide and go seek" and begin to "play" board games, chess, basketball, tennis, video games, crossword puzzles, social games, interpersonal games, war games, and simulations. Through these we develop the behaviors that help us to work well together, to follow rules, and to analyze and solve problems.

Play is also a very powerful element in all aspects of organizational development. If there is no "play" in the organization, it will tend be too stiff to work well in our changing and challenging environments. Beyond the mere clever use of words, the relationship is reciprocal. If there is no play; no wiggle room, in an organization, there will be little "playfulness" among the people.

Unfortunately, playfulness is often seen as a sign of immaturity and insincerity and thus is discouraged in "serious" settings. We are expected to toss out playfulness, along with other "childish" things.

People benefit from practice in order to learn to work well together, and playfulness facilitates practice. The lifetime works of such creative innovators as Bernie DeKoven, and Adam Blatner have established these ideas as practical reality in our world. Purposeful playfulness is intrinsic to the concept of formal Improvisation. Inappropriate playfulness is often the result of lack of effective training, understanding, and practice. The skills acquired in learning the discipline of Improvisation are extraordinarily useful tools for introducing, enhancing, or reintroducing the power and joy of playfulness that we have "outgrown".

12

Life Offers Patterns

We live in a self-organizing structure called a culture; working, playing, growing, learning, interacting, organizing, building, creating, and socializing. Our lives are ordered in accordance with conventions of our communities, families, parents, guardians, friends, and teachers. Our patterns are shaped by the styles of our learning processes, personal lives, religious teachings, gender identity, wishes, and by thoughts, fantasies, fears, fables, falsehoods, and formulas.

We live in a self-organizing human body, emerging from a DNA/RNA encoded pattern. Cells form, divide, and differentiate, creating architectures, systems, *soma*[5], relationships, needs, networks, and responsibilities. These things all work in concert to eventually result in a unique human. Each human can be, in most ways, functional, in many ways beautiful, in some ways powerful, and in a few ways incredible beyond belief.

Without our knowledge, we follow the patterns laid down before us as we develop our crawl, walk, stumble, or run. We establish and follow patterns as we learn sounds, signals, signs, symbols, syntax, and language.

Before we know it, we are molded by the patterns, codes, and conventions we have learned and inherited, into a personality, a person with a name, identity, and persona. In short, before we gain any real power or control over ourselves, or the world in which we live, we are patterned by our tribes, pre-conscious experiences, and our genetics and epigenetics.

> "The persona is a complicated system of relations between individual consciousness and society, fittingly enough a kind of mask, designed on the one hand to make a definite impression upon others, and, on the other, to conceal the true nature of the individual."[6]
>
> Carl Jung

We demand our individuality in our adolescence and, if we are loved and lucky, we are educated, trained by a reasonable code of values, ethics, and morality, and we receive a functional and human sets of basic skills and patterns of behavior. During our young adulthood, we hope, (one hopes) that we strengthen our individuality as well as our commonality, and we come to some sense of an integrated personal identity. It is this identity that we take to our extended families, friends, professions, and communities.

---

5 Defined here as the body of an organ or organism such as the whole body, or the heart, the lungs, the brain, the lymph system, skeleton, and the like.

6 'The Relations between the Ego and the Unconscious' (1928). In CW 7: Two Essays on Analytical Psychology. P.305.

Because we are creatures of patterned behavior it is common at every level of gathering to hear that things do not change, that they change too slowly, or that they change only due to disaster, or in the wrong direction. Tradition works at keeping change from happening for good and for bad. Disbelief can cause things to change very slowly. Denial of facts of dis-aster can block the ability to change. Bureaucracy and error can force changes in wrong directions.

Improvisation can help us to institute and maintain strong, viable tra-dition while encouraging change. It can help us address and dispel disbe-lief. It can shine light on inefficient bureaucracy. It cannot forestall error, yet it can generate feedback and honesty of analysis that can help us dis-cover and correct error sooner. Improvisation will also help us laugh and to become real, and to move on with what must be done once errors have been discovered and addressed.

In most of our activities, we have little formal, practical, practice in the arts of communication and organizational management. In human activity the pace of growth and change can be sudden and very fast. *Improvisation, Inc.,* explores the use of practical Improvisation techniques that will help you learn or continue to deal with this pace.

We can develop ourselves and change from being involuntary impro-visers, to being voluntary Improvisers, to becoming proactive Improvisers.

Resistance to Change is Natural

Planning, creativity, training, development, organization, encourage-ment, growth, invention, and dealing with the future all require change. At the same time, resistance to change is a continual challenge in most human settings. Improvisation, Inc. can give us tools and can lead us all to more willingness to accept, and adapt to change, and greater ability to confront resistance to change when it is needed. The following are just some of the reasons you will want to use Improvisation techniques:

- Resistance to change stems from fear of the unfamiliar and so it appears unattractive. Improvisation gives us practice in becoming familiar with new concepts, helping to overcome that fear.
- Misunderstanding creates many and varied forces of resistance. Im-provisation helps us communicate at higher levels so that lack of con-fusion can be exposed and addressed.
- Disbelief stops people from moving forward. Disbelief is usually based in mistrust, which is based in lack of knowledge and miscommunica-tion. Improvisation will help you create formats and channels of com-munication that lead to new levels of trust.
- Denial makes rational handling of current circumstances very difficult. Improvisation is being used in working in the fields of disaster prepa-

edness and crisis relief, beginning with teaching acceptance, and embracing whatever is being offered by our circumstances with the commitment to add something new.

- Fear is one of the major stumbling blocks all by itself. We will talk at length about fear in Chapter Seven.

All Resistance is Not Futile

Resistance can be a reasonable response when we face obviously dangerous, or naïve youthful, or foolishly inexperienced thinking. Off-handed change can be an unsafe thing. Thoughtless destruction of patterns can unweave useful and complex tapestries.

Our methods of adhering to patterns, to scientific constraint, to developmental planning, and deference for precedent are not all bad. In fact most of such processes have had fabulous results. They have allowed us to meander rather freely between order and chaos. We have created a world filled with health, promise, possibility, and magnificent products of service and the imagination. Most of these have been set into motion by our patterns and designs with some help from the unknown unknown.

For the past two hundred years or so, our sciences have been based on ancient principles of experimentation that have become recognized as "the scientific method". This method restricts us to knowledge that can be proved in fact by observation, weights, and measures; by success of predicted results over time, and by timed and tested sequences of events. We must produce and publish protocols (how we did it). We must be able to duplicate our results; and others must also be able to duplicate our results. Only then we can call our findings scientifically accurate, even if not true in an absolute sense, as shown by Newton's overshadowing with relativity and quantum physics. The scientific method has created systems, structures, business and economic practices, machines, buildings, tools, medicines and treatments,, all based on past proofs that work, as well as current knowledge is capable of establishing. Very many of our facts and patterns are useful and necessary for maintaining a modern, industrial world.

I do not wish to fly in airplanes built by improvisational methods. I do not wish to undergo surgery with "playful", experimental physicians. I do not wish to have my financial analyst making up trends and patterns that might be cool in a marketplace. While a well-known violin concerto played with an orchestra may not be enhanced by free-form Improvisation, Jazz and playful unfettered music can involve just as much technique, talent, practice, commitment, and emotion.

Improvisation Can Be Learned.

Improvisational Philosophy asks that we become aware of and embrace patterns that are vulnerable to challenge whether by fact, or by imagination. Its tools can be used to help the re-imaging of those structures that are especially in need of review or revision.

Even when working with plans and designs, we must almost always improvise. Often our plans do not go according to predictions: our tools or resources become depleted; the knowledge is not available or has failed; long-held ideas become challenged by new data, new circumstances, and new realities; competition, downsizing, reorganization, re-engineering, disaster, or other external pressures are applied. In such cases we either engage our innate and essential ability to improvise, or our plans will likely miss their marks.

The heart of the problem is that we have not actually studied and learned the art and science called Improvisation. We usually have merely experienced it in the midst of disaster, on the factory floor, in the classroom, when our children become teenagers, and by the seat of our pants. We have had to adjust to Improvisation in the atmosphere of chaos. Continuing without guidance is not necessary. Improvisation Techniques are always being refined and can be learned by almost anyone via a growing variety of sources and styles.

Improvisation provides mechanisms by which we can practice handling the challenges and the weakness or failures of our plans and patterns without breaking the machinery. It is a philosophy and system with which we can practice handling change in positive and effective ways. Improvisation can be developed, and it can be applied to almost any situation. Improvisation is an invaluable tool for all who must manage, grow, solve problems, build teams, resolve conflict, organize, lead, teach, or learn. A wonderful side effect is that Improvisation Skills are strengthened along with solutions to the problems they address. With this in mind, we continue here by learning some more about Improvisation as an art and science of communication and life.

PART ONE

In the Beginning

CHAPTER ONE

What is this Improvisation Thing Anyway?

While exploring the path of using Improvisation as a serious tool my hope and challenge is that you read this book with delight in the realm of the spirit, and in the search for your own creativity. Consider this.

"'Let me absorb this thing. Let me try to understand it without private barriers. When I have understood what you are saying, only then will I subject it to my own scrutiny and my own criticism. This is the finest of all critical approaches and the rarest"

John Steinbeck

The Art and Science of Improvisation

The word *Improvise* has an ancient history that most recently comes to English from the 17th Century French word *Improviser*, and from the Italian *Improvisare*. Before this it came from early French, *Improvviso* meaning sudden, and from Latin, *Improvisus* meaning unforeseen. In modern English, *Improvise* has come to mean "To make use of the tools and resources at hand without reference to expected results; to deal in the unforeseen, to take part in an act of creation."

For 37 years, it has been my joy and privilege to be able to explore the many uses of Improvisation as a very special human communication instrument as well as a spectacular organizational analysis and development methodology. The formal use of Improvisation is a recent development in the management of human interests. It is a complex concept. It can be seen as a technique, a state of mind, a frame of reference, a method of being and thinking, a technology, an art, and a science. It is a form and format capable of prompting transformational experiences.

This marvelous human skill is learned by some at an early age as prompted by disposition or by training. Most of us learn about it through experience, living life, and responding to a changing world. Because humans are very good at being human, our on-the-job training often works fairly well and teaches us some things about Improvisation in general.

We can use Improvisation as a communication model as well as a method for creating models, as a pedagogy, as a transformational learning tool, as a spontaneity generator, as a participation generator, and as a feedback mechanism.

Improvisation can be viewed: as a creativity paradigm, as a method for generating perspective shifts, as a group analysis device that surpasses that some of the most sophisticated organizational and personality testing systems, as well as an interactive benchmarking mechanism. Improvisation can be a fount of inspiration and laughter, and a source of energy. It can be used to brainstorm a solution, to define a problem, to isolate a problem, to analyze a problem, to model a problem, to play with a problem, to test a solution, and to monitor group dynamics. Improv work can be used to discover or determine group purpose, to determine risk taking ability, to manage a gathering or its subsets, to break deadlocks, resolve conflict, ease tensions, open new directions, and to bring people together.

Improvisation is a self-organizing, self-teaching, virtual reality, participant centered force for creation, learning, and remembering. It is a tool-making tool. We can accomplish almost anything we can imagine using Improvisation. You can develop it as your own personal tool as a presentation enhancement device, a toy, or the basis for an exceptionally creative lifetime of work and play.

19

Word for Word Exercise

Applied Improvisation begins as an exploration. To start our understanding of this exploration we will look at a simple structure called *Word for Word*. The form will be studied in detail in Chapter Thirteen.

This first exercise is a personal experience for you alone and requires about half an hour. It works best if you have the time and a quiet space to practice some disciplined concentration. If you do not have the time right now, read quickly through the description below and then set the time aside later to really work on it, preferably before you continue reading further.

Even if you are an experienced Improviser who has played this game many times there will still be value in the experience. The exercise can be done any number of times with new and interesting results each time.

Preparing for the Exercise

Move away from your desk, keyboard, or workspace so that there is nothing directly in front of you., Turn off your computer screen, radio, iPod, television, and any other distraction device. Try to emotionally set everything aside physically and mentally and sit up straight in your chair with nothing in your hands or lap.

- Be prepared to have a little fun.
- Your feet and legs should be relaxed and not crossed.
- Let your whole body relax.
- Try to find and become aware of your body's natural center of gravity, just below your navel and midway inside your body.
- Take a deep breath and exhale slowly. Take a deep breath and exhale slowly.
- Take a deep breath and exhale slowly.

If you can snap your fingers with either hand, practice snapping a few times, switching back and forth from one to the other. If you are not very good at snapping your fingers you can pat your knees, one at a time back and forth. It will provide more interesting results if you begin the snap or the pat with your non-dominant hand. Practice snapping or patting for a few moments. Try to do this without thinking about anything.

Getting Set

Rest your hands on your lap for a moment as you consider a simple, open ended question, such as, "What has the weather been like today?" or

"What does it look like outside right now?" or "What is my favorite vacation activity?" or maybe "What do I like best about fine art?" Try not to answer the question in your mind. If you have already answered in your head, ask another question. If you must. Keep asking new questions until you can ask without answering. This is a truly important step.

Then, answer your question and let the snapping of your fingers guide the answer by saying a single word for each snap or pat. Let the sentence form on its own.

Example: If the question is, "What is the weather like?", snap right and say, "The", then snap left and say, "weather", snap right "is", snap left "just", snap "fine."

NOTE

If you discover that you cannot do this exercise easily, take a break and try again a little later. If you discover you cannot do this successfully at first, keep working on it, and do not let yourself lead an Applied Improvisation workshop, or consultation until you can both do it, and you are certain that you can lead a group to a *Word for Word* success.

After you have made it through a sentence or two, try the same question again to see whether you can elicit different answers. Then try for a third, and a fourth answer. Seek more personal, serious and practical questions and answers. Practice as necessary. Ask and answer each question at least three times.

Evaluation and Analysis

Take a deep breath and exhale slowly. Take a deep breath and exhale slowly. Take a deep breath and exhale slowly.

In workshops this step is often referred to as debriefing. Practice doing this for yourself will pay dividends later; or in your current practice.

If you did this exercise easily and without confusion or distraction and would like to do it again, and you would like to teach it to others, then you have done well. If you did it with some laughter and joyousness, and learned something about yourself, you have begun the approach to the heightened state of a powerful level of consciousness called "Impro".

An Exercise in Application

This exercise may take half an hour or more. As before, if you do not have time right now, mark this place in the book for later exploration. You will need blank paper and a pen with black ink. Do not use a computer or

Tablet Find a place where you can sit quietly and write in response to the instructions you are about to read.

Starting the Exercise

- Inhale deeply and exhale slowly. Inhale deeply and exhale. Inhale deeply and exhale slowly.
- Create a quick list of seven ways you would like to develop your creativity. Use short answers. Do not stop to think about it; just write.
- Add three more items to the list.
- If it was not easy to come up with ten items for your list, try using the *Word for Word* that you learned above. "A way I would like to grow in developing my creativity skills is to (snap – word ‑ snap).
- Add five more items to the list.
- Look over the completed list of fifteen or more ways in which you would like to develop your creativity. Circle seven that seem the most important to you. Do this quickly without thinking about it.
- Of the seven items you have circled, pick four and write them on a different sheet of paper.
- Consider each circled item and ask the question, "What must I do to grow in this area?" Use the technique *Word for Word*, as described above, to answer this question at least three times about each item.
- When you have written three answers in response to each item, answer the question in regard to each item again, honestly seeking new, simple, creative, and thoughtful answers.
- Write the new answer; now write it again with your left hand instead of the right, or with the right hand if you are left handed.
- Try to answer the question in *Babble* (described below).

Other things to do with *Word for Word*

Try the *Word for Word* exercise while speaking into a tape recorder. Do the exercise while standing up and walking around and stamping your feet. Do it again with your eyes closed. Do it while walking backward. Do it while turning in a circle. Try some new ways that you invent. A breakthrough is available if you work for it. If you have been working for half an hour or more, take a break.

The exercise has unlimited possibilities and applications. As you work with Improvisation it may be a good idea for you to keep notes of key issues for later exploration. A good record will include personal development issues and those involved in the development of your organizations. Review your notes periodically.

Applied Improvisation is the art of communication first, last, and for‑

ever. It is a state of mind and a state of consciousness different than normal. It takes time, work, playfulness, and consistent discipline to begin using Improvisation Techniques effectively and efficiently.

The exercises and structures in this book are progressive, building upon one another. Our willingness to play leads those with whom we are working and creates a further willingness to play. Playing develops skills. The development of the skills makes everyone want to play more. The more we want to participate, the more we will want to play with other people. We can begin using Improvisation ideas and practices now, slowly and step by step, for our immediate benefit. The following chapters will help you own this tool. Proceed with joyous acceptance and you can open the doors to the deepest creativity.

CHAPTER TW0

Opening Doors to your Creativity

A basic requirement for effective use of all levels of Improvisation involves becoming engaged completely in the present moment. From here one can learn to change by opening one's own mind and spirit. Beyond actually showing up to participate, this is probably the only absolute requirement for the most wonderful use of Improvisation. Everything else is merely a guideline, a suggestion, an idea, a technique, or perhaps a best practice. It is not just a matter of being an open-minded person. Ask yourself whether you are currently attending to the current moment and to the doors and windows of your mind and soul. Are you actively engaged in a discipline that will open your being and keep you open to the current moment? It is said that, to walk in another's shoes, one must first remove his or her own shoes. Start out barefooted and see where it leads.

Organizational development for groups, for networks, and for individuals begins with opening doors: to the personal creative initiative that can enhance all efforts in human organization, to new ideas and methods that create group participation and encourage crews, teams, and project sets. Establishing open doors between people is a vital key to communication. Before we can learn or teach anything new, we must have openings. In the simple act of putting something new into a container, the container must be open.

Care must be taken with containers. A broken container may no longer be able to hold the "something new". Try to open a soap bubble to put in more air.

The mind is like a mostly closed container enmeshed in patterned responses. It is also lithe and loose when open. It also can be as fragile as a soap bubble or brittle as glass. When the mind or the heart is closed, there is confusion and stress, especially about "new" stuff.

> "If I don't know I don't know
> I think I know.
> If I don't know I know
> I think I don't know."[7]
>
> **R. D. Laing**

New Stuff is a Cause of Confusion and a Source of Creativity.

> A note on a door says,
> "I don't think I am here.
> If not, I have gone to look for myself
> If I get back before I return,
> please let me know where I am
> so that I may assist you
> as soon as I am there."
> A note is left for a friend saying,
> "I was here and you were gone.
> Now you are here and I am gone."[8]

These thoughts are like Zen teaching stories known as koans. They are designed to create a confusion of possibilities to help us reach for other

---

7 Lang, R. D., Knots, New York: Penguin Books. 1970.
8 Anonymous.

levels of listening, experiencing, observing, and understanding. The confusion of possibilities is another foundation upon which Improvisation operates. If I lead you, or your organization, to the confusion of possibilities, and you have created an atmosphere of safety, the doors to creativity can be easily opened.

Creativity thrives in states of confusion and we must learn to take small, successful, incremental steps in the direction we wish to pursue. Because people are so wonderfully complex and rich in possibility, the size of the steps they take is relative to what is happening in the present moment.

After creating an open mind and spirit, we must constantly strive to become aware of the illusive present moment.

Being in the Present Moment

Study and practice are required to learn how to discover and to stay in the present moment. This is the sort of "being in the present moment" that the pilot of a jet plane must achieve or a marathon runner must maintain. It includes, yet is more than, a "be here, now" abstract, philosophical construct. It suggests a focus on the realities of functioning in the current moment at high speed, high altitude, high tech, high concentration, striving for Olympian standards.

This kind of attention must be given to an infant in your care, to a child who is talking with you, the kind of attention you like best when it is being given to you.

Getting into the Present Moment

In order to use Improvisation most effectively, it is probably best not to assume that we are operating completely in the present moment. It is helpful to seek a physical discipline to aid in avoiding pursuing a purely mental perspective. Dr. Ginny Whitelaw tells us that the mind learns from the body.

If you already engaged in a discipline that gets you into, and keeps you in the present moment, revisit your art and reconsider your practice in the light of Improvisation.

Our ability to communicate well is enmeshed in our ability to learn and grow. Some disciplines that can be used to keep us in the present moment include active meditation, crafts, arts, many sports, a number of forms of physical training, many martial arts forms, making music, singing, dancing, and all kinds of fixing, building, making, and growing things. Other recommendations include walking prayer or meditation, bicycling, canoeing, roller skating, and more. Other useful activities include volunteering, community service, active participation in a hobby, particularly with children, and in whatever you are doing, practice, practice, practice.

Most deep practices require that we periodically use and learn new methods and techniques and that we add to our practices. Your disciplines must be effective, easy to get to, clear, simple, and something that can be done really often, maybe even every day. It is good if your disciplines are personally rewarding and can aid in leading to better health, self-defense awareness, improved balance, improved interpersonal communication skills, strength, confidence, and better self-awareness. All such things are available from these kinds of focus points. However, personal gain is not a requirement; commitment and practice is.

NOTE

Karma Yoga is a meditation form in which we may achieve high states of consciousness by performing menial labor in aid of the general good, traditionally chopping wood and carrying water, while focusing on the fullness of the moment and on the emptiness of the moment at the same time. This is best done without acknowledgement or reward.

An Exercise in Being in the Present Moment

This is an exercise used to develop the necessary skills of clearing our thoughts, and bringing ourselves completely into the present moment. There are three phases. Variations on this exercise may be used to review and analyze different aspects of your life and work, your future, your goals, and your objectives.

If you do not have the time to do this now, bookmark it and commit to try it soon. If you decide not to do the exercise right now, try the following instead: put the book down and give someone, or yourself, the gift of a laugh, or a hug. (Sure, you can hug yourself).

Another alternative is to call someone close to you and say just how much you appreciate him or her. Better yet, tell someone how much you love him or her.

Using this Exercise

It will be best for you to record this guided visualization. Otherwise, if you have a dear loved one whose voice makes you feel good, have them record the guided visualization script. You may also have this person read the script to you the first time. In any case, use a soft, slow paced, hypnotic voice. The first time recording should take about 10 minutes. After you have been using the process for a while you may wish to record it at a slower pace.

Sit comfortably in soft light with your eyes closed. Let both feet rest gently on the ground with your hands in your lap, not holding or touching.

27

The first time all the way through should take about half an hour.

If you must interrupt the visualization for any reason start again at the beginning.

Keep urging yourself into relaxation no matter what may come up.

A Guided Visualization Scrip

Releasing the Past

"Relax for a moment while you breathe in deeply, then breathe out slowly. Breathe in deeply, breathe out slowly ... Breathe in deeply, breathe out slowly."

(Say your own name) think for a moment about what has been happening around you during the last few moments. Whatever comes to mind, let the thought go.

For a moment consider anything that has happened during the past fifteen minutes or half hour. Do not worry if nothing comes to mind. If any thoughts do come, release them quickly by simply saying 'Thank you'.

Consider anything that has occurred during the past hour or two. Release these thoughts by saying 'Thank you", and move on.

Now bring up any thoughts about things you have done, or images from this whole day, from the time you woke, throughout the day, and up to this moment. Breathe, release, and move on.

Allow the events of last evening to come into your mind. Any thoughts? Any memories? Release these thoughts with a 'Thank you', and continue.

Think back to yesterday. Recall things that happened yesterday? Now think of events and thoughts that have occurred during the past few days. Remember last weekend. Breathe, release, and move on.

What comes to your mind when you think about last week? Anything at all from the beginning of last week until now. Breathe, release, and move on.

Breathe, release, and move on. Breathe, release, and move on. Breathe release and move on.

What is something that has occurred during the past two weeks? What has happened during the past month that still comes to mind?

Has there been any event in the last few months that has a place in your mind just now?

Quickly review the past year by the seasons. In their real order, where you are sitting say the words, 'winter, spring, summer, fall'. Is there any other thought that comes to mind to be honored for a moment and then released? Any thought is worthy of thanks and blessing for its presence and its reminder.

As your mind wanders over the past year, think about special events or special moments. Bring to mind Christmas, Boxing Day, Hanukkah, Kwanzaa, Ramadan, New Year's Eve, New Year's, Day, Easter, Valentine's Day, Memorial Day, summer vacation, Labor Day, Thanksgiving, Halloween, Michaelmas, birthdays, and anniversaries. Consider them, breathe in and out, and let them go.

Breathe in deeply. Breathe out slowly. Breathe in deeply. Breathe out slowly. Breathe in deeply. Breathe out slowly.

It is now time to bring last year to your thoughts. Is there anything that comes to mind?

Let the time frames become a little fuzzy. Let the thoughts go without worrying whether they were last year, or the year before. Keep breathing slowly.

From the past couple of years what comes to mind? Let the thoughts come quickly and release them quickly.

Fill in the blanks following the next sentences.

'Over the past five years, I can think of....'

'If I think back over the past ten years, I remember....'

Let the thoughts arise on their own. Let them go.

Think back to your first job, to your schools: high school, junior high school, middle school, elementary school, to the playground. Go back to your childhood, back to times as a toddler, back to times before you can remember.

Relax. Breathe in. Release it. Relax. Breathe in. Release. Relax, relax, relax, relax completely. Keep breathing. Move more quickly now. Stay only a moment in each place. You are not exploring. You are mind surfing, head gliding, flying though time.

Do you have any thoughts remaining from your past, your family's past history, from books and plays and movies about older times, or from human memory that can be brought to the surface for a brief look and a quick farewell? Think about them now and let them go.

Be prepared for thoughts that may come from genetic memory or even from the possibility of past lives.

Relax and breathe for a moment. Let the past go completely and fully. When your mind is clear of the past, it will be time to come back to the present for a moment.

Gently let your mind drift forward until you are back in the current moment.

Releasing the Future

Do not open your eyes. Do not look around. Let yourself prepare for another journey.

What are you doing after you finish this exercise? During the next few hours? How about later tonight? Let the thoughts go.

What have you planned for tomorrow? Who do you have to see? What do you have to do? Consider the coming weekend. What will be going on then? Consider the thoughts and let them go.

What about next week? How about the next couple of weeks? What about next month? Think, "During the next two months I must…."

What season, holiday, devotion, or celebration comes next? When is your next birthday? Consider. Release. Consider. Release. What comes to mind? What is an anniversary of any kind coming up?

What are you going to do next year? How about the year after that? Think and let go.

Fill in the blanks in the following sentences and release the thoughts as they come.

'During the next five years I hope to….'

'In ten years I would like to….'

'Twenty years from now I would like to be….'

'Before my life is over it would be nice to….'

'For my children there should be….'

'My grandchildren will need….'

'The next generation really needs to….'

'Far into the future, I know that there will be….'

Let all these thoughts go. If they are really important they will come back at an appropriate time.

Take a deep breath. Relax. . . . Relax. . . . Relax. . . . Relax. Prepare for the next journey.

Exploring the Present

Keep your eyes closed for a few moments and slowly begin to increase your awareness of the immediate surroundings.

Feel the temperature. Is there a breeze? Can you feel the air on your arms or face or hands?

Without using your hands, feel the clothing on your body. Can you feel your glasses or your hair on your face or neck? Feel the weight of your body. Feel your shoes on your feet.

Listen to the sounds around you. Try to hear the obvious sounds first: air conditioning, voices, traffic; the sound of your own breathing, little sounds that were not obvious when you started.

Feel the air moving in and out of your mouth and nose? Are your teeth together or apart? Can you feel your tongue in your mouth?

Allow the doors to all possibilities open.

Now notice any tension you may have in your neck, your hands, your jaws, your back, the rest of your body. Allow the feeling to pass.

Can you smell anything pleasant or unusual? Can you smell anything at all? Can you feel anything else?

Now, very slowly. Open your eyes and look around. Look around the room. Look up and down. Look from side to side. See the ceiling, the floor. Look at your hands and arms.

Look around again and find something you have not noticed before.

Breathe. Relax. Let go of any thoughts you have right now.

At this moment you may wish to rub your hands together or slide your feet back and forth on the floor in order to bring yourself back into normal consciousness and into this room at this time on this date. Breathe in your surroundings and let yourself be in this present moment completely.

Keep breathing.

Set your present level of awareness into your physical being. Rub the back of one hand with the fingers of the other. Understand that you can repeat this same small action at a future time to help you return to this level of feeling completely in the present moment.

If you have fully engaged in this exercise, you will be more fully aware of the present moment than normal. Notice the feeling. Relax into it. Choose to be here. Revel in being completely in the now, every moment.

Debriefing

If this exercise was difficult, confusing, jumbled, or just did not offer much sense, please do not give up. If you have never done this sort of work, there may be a lot of housecleaning that needs to be done. After you have had an opportunity to consider the thoughts and emotions that did come up, try doing the whole exercise again. Your next effort will be easier and will take less time. It will continue to become faster and easier each time you try it. You will become more proficient, and the process will give you new insights at new levels each time you practice.

If you truly wish to master the process, guide another through it. If you have an opportunity to take a group through the exercise you will find additional purpose and value.

As you work with this idea and this exercise, you will be able to coax yourself into the here and now more quickly using less of the exercise. Eventually you will be able to simply say something like, "Clear the past. Clear the future. Notice your surroundings". Touch the back of your own hand, and you can become truly "present".

There are a few guidelines to opening the doors to your creative self. If you are earnestly on the path to opening these doors, you will go through some levels of confusion. You will need to work diligently to keep yourself completely in the present moment. Working with all the doors and windows open is an essential element of creativity and of successfully using Improvisation. Committing to the discipline of mastering this exercise will help you to learn and to practice this very basic Improvisation idea.

CHAPTER THREE

Basic Improvisation Ideas

Community and communication can be seen as interchangeable. In both, our individual differences can be set aside in favor of a higher order. Without communication or community, our focus tends to be centered too much within ourselves. With strong community, we can garble our speech, misspeak our words, and stumble across our ideas, and allowances will be made in response to the bonds of community. Without community, elements of disbelief and misconception interfere with our ability to communicate. Improvisation itself is composed of values that create the strengths of community among the people participating. The basic practices and guidelines of Improvisation create strengths of communication among the people playing. As we play together, we grow together. As we grow together a sense of safety begins to grow.

Many people have explored the use of Improvisation tools and methods in a wide variety of non-theatrical applications. Some who have adapted Improvisation methodology to non-performance venues have expressed thoughts about how and why it works. Now, many have used it in business settings. A host of new books and articles have documented uses of Improvisation outside the theater. The ideas I present here have proven valuable to me, over time, in developing creativity and using Improvisation methods in business, community organization, and professional settings.

A First Basic Requirement

Showing up is the very first thing that is required. This also means showing up in the present moment, as well as being present for the whole process. In many business situations people bring their cell phones, or allow themselves to be called away while the work and play is going on. Do not let this happen.

If you cannot stop it then notice it, and use it in the group while it is going on and in your debriefing. Be particularly aware of what is going on when people seem to be compelled to leave. If you are working with an organization full of people who refuse to be present it may be necessary to realize that you are engaging an uphill battle that can rarely be won.

If managers and supervisors refuse to participate, your work may have little or no effect on the organization. My advice is to tell those who hired you that this is the reality, and then do not work with the group again unless at least basic participation is guaranteed.

Four Improvisation Ideas

There are certainly 30 to 50 primary ideas that will serve us in our study and work in this amazing art and science. Among them are as many as 15 to 20 guidelines that most Improvisers will accept as good, or even best to follow. One of my theories is that most people can benefit from as few as five basic ideas once they have shown up. With ten, most can create a significant difference in their lives, their families, and their working situations. With 15 or more practiced and well considered "clues" one can teach and develop the art.

The ideas I propose are grounded in my presenting Improvisation skills to thousands of business and professional people, mostly with little or no theater or performance background, as well as for hundreds in comedy performance troupes, and single series Improv students leading to a performance. Today, most Improv Theatres, and many established comedy troupes offer short series, or sets of classes leading to a performance.

These ideas tend to be valuable for Applied Improvisation Professionals, general teachers, presenters and trainers, for professional and semi-professional troupes, and for hobby Improvisers from church, mosque, or synagogue. They also apply to real life situations.

I find the following considerations so compelling that I call them ideas. ***With Improvisation, all "rules" are only clues subject to being ignored, challenged, scrutinized, and laughed at.***

In my experience the most amazing Improvisation happens when these four basic Improvisation ideas are at work. As they are not the only ways of thinking, except for being in the present moment, they may not be among the favorites of many outstanding Improvisers, both for Application and Performance.

A First Improvisation Idea

We must strive to come completely into the present moment. My first Improvisation idea is a key to what makes Improvisation work in complex and real settings. As proposed by the above exercise, when we are most effective, most clear, most alive, most joyful, and most fun we are functioning in the here and now. It is also the state in which we can produce the greatest change, fight the best fight, do the best work, take in the most information, and enjoy the greatest retention of new information.

The very fact of being completely in the present moment is a creative act in itself. New thoughts, new ideas, new solutions, new creations, new pathways, new images, new visions, new directions, new programs, new devices, new relationships, new applications, and more can come from the process of simply being completely in the present moment.

A STORY

A friend of mine once had the great pleasure of meeting Margaret Mead, one of the most extraordinary anthropologists of the last century. The setting was a non-public area of a large meeting hall where Ms. Mead had spoken to several thousand people.

My friend spoke with her for about five minutes and never forgot the experience. He said, "She was completely with me. It seemed that there was no one else in the world; she had nowhere else to go, no one to see, nothing else to do, and there was nothing else going on. I was the center of her universe." His eyes were a little shiny as he remembered the experience of being with someone who was completely present in the moment.

Other people are very good at being aware when we are not present with them. Few will accept the fact, and fewer still mention the problem. One can verify this with children. Little ones will whine and howl to demand our focused attention when it is not there. Nine-year-olds will tell us truths about ourselves if we are somewhere else when dealing with them. Adolescents will write us off or even become dangerous to themselves and others in an atmosphere in which adults are "absent" in their presence. They do this while doing all they can to demand attention at the same time they drive people, friends, and adults away.

At home, in business, and in volunteer work it has been noted that one of the first and most important reasons for personal dissatisfaction is the feeling that "no one is listening", that "people are not really there for me", "that no one appreciates how much I am putting into the work".

In working with clients, if we are completely present it is very possible to say, "No" and still retain both the relationship and goodwill. In the same setting a "yes", given with an absent or vacant spirit, can lose both.

To say we want to live or work in the present moment and actually doing so can be two different things. Getting there (here) may require discipline and hard work. It need not be so hard; yet if it is hard, that is certainly normal. It is also worth the work.

A Second Improvisation Idea

We must strive to become completely honest with ourselves. This is a tricky one. True personal honesty is a private matter. The discussion here may be a doorway into a lifetime of exploration. Only we can know our motives and motivations. Only we can absolutely know whether we are being honest with ourselves.

Many of our life struggles develop from lack of personal honesty; first with ourselves, and then with others, usually about or errors and weaknesses. Interestingly enough our lack of honesty about our opinions and our strengths can also result in negative life experience. Real honesty requires that we make the decision to look at the world with true eyes, that we make the decision every day. We often hide the truth from ourselves when we see things that we do not wish to see. Our world also sometimes seems filled with inequity and corruption, stupidity and error, meanness and obstinacy, ignorance and violence. Often we close ourselves to these truths in order to protect ourselves from such harsh realities.

Yet there are other truths as well. The world is also filled with wonder and delight. There is kindness and compassion, there are miracles and saints, and there is laughter and joyfulness. In order to maintain our sense of truth, we must look at both sides of everything and seek to understand the balance between chaos and order. We must do this to establish our own balance.

To use Improvisation to a great advantage try to overcome these influences and pressures and to work on being as honest with ourselves as possible. Being honest with ourselves also begins with operating in the current time.

NOTE

It is best to hold to the discipline that anything we do within the details of Improvisation is being done for the first time.

We advise against the use of any idea that comes from outside the current moment of Improvisation. As leaders we must demonstrate these values in all we do.

Conscious Improvisation is a uniquely human event, as is almost all complex communication. It helps us to look at and understand ourselves as human beings. We need to allow that during any event we may be afraid or elated, we may be confused or inspired, we may be right or wrong. We must strive to be available to these truths, and we must seek them and act on the knowledge that we are human as well. Among the most powerful comments from people who have done Improvisation work are the statements: "I have learned that it is OK to be myself.

It is OK to make mistakes! It is required that we learn from them."

Improvisation does not require that we become a completely honest person immediately and suddenly. Nor does it assume that we are a dishonest person now. It does require that we explore and develop our ability to stay totally loyal to the moment at hand. This is true whether we are a consultant, a facilitator, a director, a student, or a player.

The deep concepts of being true to the present, and being consistent within ourselves are the subject of almost all the religions and philosophies of the world. For effective Improvisation we must strive for honesty in what we are doing and feeling in the present moment and avoiding bringing elements from the past, from outside the now.

A Third Improvisation idea

We must learn to become completely honest with at least one other person. We live in societies that tacitly condone "little white lies." Sometimes we are allowed a little lie to be kind, or to protect one another. Sometimes we tell small lies to ease our own paths or to get our own way. (Notice the rare use of the word "get" throughout.)

As much as being honest with others is a good general life practice, and it would be lovely if we could be completely honest with everyone at all times, when there is a real emergency, especially if there are young children present, we must often hide the truth, monitor our words, and inhibit our emotions in order to protect the people in our care. Sometimes great honesty could hurt us personally. Telling an armed robber that we think he or she is a jerk, or where the jewels are kept might not be in our best interest. Sometimes it may not best to share too many personal truths with our own supervisors and managers. When people, whether friends or strangers, irritate us due merely to differences in style, it is not always necessary to tell them so, and to do so may actually be harmful to those concerned.

We expect our government leaders, and spies, to withhold certain kinds of information, and often to compromise their own personal values, in favor of the general good. Sometimes this is for the sake of national security. Sometimes it is for public safety management, and sometimes it is simply outright dishonesty. In our relations with others we are under many constraints regarding openness and "hard line honesty" often due to the existence of operating secrecy. Certain meetings must be held in secrecy, and certain information cannot be shared with a work force, the general public, or competing organizations. A lot of information must be released in portions over time in order not to place either the organization or its people at a disadvantage. In business, many laws of disclosure do not allow us to share our joy at good fortune or concerns for the bad if doing so could constitute illegal trading in various markets.

However, many philosophical systems suggest that complete honesty with at least one other person is a path to personal development, and correction of error. The Catholic Church has advanced the value of confession since its inception. Twelve-step programs all advocate honesty with at least one individual. Having a friend to tell about the trials and tribulations of our truths is a wondrous thing. At the very least a person can become completely honest with God or Spirit in the form of prayer. Possible confidants may be a spouse or a best friend or any person who will support your efforts to reach the goal of achieving honesty with at least one other person.

The quest for developing this third idea is best served by finding some confidants, people with whom we can be completely honest. It seems that the greater the number of people we have in this category, the better will be our Improvisation. I also think honesty is related to happiness. Whoever has the least to hide has the most to share.

There are generally important differences between the people who are family and long term friends or associates, and the temporary relationships we encounter on stage, or in Applied Improvisation settings. The Improvisation hope is that we will learn to be honest with others. A first candidate for this position is the person with whom we are working the most closely and personally in the current moment. If we are lecturing, choose at least one member of the audience, if only in our mind. Another best candidate could be anyone among the people with whom we are working. In the Improvisation theatre, this includes all the people who are on the stage or in a show with us.

When working as an Applied Improvisation professional, it is some times possible to recruit a specific member of your audience to serve this function temporarily. It may be that you will need to recruit someone in private, or bring an ally with you for this purpose in special cases. In any case, there must be at least one other with whom you are committed to being honest during the Improvisation experience.

A Fourth Improvisation Idea

We must offer our work for public view. Improvisation is based in activity. It has intellectual components, yet it cannot be done entirely in the mind. At the same time, Improvisation is a thoughtful process that requires great personal exploration that cannot be fully accomplished in private.

Improvisation managers and the Improvisation consultants must stand up in front of others and engage them in the exercises. This is the core of "participant-centered training", and of participant-centered change and development as promoted by training pioneer Bob Pike.[9] Without interaction with the outside world, all experience can be self-managed, and therefore ignored, stifled, or redirected from within. Thus the possible changes in behavior can be lost or veiled in apparent change.

With a plan or process, we bring order to its development and can usually accomplish much more than possible in the atmosphere of unplanned chaos. However, a plan, by definition, automatically limits the product. The perfect plan perfectly executed will give us only what we expected or hoped. A plan will give us more only if there is a component allowing for the unknown within. This tactic is similar to Improvisation, yet it will not usually invoke the same level of extraordinary possibilities.

This does not mean that we can avoid work and preparation. It just means that we have to use the Improvisation process to engage in the Improvisation process, so we have to put our work into public view.

Fundamental Preparation for the use of Applied Improvisation

One of my early Improvisation training contracts was for a regional meeting of professional executives of the Girl Scouts of America. They were gathered room nine Southern states at a prestigious and elegant meeting facility in a famous country setting. It led me to the foundation of my Improvisation philosophy. I was being offered, for me, a large amount of money for a small amount of time with a very important client, and the opportunity to influence a huge number of people. The schedule gave me three months to "think" about it.

---

[9] *Creative Training Techniques*, Bob Pike, Minneapolis: Lakewood Publications, 1991.

My first response was to begin planning. I started making outlines and listing the formats I would use. I thought of clever lines and interesting progressions that would bring the crowd to me and to my work. After a few days I realized what I was doing. I was doing all this in my head. I was not being honest with myself and my understanding of my art and science. It was not considering the others to be involved. I didn't even know who they were, and it was all being done in private. I was doing everything my understanding of Improvisation had advised against.

Improvisation was my craft and I knew it inside and out. It did not include planning the steps I would take three months hence and anything I came up with would automatically be three months old, and would also hold my mindset into the past.

From that moment forward, as thoughts came to me, I gave them a moment of consideration (from the perspective of the then present moment), and then let it go. Each day I reminded myself that I was an Improvisation artist and pioneer with full knowledge of how the process worked. It is not possible to truly understand what techniques would be most appropriate until the moment of the gathering. The people with whom I would be working would lead the way, and it would be my job to explore and learn with them. It became the core of my discipline.

In the interim I met with the executive representatives to better understand what they hoped to accomplish. When asked about my plans I spoke in generalizations of the values of Improvisational Thinking.

My next task was reading every training manual the Girl Scout organization had available. It included the professional adult training materials, all the manuals and materials for the volunteers, and books and guides offered to all levels of the children. By the time of the event my knowledge of the organization was as great as possible as an outsider.

My preparation also included a personal review of my lifetime as a volunteer, and my credentials as a professional volunteer organizer before being introduced to Improvisation.

An unexpected benefit was learning a great deal about the language used by the organization. It was not a trick, or a memorization gimmick. It had become an easy integration into my own vocabulary.

On meeting the participants on the morning of the presentation, my mind was blank. I had no plan for the first words out of my mouth. I did not know where we would go together. This resulted in participants operating at the highest levels of creative interpersonal cooperation. By the end of the day someone said, "We are working at a level that we usually do not achieve until the end of an entire conference."

It was the result of staying in the current moment throughout the development and the engagement in the program. It was the result of being honest with myself and with my fellow explorers; of building the event while putting it out for public view. It was the result of following my "Improvisation ideas."

A Philosophy of Improvisation

The sample is small in terms of the human population, and my protocols are not written. Research will never be finished. My experience, however, with Improvisational Management and Improvisational Organization ideas, has included work with around ten thousand individuals. Counting larger gatherings, the number I have observed has reached as many as 40,000. Time and again I have come to a working philosophy:

"With some assistance, anyone can become spontaneous and creative, and when an individual experiences the magic of being in the 'Improvisational Now', in a safe environment, a visible light in the eyes turns on and it can stay on forever. It is a moment of creativity as powerful and fundamental as the electromagnetic wonder that appeared at the moment that scientists call 'The Big Bang'."

The following are offered as some touchstones with which to consider Improvisation that may help in learning and developing the skills of Applied Improvisation.

THOUGHTS

Improvisation is a discipline. It can be taught.
Improvisation is a state of mind. It can be learned.
Improvisation is a tool. If used correctly it always works.
Improvisation is an ancient art form.
The Etruscans did it first.
Improvisation is a process.
It works in steps, one at a time, over time.
Improvisation is an art.
It takes desire, practice, and experimentation.
Improvisation is a technique, not a thing of itself.
It is a fun way of doing things.
Improvisation is a craft.
It has rules that will produce desired results
If they are accepted.
Improvisation is a frame of reference.
One can learn by watching,
by thinking, and by doing.
Improvisation is a science.
It has predictable elements, and
verifiable and reproducible results.
Improvisation is a way of being.
It is a way of being present in the moment

41

while being externally focused.
Improvisation is a gift.
Improvisation is a relationship.
It is a relationship with oneself and with others.
It is a gift given and received and given again.
Improvisation is a natural event
for all conscious beings.
Improvisation just is.

As a generally accepted philosophy, it is not true that the ends justify the means. Nor is it always true that the means will achieve the ends desired. The true balance of life comes from understanding the fact that the means and the ends are all of one fabric. Improvisation form and spirit are as important as the goals or objectives of the practitioner. This truth is at the heart of Improvisation.

As we explore and practice the work and play of Improvisational Being, we will discover our own ideas and insights. As we earnestly implement Improvisation Practices in our work, volunteer experience, and in our daily life, we will see and hear the changes in ourselves and in the people with whom we are engaged. As we discover more and more practical applications of Improvisational Methods, we can discover community and communication growing before our eyes. It will take work and play to achieve these results. It will take earnest, honest, self-evaluation and organizational evaluation to walk this path. If you apply the ideas and think the thoughts, Improvisation will work for you. You must also seek more deeply into the look and the feel of Improvisation at work.

CHAPTER FOUR

Improvisation at Work

Improvisation is more than a free-form, free-for-all. It is more than "flying by the seat of your pants", more than making things up as we go along. There are guidelines to follow, ideas to consider and invent, axioms to learn, suggestions to be considered, work and preparation to be accomplished if it is to work at its highest level. Mental preparation is required. You need to discover your audience. You must learn what you want to accomplish. There is even planning involved.

In order to begin an Improvisation activity and make full use of the community and communication that we will explore, a great deal of organizational planning and training can be done before we begin. A very important element of planning and training is involved in exploring and developing human feelings. If we do not feel like learning, we probably will not learn all that much. If we do not feel like changing our behavior, we probably will not change our behavior. If there is not passion in our goals and visions, there may be a lackluster performance. If there is little feeling, there tends to be little creativity in the person or the organization.

Keith Johnstone considers the frame of mind required for good Improvisation to be a special, separate, and distinct state of consciousness. He calls this state of consciousness *Impro*. This state is filled with feelings and emotions. *Impro* is achieved by entering into Improvisational Discipline with full commitment and effort. To prepare yourself for excellent Improvisation Management, it is a good idea to review your feeling in terms of both your emotions and your sensory perceptions.

Understanding the role that the senses play in Improvisation helps in developing their role in human communication and development in general.

The Physical Senses

Improvisation works best when we activate combinations of the senses. This is true of all exceptional work. When the Improvisation State, Impro, is achieved, it tends to generate deep reflections. For this reason it becomes necessary to examine the feelings and to begin to engage the senses more fully and easily. It is good to engage in this process enthusiastically, for our own sake as well as for the development of the people with whom we are working.

The more senses involved in an event, the more completely and deeply it may be experienced. The five or six or seven senses that humans use are basic, and the expansions of synergy are engaged as well.

Every one of our senses are complex and miraculous events. We will examine each of them.

To See

See: "ME: seen; French, AU, *seon;* akin to OHG *sehan* to see and perhaps to Latin, *sequi,* to follow. To perceive by the *eye,* to perceive or detect as by sight, to have experience of, to come to know, to be the setting or time of, form a mental picture of, to perceive the meaning or importance of, to be aware of or imagine as a possibility, examine or watch, read, to read of, to attend as a spectator, to take care of or provide for.

To see includes internal vision, with mental pictures and movies, symbols, and recognition.

44

To see deals partially with memory: what we saw, and what we thought we saw, what we think we thought we saw, what we would like to think we thought we saw, what we would like to think we thought we may have seen.

To see has a future tense that is linked to memory. "Seeing" what my experience tells me must come next. Prejudice is built on this.

In the past tense we can experience, "been there, seen that".

To see includes forgetting that which has certainly been seen before, as in "Never saw it. I have no memory of that person, place, thing, number, book, movie, date or formula".

To see may be influenced by others, as in, "Did you see what I saw?" "Uh, sure?"

To see in French, is expressed with various aspects of the term *vu*. When one is seeing something for the first time yet it feels as though it has been "seen before", the term Déjà vu is used. *Praesta vu*, "never seen", means suddenly noticing something that has been there all along, yet has never been noticed before.

Just for Fun

Deja you: "Haven't we met before?"

Deja who: "I'm sorry, you are . . . ?"

Deja do: You know this one. You're out the front door, or into your car and remember that you have forgotten something. You go back for it and as you go out the door again a little voice in your head says, "Didn't I just do this?"

Deja clue: "I don't know what you are talking about".

From flashes of light to flashes of word fancy, the idea of "to" see brings up a rather large number of factors and elements of its own. The more of these we engage and consider, the more fully we "see", the more fully we can feel.

To Hear

"To hear" is very much like "to see", with tactile sensory mechanisms. To hear can be thought of as a branch of touch, as hearing is accomplished by decoding vibrations that touch the inside of the ear, the skin, musculature, and skeleton. When we are not feeling good, or when our sense of feeling has been numbed by life or an experience, our sense of hearing can be diminished.

The ability of biological creatures to use sound dynamics as a feedback device is ancient and astounding. Considering the diversity and range of sound is an epic adventure that includes bacteria, fish, dogs, bats, snakes, insects, and even plants using ultrasonic and subsonic sounds, as well as the ability of whales and elephants to communicate over tens and hundreds of miles.

Fabulous extensions of hearing, using recording and electronic transmission of sound, have almost reach perfection. While it is not yet possible to create a picture in the sense of Star Trek holodeck perfection, a perfect reproduction of a symphony is very near. It is the nature of sound to be reproduced and mimicked. We can mimic many sounds that are close enough to fool humans and other animals yet the closest we come to making pictures that can actually do this is accomplished with mirrors or projections.

We talk to ourselves. We normally do this as internal sound. My friend, Jeff Justice, a professional comedian, speaker and consultant, is known to say to a crowd, "Raise your hand if you talk to yourself". When some do not respond, he says, "Those of you who failed to raise your hands, didn't you hear a little voice saying, 'Not me. No, I don't talk to myself'". Our internal voices can allow for and encourage laughter. They can also encourage mental illness, depression, social separation, and other foolishness and fantasy.

Sometimes we talk to ourselves with many voices. Sometimes we talk back to ourselves. Sometimes we talk back in what we think is silence, yet it is audible to others around us. The power of what we say and hear is tied to the foundation of civilization. The difference between, "What did you say?" and "What did you mean by that?" can be the difference between negotiation and war.

"To hear" is at least as complex as "to see". Improvisation works best when striving to fully engage in the sense of sound including vibration, and with the whole body.

Listening

Effective listening, a sub-set of hearing, is absolutely important to the quality of life. If people are not effectively listening to one another, things do not work very well. We must confirm, think about, and remember what is being said in order to listen well.

In the Improvisation structures, participants experience the effects of not listening and often realize, in public, the results of their own failure to listen. Some may actually observe themselves in the act of not listening and may come to know the silence that results. Some of the people can begin to feel and comprehend the deep and full effect of not listening.

In the Improvisation form, the underlying nature of the exercise comes back to the participant and generates an experiential interest in listening more carefully, with all the senses. It becomes useful to hear our internal voices and to integrate the life giving values of listening.

To Touch

The sense of touch is a key to understanding reasons that Improvisation works. When we are affected by our surroundings, we often say we were deeply touched"; people who walk to the beat of odd drummers are often seen as "touched"; being lightly brushed by providence or good luck is to be "touched" by an angel.

Touch is personal. No other person can truly feel what we feel. Touch is both direct and indirect, both giving and taking. It operates at both a gut level and a mind level, somatic and intuitive. It is emotional and rational ("I feel a tack in my foot" versus "I feel sad"), proactive ("I take your hand in mine"), re-active ("I feel your hand on my arm"), specific and general, internal and empathetic. Touch can encompass dozens of responses. When the maximum number of these aspects of our sense of touch are engaged, our feelings are more powerful, clear, sharper, and increasingly real.

Improvisation helps to activate the sense of touch. Improvisation systems work at a speed that requires more than mere thinking about solutions. As a matter of fact, until certain conclusion points are approached, usually referred to theatrically as approaching and reaching "end scene" moments, it is best to avoid "solution thinking".

It becomes necessary to activate other forces and channels of feelings that help us work at speeds equal to or faster than thought, which can seem to function at speeds beyond measurement. Speed beyond measurement is faster than the speed of light. This phenomenon in quantum physics was dubbed a "spooky action at a distance" by Albert Einstein, and is explored in modern physics under the title of "Entanglement"[10]

To Smell, to Taste

The senses of smell and of taste are engaged with those of sight, hearing, and touch. The vast arena of recollections dominated by smell and taste have a special power to toss us about in time and space. We are well aware of smells that may take us to the far away past in an instant. Try smelling crayons without recalling your childhood. The mention of certain foods can cause involuntary salivation and journeys of the mind to holidays, romantic dinners, school lunch rooms, family outings, and campfires with roasting food on sticks, and for large numbers of Americans, the taste of graham crackers, and melting marshmallows, and chocolate called "s'mores"[11].

---

[10] *The Age of Entanglement: When Quantum Physics was Reborn*, Louisa Gilder, Vintage Books, a Division of Random House: New York, NY, 2008.

[11] Named because everyone says, "I want s'more".

The power of smell, and perception of pheromones is its own epic exploration; set aside for another time.

As we engage completely in the activities and mindsets of Improvisation our senses are heightened. The forms help us activate our kinesthetic abilities. Full use of all our senses brings us into current time.

To Sense Surrounding Space

Another human sensory field is studied in the fields of proxemics and kinesthetics, and discussed in psychic and parapsychological circles. This sense tells us such things as when we feel that someone is looking over our shoulder or we are being followed. It is also experienced as stage sense, or sports sense, whereby players automatically stand in balance with one another and the area of the stage or move automatically in concert on the playing field.

In *Aikido* this aspect of human awareness is referred to, in the Japanese language, as *maai*. It is the art of maintaining the perfect distance from another for and through the experience at hand.

This sense has aspects of sight, sound, touch, and smell as well as awareness of what is called *ki* in Japanese, and *chi* in Chinese, which is the energy of life itself and can be expressed in the breath and extension of the energy in yoga, dance, and many martial arts. This sense is at work in elevators, where people automatically face forward and divide up the exact amount of available space almost perfectly equally. We do this also when waiting in lines and walking in crowds. When this facility is missing in a crowd a mob can be created. We will discuss a mob in greater detail below.

As we enter the state of Impro, all of our senses begin working together, literally dozens of sources of information and action become available to us. The more senses we activate, the more alive and in the moment we become and the more our learning and development stay with us. The more alive and in the moment we become, the more we can effectively be with others, the more we can engage one another in mutual quests. Our plans and organizations also work better and more efficiently when emotions are fully engaged.

A Spiritual Sense

Beyond the physical senses is a realm of exploration that adds a new dimension to all aspects of Improvisation. The sense of spirit is vital to complete understanding of the look and the feel of this deep and complex art and science. We are speaking of "spirit" in the broadest possible term, meaning everything we cannot "see" with eyes or various tools.

The nature of Improvisation suggests that we work in the spirit of play and fun and safety. To understand the meaning of this, we must look into the nature of the spirit and the spiritual aspect of human interactions. When we bring people together, much more happens than meets the eye. If we listen to the advice of *The Little Prince* we learn that "... what is essential is invisible to the eye".[12]

Very little in our world is fully known to us. Visible light is only a fraction of the electromagnetic spectrum. Sound that is audible to humans involves a tiny percentage of the available vibrations. That which is behind us, or on the other side of a wall, is out of our site. Our internal structures are out of sight. Our cells are to be seen only with extraordinary optics. Most atomic elements can only be approximately perceived with even more extraordinary optics, and subatomic particles are not within the arena of sight except by the paths they trace in cloud chambers, and in the minds of mathematicians.

We certainly cannot look into tomorrow, nor into the heart or mind of a friend, that we can only feel. We cannot see behind ourselves except in a reflection or camera. The thoughts of others are not ours to know. Our thoughts and fears and hopes and dreams are all beyond vision.

This leads us to the realization that a large part of what we deal with is out of our sight, yet still at the level of available energy, of invention and creativity. It is also at the invisible spiritual level, that the greatest resources exist. Spirit is the source of everything. In real reality it may be the only place in which anything really exists.

In view of the resources in the realm of the spirit, we should practice our arts with some reverence. We need to be gentle and thankful for all our blessings. We should be forgiving of one another and of ourselves. Whether Improvisation is a matter of the spirit or whether it is only a form in which spirit is revered, it is the same thing. With an understanding of the spiritual nature of all things, this art may help you to reach deeply into your sense of communication and organizational development and generate truly creative approach to our work and our lives.

"YES, AND ...."

This term has entered general languages across America and much of Europe and Asia during the past few years, as Improvisation has expanded around the world.

"Yes, and ..." is much more than a turn of phrase, or an Improv performance gimmick. It is the basis of a powerful philosophy, and way of life.

"Yes, and ..." refers to verbal, physical, and mental responses to the suggestions, ideas, opinions, and viewpoints of others.

---

[12] Antoine de Saint-Exupery, *The Little Prince*, New York, NY: Harcourt, Brace & World, 1943

In addition the concept is the basis of a full body, mind, and spirit response to harsh realities in a life, and world that includes serious troubles and disasters.

"Yes, and . . . " is also a very effective way to say "No!" to things that are not, correct in our opinions, or intolerable to us.

This subject is discussed here, rather than in Chapter Nine about language, because it touches a very subtle aspect of how we feel and respond in communication situations, and in our lives, and in how we teach and encourage others in dealing with the same.

Always remember that the use of this phrase can enhance every aspect of our communication and being. It is also interesting that people who have not been previously exposed to this idea can be very resistant. This resistance must not be over-looked or rushed past, or it may reinforce dismissal of the whole concept of Applied Improvisation.

The more an organization is accustomed to functioning with top down, or military type management, with control based communication style, the more there will be resistance. Most will be direct objection to saying "Yes", as a basic communication method. Some will come from those who are fearful or opposed to "Yes-people", who follow leaders blindly.

First we will look at the near opposite, "yes, but . . . ." You most likely heard someone use the expression, "Yes, but . . ." very recently. Maybe from your own mouth. These words are a common part of our speaking and communicating patterns. As noted the use of "Yes, and . . ." is becoming common around the world.

Consider the message behind the standard phrase, "yes, but . . . ." As you may know, if you tell a computer "yes" and "no" at the same time you will probably hear an annoying little beep that means, "You have broken a rule of logic." For many years I had my computer programmed so that errors activated my young son's voice saying, "Silly Daddy". That way I did not feel quite so cyber-dumb when I made mistakes. In some circumstances you will experience a crash of a whole computer program, or your computer may lock down as it runs back and forth between the conflicting messages.

You may know that if you tell a child to stop and to go at the same time you will soon be dealing with confusion, frustration, and tears. The phrase, "Yes, but . . ." says yes and no at the same time. Mixed messages do not serve us well.

In the world of Improvisation, many advocate the use of "Yes, and . . ." as a standard response to all incoming messages. Yes, and it is important for the phrase to become automatic element in verbal, mental, and emotional environments in which Applied Improvisation is being taught, and as we show the power of this stance to the growing number of people we are influencing. As a person becomes more comfortable using Improvisa-

50

tion I have advised that the attitude can be conveyed with variations such as, "Yes, indeed . . .", or "Yes absolutely . . .", or sometimes, "Yes! You are correct." At the high end extraordinary enthusiasm can be fun and effective as in, "Yes!!!, You bet the whole kit and caboodle." It is important that body language is used to convey the same message.

In some gatherings, the "yes, but . . ." conversation can bring up a great deal of resistance. Telling people that a favorite phrase, unconscious as it may be, is a mixed message can be a serious challenge to their language skills. It can feel a lot like criticizing a person's accent, or the way he or she is raising children. I have had participants vigorously defend the use of "yes, but . . ." as the only way to say something. However, it is one of the miracles of language that there is always more than one way to say anything.

Over the years I have made a concerted attempt to remove the term "but" from my language except when it is the only possible grammatical correct word. I often replace it with, "yet" if I need to separate two opposing thoughts, and never in a response to anyone with whom I am talking. In this book you will find the word "but", only within quotation marks. (I will send a free copy of this book to you if you find otherwise.)

The Many Uses of "Yes, and . . . ."

A conversation about this phrase can provide an opportunity to evaluate the effectiveness of a communication environment. If someone has an exceptional amount of resistance to the idea, there are probably deeper problems in the group with which we are working.

The following exercise can help people to replace the words "Yes, but . . ." with the words "Yes, and . . . ." This can be simple and difficult at the same time.

A "Yes, and . . ." Exercise.

Ask your participants to mill about making simple statements to one another, with the requirement that all of their responses begin with "Yes, but . . ." Then have the participants do the same thing, responding with "Yes, and . . ." Encourage people to go through the cycle between the two, at least four or five times. You may need to repeat and reinforce the instructions as you hear people saying things such as, "yes, and, but . . ." or "yes, uh, but, and . . ." Watch and listen carefully for people who may be avoiding following the instructions. This is different from misunderstanding the instructions.

Often the gathering will open to the point almost immediately. In this case, briefly encourage the elimination of "Yes, but . . ." in favor of "Yes, and

". . ." as a general practice. If there is resistance or difficulty during the exercise, spend some time in open discussion of the process and the feelings engendered by the words and the exercise. It may be necessary to re-do the exercise intermittently between debriefings, or even inventing new ways of using it by yourself.

It is at this point that the value of longer term relationships in your professional practice will become clear. Organizations and people often take some time and usually need practice in order to change behavior. The behavior of language is deeply imbedded and often take the most amount of time.

If you have the opportunity you may try instituting periodic "Yes, and . . ." hours in a given day, or day of the week. It might require a whole "Yes, and. . . . day" in the organization with which you are working. During these exercises it is important that the words "Yes, and . . ." be the first words out of anyone's mouth in response to any idea, comment, or suggestion. If this is done playfully, and in the spirit of Improvisation, it can make some real and positive differences in the ways in which people communicate.

If you have indications that your client will be difficult you can devise a virtual "Yes, and . . ." exercise to leave with the people who hired us. You will need to invent this exercise based on the paper, messaging, email, and social media culture used by your client. It can act as a semi-covert agent whose effect may manifest over time. If the resistance is strong, trying to force it will usually be counterproductive and can lead to nearly complete failure of your goals. In this case, the best plan is to recalibrate goal set and let yourself be guided by love, light, laughter, and joy.

If you are unable to move past resistance to this idea, work going forward will have diminishing effect. Please, do not give up. If we do not understand this reality, we may suffer from personal stress and self-doubt. At the least you can try to keep in touch with the client or organization, or someone within the organization who can keep you apprised of changes that occur in spite of the problems. The work of Improvisation is more subtle, and it is more powerful than anyone yet understands, even those who have been working in it for as long as 60 plus years. See the wonderful video on YouTube of the life of David Shepherd,[13] one of the founders of "The Compass Players" in Chicago in 1955.

A STORY

One of my students was frustrated by her potential clients often complaining about price. She felt that hearing a customer say,

---

[13] "David Shepherd: A Lifetime of Improvisational Theatre", Directed by Mike Fly. https://www.youtube.com/watch?v=t5wgtkgCH3A. Not made into a DVD.

"Your prices are just too high", and responding with the words, "Yes, and . . ." was not acceptable.

Not long after the workshop, she had a very important prospective client call and say, "I am sorry your prices are just too high." There was a great deal on the line. She could not say what she wanted to, which was something like, "WHAT!!! Are you out of your mind? Do you have any idea what you are saying?"

She took a deep breath and stepped into Improvisation. Her mind went blank as the words came forth: "Yes, and, uh well, uh, if you consider the, uh, the value of our personal services, food, coffee, water, fruit, and ambiance and, uh, if you factor them into the price you will find, that our real cost per square minute is more than competitive."

The potential customer said, "I will look into it in those terms. Let me get back to you." He did the numbers, came back, and signed the contract. She now says, "Yes, and . . .", if only in her own mind, to almost anything anyone says to her, as in the example,

"You are an incredible fool!"

"Yes, and the word 'incredible' reminds me of my father who retired from the military as a U.S.A.F. Historian who compiled the Air Force history of the Korean conflict, and gave me a broad perspective of life and its realities."

Debriefing

By first saying "Yes!" we merely, and importantly, acknowledge that something has been said, and at least heard, if not understood. We begin to create a positive atmosphere regarding the position of the person speaking.

We do not have to agree with what has been said. We simply use the affirmative "Yes!" to indicate that a statement has been made and heard, and the speaker has a right to speak her mind. Our next word is a commitment to add something. The word "and" commits us to something more that is an addition rather than a substitution. The word "and" may be the most important element in the power of the phrase.

I sincerely ask you to begin changing your use of the language of "no". When someone speaks to you about something with which you may disagree, take a deep and full breath and simply say, "Yes, and . . . "with more than your mouth; with your mind. Do this with the commitment that you will follow the "and" with something. I really just mean "something." Not something excellent, nor something noble, nor even something good and wise, merely something **positive**. The wisdom and goodness and truth can come from the knowledge that you are actively involved in creating a positive feeling in and around your organization. It is especially important to do this when you may disagree with the speaker or the circumstances or if the ideas being explored are unusual or controversial.

Imagine what life would be like if every time you spoke you were assured that the first response would be a simple affirmation followed by a commitment to add something to what you had to say. An environment dedicated to listening would be established along with a feeling of positive cooperation.

The fabric of Improvisation at work will lead us to our own philosophies of Improvisation. It is an entire philosophy and way of life. The improvisational way of life is filled with emotion and passion. It is filled with perceptions of the senses. The ways of creativity are also filled with sensory perceptions. It is incumbent on us to explore and develop the emotions and senses as much as we can. We can even use the methods of Improvisation to accomplish this development.

As an Improvisational Professional; practitioner, or manager, you will be served by promoting the values of being in the present moment and engaging the senses completely. You will explore and discover processes and work with gentleness. You will seek balance and develop listening skills; you will encourage speaking up, laughing, and delighting in differences; and we can all gain deep understanding of living in the spirit of the moment.

As you develop your full appreciation of this great art and science that we call Applied Improvisation, we can begin to use the fundamentals for making greater connections with the all the people in our lives.

\

PART TWO

Improvisation Fundamentals

CHAPTER FIVE

Greater Connections with Others

Making greater connections with people is a primary tool and product of the path to Improvisational excellence. Actively exploring the uses of Improvisation techniques, theories, ideas, suggestions, exercises, games, and tools are all part of the process of making such contact. When we are professionally and personally involved in human development situations, Improvisation methodology is effective in making subtle, and fundamental connections. My word forms that look like poems, beginning with "Strive to Become", these thoughts may be useful to us personally, and in practice. They can become vital to you in your pursuit of professional Improvisation.

As you read, allow the words to bring images to mind. These ideas are presented in a word form because it is so easy to rush over ideas in a list. It is my hope that you will return again and again to read these messages, for the sound of the words, and for the feelings they may bring up.

Strive to Become

Strive to come completely into the
present, in this precious moment.
Striving to stay here and now.

Attempt to be honest
completely with yourself,
honest, completely
with another.

Have you heard it before,
or said or read it,
considered, thought,
or noticed the notion?
Then do not use it now.

Keep clean and fresh,
your words and thoughts,
staying upon the high road,
the tougher road,
the road more fun.

Use the magic words
whenever you can,
"Yes, and"
"Yes, and", "Yes, and . . ."

Deny not. Say not no,
An act called blocking.
Commit and give something
new to each new moment.

Think not, first. Act first.
Respond before reacting!
Act not as though
you did not hear, nor see,
though maybe you did not.
Act not as though
you are confused,
even if you are.

It all works best
In games and play,
yet we must consider
it applies to life as well.
Listen. Listen. Listen.
Listen. Listen. Listen.
Listen. Listen.
If we become too reckless,
our effort may die.
If we become too safe,
our effort may fall.
Give more
than we take
as we seek
balance.
Breathe.
Stretch body,
mind, voice, and spirit.
Stop writing in the head.
Create relationships.
Seek not a laugh.
Seek laughter,
joy, fun, and light.
Avoid the pun.
Establish first,
who you are,
where you are, and
what you are doing.
The language of our bodies
composes most of what
we communicate.
Use it carefully.
Our presence
is a great deal of
what we say.
Express it freely.
Reach for the stars.
Should we fall short
we may merely
catch the moon.

Improvisation May Be

A
Risk
A path
A game
A technique
A path to trust
A methodology
A positive approach
An ancient theatre art
A state of mind
A way of thinking
A frame of reference
A way of not thinking
A process
A pleasure
A discipline
A team effort
A living thing
A way of being
A current event
A matter of timing
Unplanned
Scene work
Spontaneous
Out of control
A lot of laughs

Improvisation is Probably Not

A
Gag
Jokes
Mean
Negative
Scatological
Role Playing
Potty humor
Script writing
The easiest path
Stand-up comedy
A one-person show
(except sometimes)

Improvisation is definitely not

That which has been said before
That which has been done before
That which has been heard before
That which has been thought before

Do Improvisational Things

Play
Give
Listen
Receive
Support others
Engage in feelings
Relax, enjoy yourself
Accept what is going on
Even now keep yourself saying
"Yes", and "Yes", and "Yes, and ..."
Add something each time you act or speak
Say yesss. Keep saying yes. Inside and out
Improvisation
Works best
When everyone
Is trying to help,
Everyone else looks good
"Resistance is useless"
Respect and acknowledge all words and ideas
Bring yourself into the present moment
Be honest about what is going on now
With yourself and with others
Laugh again and again
Laugh some more
Be respectful
Be care-full
Be play-full
Play

Connections with People

Making greater connections with people and maintaining those connections is a most important factor in excellent life and leadership. Excellent leadership is a key element in organizational development and is required in successful professional Improvisational Consulting. Each time an organization experiences a change in programs, directions, materials, structures, personnel, or procedures, the job of maintaining or remaking connections becomes the next priority. Each time subject matter is added or changed in your presentation or work, the job of maintaining, reestablishing or reinforcing connections comes next.

With greater connections between us and among us, whatever the sort of gathering or organization, anything that is introduced has a better chance of working, learning is enhanced, skills are gained, and personal responsibility is strengthened. When there are great connections, feedback becomes overt and readily shared, and the involvement of people working well together becomes more spontaneous and effective. When there are great people connections, problems that are encountered surface sooner and solution thinking is usually activated at the same time. When people connections are greatest, resistance is reduced, communication is clear and open, and all efforts are more productive.

Classroom students who are encouraged to know one another learn more and earn better grades than do those in which there are no connections made between the individuals.

People do not awaken great connections at the level of the mind alone. Ideas may gather us together in a forum, yet the ideas alone have minor power. Connections must be learned and turned into behavior. It requires action and interaction to bring people together and thus to integrate information and effect behavioral change. The primary elements for opening doors that bring us together are our feelings. The Improvisation Process works on a level of activity and interactivity that automatically brings emotional content, people, and their thoughts together before the arena of ideas is engaged.

Data Versus Process

Among the reasons that people have difficulty making connections is that the detailed information is often given too soon. We tend to present our ideas, planned out or mentally prepared, with hard information as the first and foremost element.

It is easy to get ahead of ourselves. It is easy to become so focused on our goal, or on the vision, and the data that value for the participants is diminished. It is very easy to become caught up in the purposes of the organization or the program with which we are involved. It can so easily become more important than the people who must work with the program.

When working with important materials, vision and process are necessary, and the process must still be considered first. When working with buildings, plans are quite important; yet unless the process is fluid, realistic, clear, and as simple as possible, the result can be cumbersome and stiff.

A STORY

For many years I worked in the Marin County, California, Civic Center, the last public building designed by Frank Lloyd Wright. It was beautiful and a marvel of architecture. The building was built after his death and was originally designed to be constructed in the desert of the Southwest. It was placed instead in coastal Northern California, and its functional internal layout was designed by people who did not fully consider people and process. The place was cumbersome and made many services virtually inaccessible to those who needed them. Mr. Wright had envisioned it as a wonder of ease and efficient communication. All who used it found it to be found difficult and confusing.

THE LAST, MOST IMPORTANT ELEMENT!

Information is the last, most important element in a communication.

This is an Improvisation concept as well as a basic tenant of public speaking, and of general communication. This statement makes some people shudder, while others seem to go quite mad: "How can you possibly say such a thing about my precious information." or "I have spent years learning of this information; how dare you challenge it?"

This statement is not a challenge. It provides a functional frame of reference that supports effective sharing of information. We assume that our information is right, and good, and true, and very important, and we must transfer the information from our brain into the minds and lives of others or it has no value.

An Analogy

Considering the computer as a means of communication it does not matter how good, right, and true our information may be, if the computer is not plugged in, we cannot access the wonderful data. The same is true if the computer is plugged in and there is no power to the outlet, bad luck. If we have power and our keyboard is not connected, it does us no good. Have you ever had your fingers positioned one set of keys to the right or left on

62

the keyboard? It gives you an opportunity to work with "Babble." If your fingers are shifted to the right, your next words could look something like this, "eo:: ;ppl dp,ryjomh ;olr yjod" so if we have no monitor with which to see our information., it can be very difficult to proceed. Try translating the phrase.

If we have neither printer nor modem, we may as well have our information locked up in our head. All these things must be in place if we wish to begin to communicate. Then we must deal with the strange realities of language.

To begin with, if we are speaking different languages, it can be difficult to impossible to communicate except in signs and unstructured sounds. Even given the use of the same language, there are problems of dialect, accent, idiomatic usage, jargon, technical or professional language, variations between countries apparently using the same language, and even differences in the time frame in which we learned our first language.[14]

If are there are problems syntax *liable is to be understanding difficult.* With made up words how quixotic will our exsubstantial delictions be incredulated? If our punctuation! Does"-); not allow: the true" meaning of {} our wo,rds? to appear-what will(; others make of.' our? ideas!?!?!?. To top it off, spelling alone can create a nightmare rather than a communication.

Beyond all these considerations come issues of belief and trust. If we do not believe what we are saying, unless we are capable con artists or actors, many people will not even hear us. If others do not believe we are credible, or that our emotions do not match our words, or that the information we are presenting is just too far away from their own understanding or belief system, or if we do not speak in the words used by our own culture, neighborhood, religion, or profession, or if we seem to be speaking of things that do not seem relevant to their concerns, communication may not happen, no matter how important our information may be.

A STORY

A good friend was with his five-year-old daughter, and they had to wait for the mom to finish an errand before they could do other things. Andy said, "We will go to the store as soon as Mommy is finished. In the meantime, let's play with your toys." She looked at him through the corner of her child's eye and said, "Daddy, why do we always do things in the mean time? Why don't we ever do anything in the nice time?"

---

[14] A friend returned to Germany for the first time after a 50 year separation while living in English speaking countries. He found that he had a very difficult time understanding his birth language.

The more important our message, the more important it is for us to understand that: *Information, or data, is the last, most important element in a com munication.* Careful use of language can be vital to creating bonds between ourselves and those we are assisting, and among, well among everyone actually.

The Name is Bond; Human Bond

Bonding has a kind of mysterious magic to it. We talk of something that "resonates" with us. It vibrates at some compatible frequency. In music this is called harmony. In Spanish, the word simpatico touches on the idea. It translates roughly as "agreeable" or "pleasant", yet it connotes more than that. In French the term *je ne sais quoi* literally means, "I know not what". The sounds, facial and body expressions, and the gestures that accompany these words say more than the words themselves.

There is a laboratory experiment that illustrates a powerful point about bonding. Two pieces of living heart tissue are placed near each other in a petri dish. They are not touching nor connected by any material that could conduct electricity. When one piece of the heart tissue is given an electric stimulus making it pulse, the other will pulse as well. The same experiment done with brain tissue or bone tissue produces no such response.

There are studies that indicate that bonding between mother and child may have a great deal to do with the proximity of the hearts in utero and during breast feeding. A good, full-bodied, hug can produce mutual palpitation without regard to the relationship between the partners in the hug.

When there is a bond, it is not necessary for two parties to be in the same room, nor even the same town, to feel connected. As a matter of fact, it has been suggested that when the involved parties must be present to one another in order to be responsive, it creates an "attachment" rather than a bond. Attachment behavior can be the basis of dysfunctional relationships.[15]

Understanding bonding at the level of the heart makes the introductions of new leadership, new material, new programs, and new systems easier. Creating a connection at the heart level makes motivation easy. Heart level connections help everything.

Four fundamental Improvisation ideas seem to be critical in the process of helping people make connections with the heart. Remember that these ideas suggest striving toward being present in the moment, being honest with oneself, being honest with another, and putting it out for pub-

---

[15] Joseph Chilton Pearce, *The Magical Child Matures*, New York, NY: Bantam Books, 1985.

blic interaction.

Among the best ways to encourage connections is in the sharing stories from our own lives. To find the best stories, one sure method is to search honestly through our own life and reflect on and record what we have learned. It is fun and productive to look for especially odd, strange, and silly tales, and maybe some of our young or foolish escapades. Stories that are the most important are not merely ones that illustrate our point. More important are the stories that help us tell who we really are.

Besides leading us into wonder and delight, Improvisation exposes us to fear, failure, silliness, embarrassment, illogic, and confusion. Stories that demonstrate that we are human, that we too have been embarrassed, lost, confused, and sometimes just plain wrong, as well as that often we can be quite wise, and powerful. Chapter Sixteen will explore Improvisation story telling more fully.

Connections Require that We Shift Gears[16]

In my younger years I was hitchhiking in California. My friend Sean and I caught a lift with a truck driver who had dropped off the trailer, the cargo portion, of his eighteen-wheeler, and was taking the cab back to his original destination.

I got into the cab and he said, "Hang on, young fellas, this here rig ain't got no brakes!" He proceeded to take us forty miles, through six or seven small towns, including a good number of stop signs and lights, using only gear shifting up and down. He never touched the brakes even to come to a full stop.

Making connections with people in organizations is helped by appropriate and successful speeding up and slowing down. Successful acceleration and deceleration in Improvisation requires moving smoothly between the changes. To be off the ideal speed is to be out of current time. We must move quickly, yet not too quickly. Go slowly, yet not too slowly. This idea holds true in working with people in any capacity. It is true whether we are working with one or with many.

Thoughtful action, clear consciousness, good listening, sensitive feeling, quick learning, fast decision making, reasonable planning, easy slowing, smooth acceleration, and trained reflexes, which are made possible by quick gear changes, are all skills that develop and keep strong connections between our participants. These skills are used to manage speed changes, and are imbedded in Improvisation.

---

[16] If you do not drive, or do not drive a standard transmission car, this section may not be of use to you. However, it can be an excellent human understanding exercise to learn that skill.

Speed

Speed is a straightforward thing in nature. Light has a constant speed through a vacuum. Sound has a predictable speed, moderated by the medium through which it occurs. A falling body has a constant acceleration in reference to the larger body toward which it is being attracted. A projected object has a predictable rate at which it slows based on gravity and the laws of aerodynamics. (Keep in mind however, that according to some aspects of the laws of aerodynamics, the bumblebee cannot fly.)

Acceleration rates of biological entities are a fairly clear matter. The top speeds of most living things have been measured or calculated. The top speed for an unaided human being is currently 27.89 miles per hour (mph) or 44.64 kilometers per hour (kph). The cheetah can move at 70/113 mph/kph, the lion at 50/80.5 m/k, the hyena at 40/64.4 m/k, the domestic cat at 30/48.3 m/k, the black mamba snake at 20/32.2 m/k, the chicken at 9/14.5 m/k, and the garden snail at 0.03/.048 m/k.[17] Slowing down usually has to do with either getting tired, or running out of fuel, or motivation.

In living things, speeding up and slowing down is a fairly straightforward matter. Adding or subtracting energy speeds us up or slows us down the same way a dimmer switch turns a light up or down. In mechanical things, we must learn to deal with the shifting of gears. Human interaction and communication is a mechanical event that moves the speed of thought which is the speed of group dynamics. Some theorize that these velocities may exceed the speed of light. We must attend to our accelerations and work at the art of shifting gears helps us do this. Improvisation gives us practice shifting gears.

Acceleration

Improvisational work can accelerate in a variety of ways. During a specific format, individuals, and sometimes the whole gathering, can "absorb it" and spontaneously begin to change levels of exploration, understanding, application, and interaction. Issues that have previously inhibited the organization can suddenly be made clear, and can spontaneously disappear. People can begin to desire work in larger settings in which there is more public exposure. Participants can become more comfortable with smaller sets, in which detailed problems may be resolved, and in which issues of intimacy are more critical. Risk may become suddenly easier. Ideas may begin racing through participants' heads. Conversation, problem solving, and brainstorming can erupt among the participants. Sudden and unexpected feelings of well-being may appear. There can be a sudden rise in

---

[17] *The World Almanac Book of Facts*, New York, NY: World Almanac Books, K-III Reference Corporation, 1998.

the general energy level of the individuals and the entire organization. New channels of communication and new levels of interpersonal comfort can suddenly appear. These are all signs of the advent of the state of "Impro" and the resulting acceleration.

Thoughts about Gear Shifting

A very realistic question is, "Do you really want to accelerate?" If you are headed downhill on a slippery road with a heavy load of precious cargo, you may not want to go any faster. It may be necessary to slow down.

Whether accelerating or slowing down, it is normally necessary to shift gears along the way. Changing gears may cause a stall if the process is not correctly accomplished. We may break the transmission or engine by operating at a speed that is too fast for the vehicle. With errors in any of these areas may cause us to lose people, or to tax ourselves and our participants to exhaustion and burnout, or we can merely become less and less efficient and, as in an automobile, fail to realize the mileage that is possible with efficient running.

When we are planning to change gears, we must first decide whether our purpose is to slow down or to speed up. Sometimes in order to speed up we must first slow down, shift into a lower gear, speed up in that gear, and then shift again into the next higher gear.

People Require Shifting Gears as Well

With a group of people, first gear is the initial introduction of an idea or a startup structure. Adding details to the idea or asking for basic feedback will function as second gear. Having participants become physically active or interactive touches on third gear. Having them play with the issue as a game at higher levels, or with more relevant or more risky topics is fourth gear. Giving the process to the people to let them run with it is fifth gear, and includes offering the clutch which allows for up or down shifting as needed.

Neutral

Any change in the gear ratio requires navigating through neutral to move from one level to another. Without going into neutral, it is difficult to shift ourselves out of the gear we are in. This is especially true the faster we are going. Moving into neutral is not always an easy thing. Most of us are dedicated to our ideas and often emotionally attached to them. For humans, shifting into neutral can be a physical, mental, emotional, social, and a spiritual event. Each step can require a number of complex levels of thought, action, compassion, and communication. To begin we must listen, consider the past, consider the goal, participate, work as an individual, and work as part of the group.

When working with people, it is most effective to lead by doing. When we come to the conclusion that it is time to shift gears, we must make the decision as to whether our goal is to speed up or slow down, to gear up or to gear down. We need then to take an action that moves us through our own personal state of neutral.

It is wise to practice compassion with ourselves as well as with our audience. Some leaders and trainers become upset with themselves when they have to change gears suddenly. Some executives become upset with their work force simply because gear changes become suddenly necessary. Being upset is not a neutral position. We do best to focus and to help others to become entirely disengaged, and into the current moment.

We can warn the participants that we are about to change things. We may ask them to shift into neutral with us. We may allow them time to move into neutral and help facilitate this by the way we move and act. Our posture, our gestures, the position of our head, the set of our mouth and jaw, our expressions, and the gestalt of our physical being must all express and signify coming to and moving into neutral.

Neutral really means we are neither adding energy to the system nor taking it away. On a flat or uphill road, a car in neutral will slow down by itself. On a downhill road, a car in neutral will tend to pick up speed. An audience in neutral will do the same. As professionals we need to recognize this and admit that we may be doing the same.

Managers sometimes try to shift into neutral by explaining things, by analyzing the situation, or by changing the set structure. These are all additions of energy. These all change the level of the road or the amount of gas. They do not bring us to neutral.

Some try to move into neutral by calming the audience down. This can function as an addition of energy. Trainers sometimes try to make changes by asking questions or setting up new problems rather than by seeking a neutral gear first. These are all additions of energy. To achieve neutral, it is necessary to reach deeply within one's self and come to the point of neither adding nor taking away energy.

People usually slam on the brakes when they need to change gears in a hurry. This is not neutral. It is the removal of energy from the system. Tapping the brakes, giving the vehicle a little gas, and engaging the clutch may be interim steps in achieving neutral. To repeat, slamming on the brakes is not.

If we do not feel calm, peaceful, content, at ease, and happy, we are probably not working with neutral as an element of change. If we do not feel as though we are in neutral, we are probably not in neutral. If we feel that we are accelerating on an uphill road or slowing on a downhill road, or vice versa, we are probably not in neutral.

If we have a sinking feeling that we are not in control, we may not be. If this happens when we are trying to change gears, we are probably not in neutral. If we cannot say, "I think that I am just going to let providence or the universe take over for just a moment, we are probably not in neutral".

If we are not in neutral, our gathering is not in neutral, so changing gears is going to be a problem. If changing gears is a problem, there will almost certainly be problems in effectiveness and difficulty in keeping the connection with our group.

The Fast Lane

In the movie "Star Wars", the Millennium Falcon spaceship jumps into "hyperspace" on a screen filled with extending lines indicating that the ship has gone into some new dimension and crossed vast distances of space in an instant.

A similar event in the human being can be experienced as a cognitive leap. Religionists tell us of a transition that is called an epiphany, a sudden manifestation or perception that makes everything new to us. Events like this happen in Improvisation with a sudden breakthrough experience resulting in new levels of understanding.

Beyond mere acceleration, in an organization, or a training session, the same kind of event can occur. I call it "moving into the fast lane". The gathering has been learning as a unity, or the organization has been working particularly smoothly; there is healthy laughter, the participants are following directions with little effort, and they are helping one another. Moments of brilliance have become common, shy participants seem to be coming out of their shells, difficult or strong participants seem to relax into easy cooperation, and suddenly there seems to be an internal flash of bright light, "shazaam!", warp speed!

It is wonderful to watch it happen. The participants become calm and relaxed at the same time as they are being energized by new feelings and understanding. Suggestions are readily accepted by all, the members of the gathering take control, and the activity moves to levels that could not have been planned. The happening is so quick that it is unpredictable.

These events usually have additional elements in common. The executive leadership is relaxed and confident and operating in the perfect present moment. The facilitators are focused on relationship and take delight in the people with whom they are working. There are feelings of safety and security. There is a sense of seriousness of purpose accompanied by a feeling of playfulness and fun. Participation is at or near 100 percent. People are either active or very attentive. Energy has been growing on its own. The state of *Impro* has descended upon the gathering.

It has been said there are a number of things that are difficult to achieve or hard to sustain if directly sought for their own sake. Among these are fame and fortune. Achieving the Improvisation fast lane is another desired objective that cannot be the goal. The path seems to be a product of generating a critical mass of Improvisation elements, engaged in by a critical mass of the participants, functioning in a critical mass of feeling, led by an Applied Improvisational professional who is seeking and encouraging excellence at every level.

Connections among the People in your Group

The pace at which an organization moves can involve a variety of measures. Smooth and quick movement indicates that the connections are strong and building. Jerky or slow response tells us that some connections are breaking down. Carefully observe the people with whom you are working, and hopefully playing. How quickly are they warming up to you? How fast are they accepting information? How quick are they to complain? How quickly and smoothly are they taking part in activities? How fast are they moving physically when they are shifting to new positions or locations? How quick are they at understanding instructions? These are some things we must know to track the connections among people. Add to the list as you continue looking for and learning other indicators.

Being in the presence of another is truly more than physical, or emotional. The Improvisation axioms support bonding between people. Bonded relation-ships have the strongest connections. Understanding the relative position of the information or data involved in our communication helps us to maintain our connections to people rather than merely to ideas.

If we remain conscious of the speed and tempo of shifts in events and organizations, it will help us to maintain, develop, and enhance bonding among people. To build and keep bonds, and therefore to encourage greater connections, we must do real things at physical, social, spiritual, and emotional levels. When we are dealing with such elements we will discover patterns in behavior. Some patterns are good, though many are not. We must learn to approach patterns actively in order to summon the exciting changes that are possible.

CHAPTER SIX

Patterns and Changes

Patterns are useful and necessary to accomplish many things. They work best when the environment in which the patterns were created can be duplicated, or nearly so. Patterns can help us find good uses of our past experience. They are also capable of strangling creativity. Patterns may also inhibit bonding, and may reinforce attachment behavior.

When working with "people patterns", we must rely on benchmarks and other measures. When working with people, measurements are more difficult than when working with more concrete aspects of life. In businesses, measuring performance, and identifying and measuring business practices, is very important. Observing people in the act of Improvisation gives us valuable insight into patterns of communication and interaction. Improvisation can be used as a measure of performance, and thus to develop all important best practices.

Qualitative research is viable and universally recognized as a primary method of discovering truths and verifying reality. Improvisation can be used as such a qualitative measurement system. It can be effectively used to keep track of the way people respond to slowly increasing levels of instruction, responsibility, freedom, creativity, pressure, and confusion. Improvisation provides an excellent device for measuring the capacity of people to change, to challenge patterns, to grow, or to work together in new situations and environments. It is a good device for measuring the effectiveness of communication, listening skills, comprehension, and repeatable process. When such important information has been gathered, we can begin to approach our negative patterns and to engage in positive changes.

Almost any pattern can become a problem if we hold onto it for too long or find that we simply cannot let go. If we, as leaders, hold onto our own patterns, our participants will follow.

We know that it is impossible to add to a full cup. In the same way, it is very difficult to introduce change, or to give people new information when either giver or receiver is holding onto an old full cup. Letting go, however, is sometimes difficult. Changing patterns and accepting change are not necessarily easy and the process must be learned.

The human body and mind seem to be built to hold onto things and to grasp tightly. The body's physical structure curls into itself. Our fingers can grasp and cling until they are frozen in position, incapable of opening without pain. Our bodies and minds can settle into cramped positions, making it difficult for us to move or stand. Our muscle tissue and our connective tissue are designed to clamp down and hold tight. Engaging patterns, and making changes are learned skills. Use of Improvisation will help develop these skills.

Challenging Patterns

In some of the fine arts there is a tendency to approach the idea of challenging patterns directly. We "let it all hang out", we search for "it", we reject analysis and allow for exploration of feeling. Even in the arts, however, there is an amazing adherence to form, pattern, convention, and function.

In writing, we explore poetry, fiction, science fiction, fantasy, and invention. Still the words must be spelled "correctly" except by the occasional Mark Twain who "never could trust a man who wil spel a wrd the sam wae twize". Our grammar and punctuation are required to be carefully organized and developed following acceptable forms. The exception is the occasional e e cummings.

Stories about artists are filled with tales of those who challenged the patterns of convention and starved or lived outcast lives, in body (Gauguin), in mind (Van Gogh), or in soul (Bosch). Our musical greats have led us through fascinating paths, ranging from great pattern consistencies in Beethoven, Mozart, and Liszt, to extraordinary pattern innovation: Charlie Parker, Duke Ellington, and Django Reinhardt. Western music, which includes a lovely amount of Improvisation, is actually imprisoned in the model of a twelve-tone scale. Deep work in Improvisation has challenged the field of music with the microtonal work of Jon and Jonathan Glasier[18], and Harry Partch[19].

NOTE

The music system which is most familiar in music in the western world is based on the twelve tone chromatic scale, G, G#/A Flat, A, A#/B Flat, B, C, C#/D flat, D, D#/E flat, E, F, F#. It is based on dividing the octave into half tone intervals. This is a very flexible and powerful mechanism for exploring the extraordinary ranges and intervals of sound available to the human ear.

The traditional octave can be divided into a variety of intervals including the fairly well known even temperament, diatonic, and pentatonic scales. In addition, there are at least 54 other recognized scales and modes.[20] However, the 12 tone scale is limited by arbitrary divisions based on the size of the average musician's hand when the first string plucking keyboard instruments were invented.

The healthy human ear is capable of distinguishing up to 1,500 tones within a single octave. There is a vast field of music exploration used in working with other intervals in the octave. This field is referred to as microtonal music.[21]

Dance has generally been dominated by adherence to such patterns as classical ballet, ballroom, tango, samba, swing, folk, international folk, various cultural dance forms: clogging, hora, Greek, and country line dancing. Even with personal variations and innovations, these all have set patterns on which they are based. There have also been major pattern challenges in

[18] https://www.linkedin.com/in/jonathan-glasier-569b7024.
[19] *Genesis of a Music: An Account of a Creative Work, its Roots and its Fulfillments*, Da Capo Press: New York, NY, 1974.
[20] http://en.wikipedia.org/wiki/List_of_musical_scales_and_modes. *List of Musical Scales and Modes.*
[21] https://www.princeton.edu/~achaney/tmve/wiki100k/docs/Microtonal_music.html. *Microtonal music.*

forms of jazz and modern dance inspired by wonderful people like Martha Graham,

Isadora Dun-can, Merce Cunningham, Twyla Tharp, and Mikhail Barishnikov.[22] Pure improvisational dance has also appeared with the work of Susan Greer Essex[23] with "Dance Jam" and "The Movement Choir" Improvisational Dance Theater in San Diego, California. Contact Improv Dance from New York, NY is a worldwide event today.

The late 20th Century experienced a steady attack on conventional patterns in representational art. There were "happenings", performance art, ice sculpture, and junk sculpture. Salvador Dali madness and M.C. Escher perspectives delighted and confused us in the directions of pattern manipulations and destruction.

In daily life, abandonment of patterns by breaking rules and standards runs rampant in our schools, on our streets, and in many of our institutions. With Basquiet, heroin inspired graffiti was lifted to the level of museum art. Yet there is little that is truly new in these things except perhaps in the negation of convention, which is actually a pattern of its own.

In order to attack our patterns and realize real changes, we must first learn to let go. Then we must train in and practice the art of letting go.

A Lesson in Letting Go

I grew up where there was no snow, and it rarely rained. When the rain did come, the roads became slick with a layer of mud that made it like driving on ice. Drivers went a little bit mad. Skids would be accompanied by panic, hands gripping, feet stomping, over-correcting, frantic attempts to regain control, more panic, and the crashing and littering of cars, monuments to those who did not know how to handle wheels loosened from gravity.

My father took me out into the rain to teach me how to handle a serious skid before I got my license. He taught me that the trick to controlling a skid was in learning when and how to let go. Let go? Yes, let go! Let go of the steering wheel and take your feet off the pedals. To demonstrate his point, he stomped on the brakes and put us into a major spin. Even as a passenger I nearly panicked. His hands never completely left the wheel, they simply loosened so the wheel could move on its own; and though his feet left the pedals for moments, they were tapping the brakes and letting go over and over, and ever so gently, pressing and releasing the gas pedal carefully as he shepherded the skid to its own conclusion.

The first time I put myself into my own practice skid I started to exp-

22 "Push Comes to Shove", Mikhail Baryshnikov, Choreographed by Twyla Tharpe, 1976, http://www.youtube.com/watch?v=w_aEbEqpLdc.
23 http://www.expressiveartsinstitute.org/about/.

erience the pattern I call LMOLPC (loss of control, manic attempt to control, over-correction, loss of control, panic, and crash). Thanks to the early lesson from my father, I intervened just before "overcorrection." I let go and guided my car through its own path; there was no crash.

Over time my body began to respond to the simple command, "LET GO". The first time I faced a truly unexpected skid I really let go. There came a wonderful sense of relaxation, calm, and freedom. I learned to let go with my real body in a real situation and it worked. Since then I have experienced this feeling of freedom most often working with people in Improvisation.

The feeling is that of "popping into current time". I have become aware of and comfortable with the fact that I am not really "in control" of anything. Letting go requires that I enter into a real-time relationship with my surroundings. The result is most startling.

Over time I have learned to give the people I work with as much freedom, respect, responsiveness, and consideration as I give an automobile and the road. I have learned to guide and direct, as well as to let the people do their own work with their own relationships to time and space. I have learned to let go of my immediate control and goals in order to reach a true and natural destination with everyone aboard.

If we have been moving too quickly with your associates or we have changed lanes too quickly; if we have become distracted for a moment and have lost control; if we have overestimated or underestimated the capacity of our participants or the gathering, we may experience dangerous skids. The only answer is to become extremely honest with the situation, and with yourself, and to let go in order to regain control.

"There's a signpost up ahead."
Rod Serling

Rod Serling made this phrase famous in the TV program "The Twilight Zone". It was a warning that we were entering new and interesting and perhaps difficult and confusing territory. As one works with Improvisation it is a good idea to keep this in mind.

The best way to keep out of trouble is to simply know that trouble is coming. There are sign posts that the Improvisation process provides by its own form. The first of these is silence. The next is lack of healthy spontaneous laughter. Another is odd laughter. (See Chapter Ten, "Wholesome Laughter Leads the Way".) Next comes increased resistance by individuals or sets of individuals. Then look for failure of physical participation. Listen for chatter or noise or unrelated conversation on the part of the participants.

Notice confusion anywhere in the event. Obviously, hostility or direct challenge to the presenter or trainer, the information, or the process gives us clues that there may be trouble ahead. Use your own experience to add, or to discover other signs. When we see or feel one coming be prepared to let go, and then let go. Take a step back. Change gears. Slow down or speed up. Change form. Let go of the goal. Focus on the process. Just let go. Blaming participants is counterproductive.

The pattern of blaming the people with whom we work can occur in all leadership, teaching, and training situations. The pattern may come from the leadership, or even from participants.

As soon as we think of placing blame on the people with whom we are working, we need to stop, look, listen, and reconsider our position, and we must do this on the run. Assigning blame to others becomes a very important red flag. When we observe ourselves engaged in this behavior, we should immediately do anything we can to let go of the ideas, patterns, and emotions behind it.

The moment we begin to blame the gathering, or the participants, we are almost certainly involved in some problem of our own. Perhaps it is our own creation. Even if it may have been created by others, it does not matter. You are now in it and it is your pattern. You need to release it. Also release the thought that something outside yourself is to blame.

NOTE

If there are real problems with individuals, or with organizations that are operating in self-destructive manners, we must realize that we may not be able to engage effectively in deep Improvisation games. In such a case take very small steps, use simple structures, and work on applying these lessons to your own life.

A Thought

If others are really the problem, we are still the only ones
who can actually change, so we must work on ourselves.

Ups and Downs

Improvisation is about more than laughter and joyous successfulness. As with any serious work, there are ebbs and flows. It often happens that several really good units of activity will be followed by a slow or difficult set. Sometimes the participants do not laugh as much. There may be a growing sense of struggle or resistance. In these situations it becomes very important to avoid blaming the participants.

It may be that a deep level of reality has been reached and that internal work is being done by a significant number of the people with whom we are working. Because of the nature of Improvisational work, it may be that the group has pushed past a barrier, has reached a plateau, has touched a hidden nerve, or has activated some dormant hidden resistance. It may be that people are becoming tired, or are merely distracted by having been so completely in the moment for an unaccustomed length of time. These are all extremely important elements of the Improvisation process that require immediate attention.

The difficulties may be individual and personal, or there may be resistance to the material, the organization, the trainer, the gathering, or life in general. Whatever the source or the nature of the apparent problem, it must be handled first by letting go.

The Truly New

People have an automatic sense of confidence in an experienced guide. Your stories and memories can establish your authority even before the journey begins. You can draw maps and paint pictures. Paths and mountains may be named after you. If you have actually been somewhere before, people can hear you say such things as, "Come, this is the way, I remember it well", or "Ah, it is as lovely as ever. Come with me and I will show you". It can be easy to lead others to places you have been before. Leading into the truly new has few of these perks. New is . . ., well, new. This is simply the truth. If no one has been there before, then how do we lead others there?

In the martial art of *Aikido*, there are unlimited numbers of response options to an unlimited number of conflict situations. This is also the reality of life. With *Aikido* we deal with the infinite possibilities and focus on a defense technique called *ikkyo*, meaning "first teaching" and a mode called *irimi*, meaning "to enter". We go back to *ikkyo* and *irimi* again and again over many years. It can take a lifetime to master either. As practitioners of *Aikido* return to basic technique, as musicians return to basic scales, Applied Improvisation professionals are served best by going back to simple structures, to first ideas, and to basic techniques in order to reinforce our foundations and conditioned responses.

We can begin by understanding that Improvisation is an ancient art used to generate creativity. It creates true, real, deep, personal, wholesome, healthy, vital, delightful, fascinating, powerful, long-lasting, and sometimes frightening creativity. The territory being explored is new to everyone, including the leadership.

As we deal with ups and downs, it is the job of the professional to lead the participants to whatever the next level may be. The next level is, by definition, truly new.

Leading into the truly new is the great work of Improvisation. One leads into the truly new by taking small, successful, incremental steps toward a vision. This requires starting with the creative challenge of patterns that ultimately must be abandoned. Leading Improvisation gatherings requires us to promote great connections with people, to build on disciplined patter-ns, let go of the patterns, and to then walk fearlessly into the truly new together with our co-workers.

Being Together,
Moving Together
Into the Truly New
Being.
Being? Being what? What being?
Together? Too gather? Two gather? Together.
Moving! Moving into! Moving in two!
The truly new? The newly true?
What is true and what is new?

Make the change! Let go. Make the commitments! Let go. Make the connections, engage in mutual goals, allow for spirit, open doors, invite creativity, let go. There is that extraordinary higher state of consciousness that we describe as "The Improv" or *Impro*, or Alpha state of mind, being in the zone, or just being hot! The use of Improvisational ideas can help us get hot more, and more often.

Having made the commitments, we can also help our gathering achieve the condition we call "together". As an organization or group separates into factions, it becomes increasingly difficult to achieve this special state. If we encounter separation into groups, we must implement activity to overcome the natural separations. In Improvisation these management activities can be referred to as games, techniques, exercises, axioms, rules, suggestions, directions, or instructions.

You are the primary participant in Improvisation. You, the executive, manager, leader, mentor, presenter, teacher, or trainer; you are the leader in the reality that we are all in this together. Being in this together is about more than attending a meeting or a conference, more than being part of the same company, the same business, not-for-profit, governmental, industry, or educational organization. It is about being humans and working and living together at the highest possible levels.

We all live on a tiny planet inside a delicate, small, and profoundly interconnected biosphere. We are all connected by the magnificent mystery of life. We are all defined by mysteries of DNA coding and neuro-styles. We are all associated by our similarities. We all have bodies that must breathe, drink, and eat. We are subject to health and to illness. We are families, communities, and peoples. We share the abilities of our emotions, our joyousness, and our fears. We live in alternating light and dark. Brilliance is followed by confusion, by moments of clarity, by strengths, weaknesses, hopes, and dreams. These are also the things that bring us together.

Sometimes during our most busy and complex days we forget that it is the similarities that are making it possible for us to be engulfed in deep connections, and thus to share information and experience. It is with our connections that we can accomplish things together, learn, teach, engage in projects, or conduct business. Walking our lives and talking about our lives with the deep self-assurance that we are truly in this together can provide enough of an example for the entire gathering to begin operating as a unit. This is basic in leading into the truly new.

Human Tools

Complex modern communication tools include the availability of computers, laptops, cell towers and smartphones and satellites, iPads, varieties of paper, projectors, screens, cables, Wi-Fi connections, printers, photo labs and 3D copiers. These items do not have free will. We do not have to ask them to participate. We do not need to explain that they are parts of a network. We do not need their cooperation to function. They must simply be introduced with correct interconnections, and then we turn them on and off and use them as we will.

Communication works in a system that includes mind and brain, memory and language, numbers and symbols, emotions, meanings, voices, ears, and fingers. People have personalities and free will. We must be asked to participate. We are unlike machinery in that we must be reminded that we are part of a network, or we can fail to connect, or tend to drift away.

Start the Moving

Once Improvisation basics and communication elements are in place and working, we can best begin moving together into the truly new by asking for permission. Simple words should be used, such as:

"Shall we go to the next level?"
"Are we ready to try something new?"
"Shall we see where this leads?"
"Let's see what there is to see."
"Let's try this!"

Things Can Go Wrong

If we miss or ignore signs and signals and try to push our original goals, sometimes it works; often it does not. Allowing gaps in Improvisation methodology will often initiate things going wrong. Sometimes we try to skip to another process, leaving a miss or a mess behind. We may try to leap across gaps, catch up later, let time heal small wounds, or simply let holes in the process stand. In organizational development these events can cause structural damage to the fabric of the connections. This can be dangerous to the development of basic understanding and behavioral change. A great teacher taught me that if I read something that does not make sense, I should go back over it to look for any word I do not fully understand. She said I must then learn the meaning of the word and read the passage again. She said that with difficult materials it may be necessary to do this with each word we do not understand completely, even when we know the basic definitions. Sometimes we must go over words we really think we know. It is a great exercise for an individual or a group to look up such simple words as "the", "at", "in", or "play". There is much to learn. We cannot afford to leave gaps of reality in our work.

Responding to the Response

Listening is an important matter. Actively responding to the words of your participants is a basic demonstration of good listening. Sometimes an executive or presenter will ask questions and neither respond nor react to the responses. It is best not to ask questions merely for the sake of form.

When we move into the truly new, a form of consensus is required. There must be 100 percent willingness to go along.

"100 percent willingness?"
"Yes, 100 percent willingness."
"Are you crazy?"
"Maybe."

Willingness to go along merely means that there is enough understanding, agreement, or cooperation, and that the organization can move forward with everyone aboard. If we cannot generate this level of consensus, we may be taking too large a step. Consensus does not mean that everyone agrees on every point merely that they agree to go along. There may be in fact, probably will be, resistance, fear, timidity, ambivalence, doubt, and even grumbling. We may need to scale back and seek a smaller step. We may be accelerating too quickly.

Your gathering, in terms of set design may need to be altered to create more safety, comfort, and network alliances as will be noted in Chapter Eleven.

You may be working too far ahead in your language. Imagine describing a kiwi fruit in order to convince a person to set muscle and tools to

80

work in order to cultivate land, and to plant seeds to grow them. It would be a little like trying to convince an executive that a single ropes course would help the bottom line if you have not made the personal commitment to take the step yourself. You must demonstrate the need to take the step.

Improvisation works most effectively when we are taking small, incremental, successful steps toward our goals. It is not necessary to obtain acceptance for our entire program and all our ideas. All we need is 100 percent willingness on the part of the participants to enter into the next arena. With careful work we can establish an attitude of willingness to participate within the gathering.

A Desire to Participate

Extraordinary clarity, confidence, charisma, and charm can compel a crowd to go along with us for a little way. Generating wholesome laughter as we proceed will accomplish miracles in helping people follow.

A simple technique of asking the audience to stand up and then sit down again can begin full participation. You may say, "Stand up, turn around to the left, then turn around to the right, and then sit down. "Having the participants stand and introduce themselves to someone next to them serves purposes both of icebreaking and of generating activity on the part of all the participants. As we do these things, we must be careful to note whether there are any members of the group who do not take part in such a simple exercise. The greater the resistance, the more we must work with great intelligence and care.

Asking questions and requesting that hands be raised in response is an easy method of generating physical participation. Ask a simple question such as, "How many people here have been through an organizational reorganization? Let me see a show of hands". Notice how many hands are raised. Then ask the opposite to the question, "How many people here have not been through such reorganization?" Notice the hands again.

Even if you are absolutely certain that 100 percent of the participants raised their hands for one of these questions, say something like, "OK, how many have been through too many corporate reorganizations and are just too tired to raise your hands?" Then say, "Anybody who has not raised your hand yet, please do so now."

Sometimes it is good to debrief this question and answer process with the participants in order to shine the light on the fact that we want full participation, and that it is important to us, to them, and to the process.

At later points in our work we can use the questions and answers process as a gentle reminder. You will usually receive some laughter when the gathering recognizes the pattern. If you do not, it may be time for a break.

In another set of techniques used to obtain full participation, writing is required. Ask the participants to take out pen and paper. This is a 100 percent activity all on its own. Ask them to print one goal, or a vision, or dream on a single sheet of paper. If they go along with this, ask them to print two goals, visions, or dreams on another piece of paper. If this works, ask them to print three of each on still another piece of paper. There should be no names on the papers. It is important that you ask them to print. There are a number of things we can do with these papers:

- Gather them up and redistribute them randomly.
- Arrange them into stacks for random review through the day or the week or the month.
- Tear them into little pieces.
- Ball them up and have a paper snowball fight with them.

Each of these activities will generate energy and will create small participation steps. These simple steps can be used and reused with many variations.

Do as I Do

Simple personal demonstrations of Improvisation techniques can accomplish a great deal in helping people move along with you. It is best to use simple steps. Present a demonstration yourself, then let the group play a little; demonstrate with an assistant, then let the group play again. Then have two participants from the audience do another demonstration. These demonstration processes will help to create unity between you as the leader and the group. Repeat or expand as you feel the need. Once this process has been done, it becomes easier to move forward together.

Assailing patterns and making changes requires careful selection. Patterns are often fundamental to building and growing things. However, when your patterns are negative, or produce unwanted results, we may need to identify and attack our own personal patterns in order to lead the way for others. As we develop the use of Improvisation methodology, we will need to let go of many of our own ways. As we lead people through these explorations, we must not diminish the realities of others who may be holding onto patterns of their own. When we are moving into that which is truly new in our gatherings, we must bring people together so we can help them to move forward together. When things go wrong, we can fall back on the great connections we have made and work toward experiencing even greater connections. Generate cooperation and participation by the way you act, and by your own example.

Once we are moving together, breaking non-working patterns left and right, we can move unhindered into the truly new. The only thing that must be dealt with then is fear of change, fear of the new, and as always, fear of fear itself. Improvisation can help you learn how to better manage, or even make use of our fear.

CHAPTER SEVEN

An Exploration of Fear

The use of Improvisation creates change. Change can generate fear. Fear can interfere with our connections with others, or can even destroy them. When we become afraid we tend to fall into patterned responses. Unless we have training and guidance, the negative effects of fear are unavoidable so we must learn to manage our fears.

Management of fear tends to have three major elements. The first is admitting the fear; engaging with it, bringing it to the light, and exploring it. The second requires working through fear in the present moment. The third calls for using some discipline as a structure upon which to hang and distract the fears as we work through them.

Bringing Fear to the Light

To manage fear we need to bring it into the light. We can use Improvisation techniques to learn to take small, successful, incremental steps that allow us to bring up fear in portions that can be handled. The idea of putting Improvisation out for public view is part of bringing fear into the open where it can be managed.

Exploring Fear

- The more serious the subject matter, the more there can be fear.
- The more difficult the subject matter, the more fear it can bring.
- The newer the subject matter, the more fear.
- The more complex the subject matter, the more fear.
- The more personal the subject matter, the more fear can be imbedded.
- The more public, the more fear.
- The more abstract the subject matter, the more fear.
- The more taboo, the more fear.
- The more real ....
- Fear factors can be increased or decreased with the size of the gathering.
- Some fears are phobic and without rational sources.
- Some fear is internal and without discoverable sources.
- All fear is in the mind, and body of our emotions
- We measure things in order to understand and encompass them and to thus be less afraid.

Measurements

Time and motion studies early in the 20th Century developed human measurement tools that were intended to help factory managers promote more efficient work processes. While some of the physiological responses to fear can be measured, the communication and interactions of people are simply too personal and too complex to study with simple time and motion measurements. People and organizations are living, changing, holographic, analog organisms. They can be observed and annotated, recorded and viewed; yet chart and graph measurements do not give us complete enough pictures to quantify them in a truly realistic way. However, Improvisation can function as a methodology for conducting qualitative analysis.

Improvisation is composed of living, changing, holographic, both analog, and digital processes that we can observe, record, and compare. We can change various elements at will and record the responses with your mind and memory. You cannot write your impressions down while you are working, and notes made later will be out of current time so information gathering and analysis need to be immediate.

From the very first exercise, we can observe, and reliably measure, the abilities of the group, and of individuals, to move together, to change, to communicate, to laugh, to cooperate, to learn, and to alter behavior. We may even be able to observe aspects of direction and speed.

If we wish to learn about the effect and effectiveness of any Improvisation activity, we can move to the next level of complexity or the next level of seriousness or reality, and there will be observable responses. We can see the changes that have occurred in the group's ability to work together. We can then move back to a previous level of complexity and seriousness to compare and verify our results. Simple changes in your presentation will give us the ability to move back and forth while observing the response of the group. If we can demonstrate faith in the group as a learning and changing entity, the levels of fear that are present will be diminished.

As we learn about our fear, we bring it into the light. In the light we can manage the fear; call on allies to help us begin to work through the fear and lead your organization into strength.

Working through Fear in the Present Moment

Clear analysis and understanding of reality are difficult in the face of unmanaged fear. Understanding information, study, and research can also be difficult when one is afraid. Management of fear is rarely taught and seldom practiced. It is usually handled personally and covertly in the real world, which can be a difficult and expensive training ground. Some exercises are serious enough to simulate fear so that its management can be practiced in artificial settings. As a naval officer, I was placed in frightening and dangerous simulations during fire-fighting training in order to practice prior to a real crisis. That sort of system is usually a little drastic for those working in hotels, offices and board rooms. Outdoor challenge programs and "ropes" programs have been used to "build teams" and to give organizations practice dealing with the unknown and with fear. Such events require specialized surroundings. Improvisation has been referred to as an "indoor ropes course" by some participants.

Thoughts on Working through Fear

- Improvisation provides a practice tool for real-time training in fear management.

- Improvisation works best in the present moment, where fear resides.
- The management of fear requires discipline. Serious Improvisation is a fine discipline form.
- The work of Improvisation functions at different levels than mere exercise or philosophy.
- The rules and attitudes practiced and followed while playing with Improvisation can be used as daily discipline in fear management.
- The practice of observing the people in your organization can help us improve skills in observing and measuring fear management realities.
- The processes can be used to address the topic of fear management, as well as other general concerns based on the realities of the matters at hand.

Hang the Fear on a Structure

The third element in managing fear is using a structure on which to hang fears as people work through them. It is simple truth that fear is a difficult aspect of life. Improvisation is a microcosm of life and has within it both fear and its resolution.

As an Improvisation Professional it is good to say such things as:

Please, stand up with a group
of the people around you.
I have no plan nor idea of what
you will be asked to do or say next.
We are going to work on real issues
and real problems together.
We are all going to watch together
as we work our way through the problems.
We will talk about what we have done and learned.
We will create plans to implement some of the new skills
or good 'bits of information that we have observed.
We will measure and benchmark ourselves
to see how we have improved.
We are going to bring fear into the present moment.
We are going to bring fear into the light.
Together we are going to learn to manage fear.

The Discipline

- Working with games, structures, and exercises in scheduled and monitored real time, with real people and real feedback, provides a foundation for the discipline of Improvisation.

- Integrating Improvisation into our daily life is another form of the discipline.
- Integrating the attitudes and ways of Improvisation into our family and community life is the work of the discipline.
- Bringing activities, techniques, the philosophies and agreements of Improvisation into the life of your business and organizational practices is the value of the discipline.
- Improvisation engages sources of creativity.

By engaging in a discipline, you will create a structure on which fear may be placed for display and managed by the whole gathering. The fourth Improvisation idea asks that we put ourselves out for public view though fear of speaking in public is very strong. If you try something new and it does not work, we say that you "fell on your face." This is also the fear of falling.

Improv processes and structures create results we cannot see, even though they are right in front of us. This is certainly like fear of the dark. Comedians talk of trying to be funny and having the attempt fail. They call this "dying on stage", which equates with fear of death. I guess that just leaves fear of spiders and snakes. Improvisation is, by definition, the act of entering the truly unknown. We fear the unknown.

> "The only thing that makes life possible is permanent intolerable uncertainty, not knowing what comes next."
> **Ursula Le Guin**[24]

Overcoming Fear with Improvisation

The ability to be afraid is a wondrous thing. Along with hope and determination fear has helped humans to thrive against all odds. At the same time, fear can stop us in our tracks and cause us to freeze in the face of real danger. All kinds of fears show up in life and during an Improvisation process.

Afraid? Of What?

Fear of being looked at, fear of being seen,
fear of being embarrassed, fear of being bold,
fear of being noticed, fear of not being noticed,
fear of being extraordinary, fear of being common,
fear of feeling alive, fear of feeling not alive,
fear of judgment, fear of self-judgment,

---

[24] Ursula K. LeGuin, *The Left Hand of Darkness*, Barnes & Noble: NY, 1969.

fear of letting go, fear of holding on,
fear of knowing, fear of not knowing,
fear of being wrong, fear of being right,
fear of having a good time, fear of having no time,
fear of freedom, fear of change, fear of failure, fear of success,
and fear of fear, or of fear of fear.

Distinguishing Good Fear from Bad Fear

Extraordinary things have often been accomplished because an individual has been fearful of loss or failure, while equally great plans have never gotten off the ground for fear of loss or failure. We are often as fearful of success as of failure: success means that people will really notice us. Success usually requires that we repeat ourselves, and then success is expected even before we begin. A single success may have been luck. What if we are found to be lucky instead of good? Success can also generate jealousy and competition.

The worst aspect of fear is that it begins deep, in the quiet darkness of our insides, with a tightening of the blood vessels, and changes in the heartbeat. It comes with constricted breathing. It begins to change its nature as it travels along the nerves and makes the skin tingle, the palms sweat, and the mouth dry. At that point we can know it for what it is; just plain fear. It creeps into the mind, and we then have two choices. The first is to send the fear back into the dark internal world where it can hide and grow evil, like Shelob in her lair from Tolkien's *The Lord of the Rings*, or we may bring it out into the light.

Good Fear

Fear is a powerful force in real life. It gives us warning of real danger and eminent consequences. It comes with, or is caused by, a flow of adrenaline, giving us extraordinary strength or speed. Adrenaline can help us to deal with real or imagined emergencies. My very tiny grandmother once rescued a fifty-pound barrel of nails from her burning house. After the fire she could not even move the barrel. (She was never able to explain why she chose to save nails. Perhaps it was an affinity with toughness.)

Good fear can also be a valuable motivator that forces us to reflect carefully on choices and on consequences of wrong or slow decisions. Here the adrenaline may help us to think more clearly and more quickly. Fear may startle us out of inaction or lethargy when consequences may not be extremely serious yet lack of action would create uncomfortable results. Improvisation helps us practice working with fear at these levels as well.

Good fear may be valuable as a motivator that can push us slowly out of patterns, beliefs, and behaviors that may have taken a long time to develop or cause problems in our lives.

For years I had insisted to myself that I was terrible at math. I had allowed this belief to keep me from several goals. Later, working for a manufacturing corporation, in spite of my "math disability" I performed complicated financial analyses of prospective customers. My work was good, my results excellent, and as my responsibilities increased, the complexity of the work increased. In response to this, the company purchased an expensive correspondence course in "Financial Analysis and Risk Projection". I received the first lesson, saw that the math was difficult, and set the lesson aside to try later. Lessons piled up on the "to do" shelf.

The final unit arrived and I had one weekend left in which to have all the lessons done and into the mail. If they were not done, all that would be left was to explain to my next prospective employer what had caused the termination of my last job.

Good fear set in and when I sat down to work, the math suddenly seemed simple. A greater fear had driven a lesser limitation from my mind. I put the whole series of lessons into the mail on Monday morning and graduated with honors. My math skills have been just fine since that day.

Fear and Learning

On the other hand, a great deal of learning difficulty is based in fear. There is the fear that we cannot learn, fear that we are not good enough, fear that we will forget, fear that we will fail when tested, fear that we will remember the wrong things, fear that we should have known it already, fear that someone will discover that we do not know what we should know, fear that it doesn't really matter anyway, and many other forms of just plain fear.

All these aspects of fear take us out of the present moment. They all create distractions and inhibit focus. The stronger the fear, the more likely it is that surges from the endocrine system will stress the body and mind into the posture of "fight or flight" where we will even run rather than learn or change.

"Not Good" Fear from the Past

"Not good" fear is sometimes in league with good fear. It arrives from another dimension. "It is a dimension neither of sight nor sound, but of mind".[25] It is also a dimension of time. "Not good" fear comes also from both the past and from the future. It clouds the thinking and slows the reactions. It is a little like neurosis. It speaks to us in voices from our heads, and those voices often have little or no association with reality. An understanding of Improvisation processes will be served by a further look into these fears.

Fear of Public Speaking

Fear of public speaking, glossophobia, forces me to tilt my head in wonder. All speaking is public speaking unless we are talking to a higher power ourselves. Yet we know that fear of public speaking is near the top of the list speaking, in front of fear of death.

Some number of people must certainly have been humiliated at early and impressionable ages in public speaking situations. I suppose that more have watched such an event and have learned fear from that. Some of it seems to come from the "ether". I have been speaking in public for 60 years, and for more than twelve years taught public speaking classes at Georgia State University. I have never seen an audience attack a speaker.

I have also watched people sit down, after excellent presentations, with their breathing heavy, hearts racing, and lips swearing that they will never do that again. It is interesting to note that most often in these situations the audience demonstrated high levels of support and appreciation, in direct contrast to the feelings experienced by the speaker. A reality of the fear of public speaking is that it requires one to be removed from present time in order to do its job. When people are in the present moment, they forget this fear. There is actually no room for fear in the present moment. We can fear only what could be, based on what we decide has been.

Fear of the Unknown

Fear of the unknown also confuses me. It is a simple truth that we cannot really predict the future. Horse races and dice games have been proving the unpredictability of the future since humans had a minute to spare on frivolity. The weather service also comes to mind. It has been suggested in chaos theory discussion that even if we had grids of weather data receivers stationed one foot apart, six feet high, completely covering the globe, we still could not reliably predict rain in a certain place four days from now.

The closest we can come to predicting the future is to analyze as much data as we can gather, as with supercomputers cloud networks, and on the Internet in general, where we are creating and linking extraordinary

---

[25] Rod Serling. *The Twilight Zone.*

amounts of information, and then putting our trust into the probabilities of pattern repetition. We can operate with what help statistical odds give us out, and supposing the odds were in our favor, and the predicted event happened, then we can take credit for knowledge of the future.

Always, and all the time, the next moment is unknowable with few exceptions, such as knowing that an item dropped from a high place in a closed gravitational field will continue to fall until something gets in the way, so far as we have experienced. Life is the next moment revealing itself again and again. Fear of the unknown is fear of life. This is a "not good" fear.

As with all such fear, it is a waste of time at best, and can be destructive if allowed to grow. It takes us further and further out of the current moment and robs us of our strengths; it robs us of our Improvisation. This is commonly called anxiety or future phobia and it robs us of our Improvisation. It is interesting to know that the Latin word for future is *future*. My understanding is that it is fear of life, and living.

Learning, Memory, and Not Good Fear

When the people with whom we are working are essentially attentive, and the communication methods are realistic and reasonable, poor retention of information is usually the result of at least two things: lack of relevance, and fear. Fear is the more destructive. As easily as fear can implant a memory as a phobia, it can also diminish and distort recall of information and experience.

"Not good" fear starts in the guts and expands to fill the available space. More accurately its beginning lurks above the "guts" high atop the kidneys in the glands called adrenaline. After the tummy responds, some of the next space filled is the chest and heart, and then that reserved for memory. The next space to be filled can be the entire inside of our body, and then it expands to anything that can be touched by person, thought, or spirit. Fear can fill the area surrounding the body. It can then spill over to another body and from there to fill a room, a meeting, a town, a nation, or even a world. It can become infectious to the point of uncontrolled mob violence. "Not good" fear is a product of the flip sides of memory and imagination. Not good fear comes from a time other than now, a place other than here, a realm other than the actual. It is the antithesis of Improvisation.

Fear in Reality

All our fears, whether they are based in substantial reality or not, whether they are good or not good, use the same channels to invade us. Unless fear comes from a source of true danger, we are jumping at shadows and leaping into unnecessary old patterns of fight, flight, grapple, diminish, resist, and struggle.

My *Aikido* practice included many years teaching classes, participating in public demonstrations, and presenting the results of my training in periodic public tests. At the higher levels, these tests include attacks from four or five trained people at one time. The process is called *rendori* which translates as "seizing chaos". These tests are performed in an arena composed of peers, the public, and before a panel of senior Sensei. The single most important and most difficult skills are the abilities to relax, to continue breathing normally, to accurately assess the situation at hand, to accept the situation, and to become fearless in the face of danger. This fearlessness must be developed with real-time training and practice in the principles and techniques of *Aikido*. Improvisation work will give you similar real time training and practice in learning to relax and to become fearless in the face of many possibilities.

Accepting Our Fear

As executives, managers, trainers, presenters, teachers, and leaders, we have faced all our fears, and for the most part we have put them aside. We have managed our fears of success, and of failure, and are focused completely on the needs of our participants. As my then eleven-year-old son said, "Yeah, right!"

Each time we enter the arena of our work, we face higher levels of expectation. We often impose these expectations on ourselves more than others impose them on us. We can become expert in hiding our fear. We can begin to believe that if people feel our fear, they will think of us as incapable or incompetent; if they know we have fear, they will become fearful. This is far from the truth. The denial and ignorance of fear infects the surroundings of others.

If we do not acknowledge our fear, at least to our self, we also teach those we influence to hide their fears. If we are not fearful in new and challenging situations, we may teach our participants to think of themselves as beyond such human frailty as fear. This either alienates or intimidates others and teaches them to value things that are not true.

Acknowledging our fear does not require that we fall apart and collapse, nor suddenly become a fearless superhero. However, those who say fear is absent in their lives are often admitting the absence of feeling, or the absence of awareness or common sense. This is especially true with Improvisation as it shines a light on the process.

If I am never afraid, then there is an assumption that I am not being challenged beyond my sense of comfort. If we do not challenge ourselves enough, we must ask, "What is really being learned? Are we leading participants into a failure to challenge themselves?"

As Applied Improvisation leaders we must allow ourselves to know and to experience our fear. We must admit that the fear can be real and that it is normal, and that by acknowledging it there is a possibility of working through it. It is also good to admit that the fear can be unreal and that it may not be normal, yet it can still be acknowledged and worked through.

The second Improvisation idea is to strive to become honest with our self. If you are trying something new in public and there are consequences for failure, it is probably irrational not to feel some sort of fear. We must be honest with ourselves about this reality.

The third Improvisation idea suggests that we learn to be completely honest with another person. We may accomplish this when we tell someone we are afraid. Better still, engage in it with the whole audience and move ahead anyway. You may as well "shout it from the highest hill". It is our job to create an environment in which fear may be released into the light and laughter of the moment.

Whatever You Call It

Fear or uneasy trepidation or extreme hesitancy or resistance or unnamed discomfort or timidity, or any other name for fear has to be acknowledged by both the Applied Improvisational leader and the participants. It must be brought into the light to be worked through by all who would learn a new thing. If this is not done, it becomes very difficult to accomplish learning and behavioral change.

Sometimes, as leaders, we find ourselves in the interesting position of being afraid to generate fear in our gathering. Sometimes when fear does surface in our participants, we become co-dependent and attempt to "fix" it, to make it better for them. Both these responses result from an attempt to become comfortable. Pretending to be comfortable, we teach comfort; everyone remains comfortable; comfort begets comfort; and nothing changes at all.

Exploring the Field of Fear

As Applied Improvisational leaders and teachers, it is good to realize that people can be filled with fear, surrounded by fear, motivated by fear, stopped by fear, and lost in a universe of fear. Our minds, the media, our friends and family, our co-workers, and our culture sometimes seem to conspire to focus on that which is fearful.

We live on a planet on which an undefined thing called gravity holds us upside down and skittle sideways, on a thin layer of loose dirt and rock that is spinning rapidly through space, propelled by some unknown force. We live in a body that is only a single heartbeat away from stopping. Our bodies are made of more than five billion cells, and only a single cell gone wrong can create a life-threatening cancer. As we can all see, some fear is rational under the circumstances.

From another viewpoint our entire culture can be seen as being built on the idea that a percentage of error is acceptable. In any given year there should be 35,000 automobile deaths, so many airplanes are expected to crash, and lightning may strike at any place or time. Terrorism stalks us, financial disaster lurks, technology looms, and fate laughs. "Yet for today, for this day's task, let's put that all aside and pretend that we are not afraid." Not without consideration and practice.

Improvisation techniques and process can activate the gathering of all our senses as one single manifestation called fear. If the various levels of Improvisation fear are not acknowledged and brought into the light, the people with whom we are working may do the same thing with Improvisation fear that they do with life fear. They may submerge themselves in it, or ignore and suppress it, or act it out either actively or passively. We may steel ourselves in the face of fear, freeze before it, forget everything that happened while it was present, or we can let it control our next steps. We can also grasp it, accept it, enfold it, use it, and understand that it contains the energy needed to climb to the next level of uncertainty, the next level of intelligence, the next level of relationship. It is a major responsibility of Improvisation Professionals to be alert and aware of such phenomena.

Fear can be cumulative and contagious. Sometimes the larger the gathering the more potential there is for fear, as there is more potential for excitement and experience and relationship exploration. It is also very interesting to note that the larger the crowd, the greater the tendency for people to suppress or expand their fear, to internalize it or externalize it. Any of these possibilities can be positive, negative, structural, or can provide resolution to many things from the past, including fear.

Sometimes the smaller the gathering, the more the potential for fear to be recognized and dealt with, which can be fraught with wonder and the need for care-full-ness.

In "civilized" meetings, where our purpose is general, the odds of the fear growing wildly or getting out of control are pretty slim. It is possible to generate an atmosphere in which resistant participants seem to gain control of a gathering, yet that is about the worst we will experience.

Few working meetings have turned into mobs or riot or a general panic. Today workplaces and all levels of schools, secondary, elementary, university, trade, graduate, or internship, there is a growing chance that an act of violence might be a response to fear. I guarantee that violence is the result of fear at some usually complex and cumulative level.

It has been my privilege to have used Applied Improvisation in a number of prison settings, and with my small sample have found that the structure, the laughter, the presence of an interest in listening and of providing a real opportunity of relating to others creates a place and atmosphere of safety, which is necessary for magical learning and personal growth.

A very normal experience in reaction to fear in a large crowd will be suppression, which can cause a great numbness and peer pressure toward covert isolation. This will eventually allow the entire group to deny that anything is going on.

NOTE

Thoughts regarding larger emotions are not for disaster or panic situations. Knowledge of these factors can serve first responders just as incorporation of Improvisational Thinking began being used in disaster relief, and preparedness in the Philippines in 2013.

It has been said that there are really only two emotions: love and fear. If we are not actively working in the direction of love, we can either drift or plummet in the direction of fear. If we hide and suppress fear with effort and care, the people will smile and express gratitude for a good time had and done by all, and everyone will go home much the same way they arrived, little touched by the people, the experience or the change in learning. Sometimes we will be so pleased with our own comfort and lack of change that we will plan an even larger program, just like it, for next year.

Using Laughter against Fear

The most effective Improvisation fear management tool is that of laughter, a nearly uniquely human gift. Other often used methods of managing fear include avoidance, resistance, and suppression. Running away is sometimes mistaken for fear management. Improvisation offers a path paved with laughter as an alternative approach that allows for encouragement of the presence of rational fear that can be managed by the very process being experienced in the seminar, or workshop, or work/play place.

Laughter is a natural product of Improvisation. It is the product of such elements as surprise, reduction, re-imaging, re-imagining, simple emotional release, *déjà vu*, seeing things with new perspective, seeing others expand and contract in our eyes, making odd connections, word play, known people revealing themselves, being led into unexpected turns, suddenly being really listened to and engaged with as our real self. By encouraging wholesome laughter, we have a natural balm for the fear that occurs when we deal with learning and growing in public. See Chapter Ten, Wholesome Laughter Leads the Way, for a discussion of this wonderful healing aspect of Improvisation.

Most kinds of laughter help to dissipate or reduce fear. Hearty laughter may actually release internal chemistry that counteracts fear. Original and spontaneous humor carries a power beyond that of a joke or a story. Its suddenness and the fact that it must be based in current relationships gives it even more power to act positively on fear.

Even when fear is based on reality, laughter can relieve some of the stress and can help restore perception and perspective. When fear is in the mind (the imagination, or the memory), really delicious laughter can actually relieve fear completely and permanently. When I teach self-defense classes to teachers, I suggest that leaving the building in an emergency can be made safer by laughing joyously along the way. Whistling is also nice if done with assurance and power.

While Improvisation may bring some fear, it is also a generator of spontaneous, relationship based, hearty, wholesome laughter. Managing fear can be a simple matter of walking through it. One of my many teachers once described fear "a film like the surface of a soap bubble." She said that all one must do to pass it by is to walk through the film. The hard part is taking the step. Getting through is easy. How does one take this step? It is a little like letting go. You lift up one foot and put it down in front of another. Repeat the process until you are through the film.

Fear has the capacity to paralyze us. Walking through the bubble of fear requires movement. Improvisation generates movement. I have watched boardroom executives and middle-school children walk through walls of fears using these tools of Improvisation. They can usually just step through without noticing the fear when it is wrapped up in wholesome laughter.

If we stick with the ideas, and commit to emotional commitments, Improvisation can provide the environment needed to bring us together with our friends and family, with our co-workers, our visions, and our goals. Being together helps us to create a safe environment in which we laugh together without regard to our differences. Laughter and laughing together are forms of internal movement that help us to progress as individuals and as groups. Given various Improvisation processes, the paralyzing effects of fear can be overcome and the power of fear can lead us to fearless action, to serious fun, and to very fun, serious work. As the walking begins, the bubble of fear begins to thin.

With the light, with the power of the present moment, with discipline and practice, almost all fear can be turned into good, clear, real, motivating fear. By accepting the facts and realities of this pituitary, adrenalin steroid producing body response to imagination, we can approach the entire field of fear rather than single, isolated moments that can lock us in place. With playfulness and laughter, we can learn to walk through all the bubbles and on to the business, work, and play of life.

CHAPTER EIGHT

Feelings and Emotions

Managing with the creativity of Improvisation involves exploring our feelings and emotions. A lot of our time is spent in our minds. We consider our problems and difficulties, dream about and plan the future, think over the past, and consider problems. We spend time learning, remembering, analyzing, collecting, and organizing data. The unfettered, free expression of emotions is often not acceptable in surprising numbers of human settings. Feelings and emotions are often difficult to deal with in any circumstance. Our feelings can be confusing and complicated. Emotions are usually activated before logic. It can also be difficult to distinguish thoughts from feelings. These realities, among others, help to repress the presence and effective use of feelings in some of our most serious situations.

At the same time, it is clear that "gut level" feelings are major tools used in the development of creativity leading to more effective management. Invention, imagination, implementation, visualization, adjustment, problem solving, and crisis intervention are often the result of activating feelings while the statistical and logical factors are being interpreted. It also happens that a logical solution, the one that ought to have worked, that was planned and made ready, simply did not work, or worked in an unexpected way.

In order to develop the best Improvisation management skills, it is a good idea to feel our way through the realm of feelings and emotions. We will begin with thoughts and a personal survey.

Thoughts about the Idea called "Feeling"

Consider again the sense of touch: pleasure, pain, pressure, temperature, vibration, tickling, soothing, stickiness, and oiliness. The memory of any of these feelings may be activated by any of the other senses. Such memories are truly composed of thoughts. Even while the memory can actually cause a physical response such as a tingling, a rash, a temporary paralysis, or unconsciousness it is still a matter of thought.

Another level of feeling includes the somatic and kinesthetic. This has to do with the way whole body systems respond. Examples of somatic units and their responses are: the whole body kinesthetically (it can shudder as a unit or may experience a hot flash or a chill), the skin (may tingle or "crawl" as a unit), the stomach (can tighten or chum with tension), the heart (can beat quickly or palpate), or the jaws (can tighten along with the back of the neck and skull muscles). Also, the head aches, the hands shake, the blood boils, the ears ring, a muscle cramps, and the lungs fill or empty suddenly (gasping and laughing). Each of these events may also be triggered by thought.

Another feeling is composed of emotions themselves. When asked how we feel, we may respond with abstract and subjective words; "I feel sad." Other abstract words include "feeling" tired, bored, happy, sad, frightened, crisp, and clear. As the words become even more abstract and personal and thus less generally descriptive, the line between feeling and thought becomes more unclear. The names of the emotions can replace the feelings themselves.

Another level of what we think of as "feeling" is purely in the mind. It is indirect, abstract, imaginary, and can be "fantastic". When asked how we feel we may respond with words that have no meaning beyond some personal thought process. We use such words as, OK, fine, good, "so-so", bad, upset, silly, or lost, all of which withhold true feelings and emotions.

A Survey of Feelings

The purpose of this survey is to support your thinking to open yourself and others to experiencing and sharing a broader range of feelings and emotions, to learn more about the possibilities. The following may be done as a personal exercise and used as a group development tool. The exercise is best done with paper and pen. It can take as little as 15 to 20 minutes. I suggest that you be conservative regarding the time you spend working in this area.

Complete each statement once, then complete each one four more times. Use a pencil so you can erase and reuse the form

I feel _____

I am _____

Complete each statement as you come to it.

My feet feel like _____

My hands feel like _____

My stomach feels like _____

My mouth feels like _____

My_____feels like_____

Complete each statement below once. Then return and fill in each blank four more times.

I am_____

My feet are _____

My ears are_____

My nose is _____

My toes are _____

My eyelashes are _____

The most pleasant feeling I can remember was when

_____

The worst pain I can remember occurred when

_____

After you have completed this chapter, I encourage you to come back to this survey. I also suggest that you do it again after finishing the book and after major experiences using Improvisation. Fill in the blanks in different orders and a numbers of times. Create your own questions. Explain your understanding of feelings and emotions to your children or siblings, or to other family members, or to a group of 12-year-old people. You may also wish to use this exercise before you begin working with people in your organization.

Analyze your Answers Different Ways

Take some time to reflect on your answers to the questions in the exercise above. Especially observe differences in the kinds of words you used in the various question formats, and over time. Notice what categories of words you have used in describing your sense of touch. Have your senses of touch grown stronger or have they taken on more breadth? Are they becoming more engaging; both more and less sensitive as appropriate to the wonder of touch itself? Consider your thoughts and reactions to these responses. Are there differences between your thoughts and your physical reactions? Are you willing to share any of your responses with others?

NOTE

Be careful with this suggestion. Improvisation is not therapy and should not be used in a therapeutic fashion except by qualified, credentialed professionals.

This exercise is intended as a mental focus process that will help you and your cohort group to begin learning with more of the physical body involved and with more honesty. This exercise can also be developed into an entire training session or program with discussion and feedback groups. Such events require high levels of facilitation skill.

If you choose to have participants share responses and reactions, the gathering may take on a life of its own. You may need to be prepared to abandon some of your earlier goals for the session if this happens.

Group Centeredness

Complete understanding of feelings also requires Improvisation Professionals to be, or to become, fully participant centered in support of everyone becoming group centered. Many people become self-centered when faced with a stressful situation, an audience or an organization. Self-centeredness is a primary source of the fear of public speaking. It is also the source of the droning informational meeting, or discourse with strict adherence to an agenda, script, plan, or pattern and little or no interaction.

If we do not understand our material at this level, then we are liable to feel quite vulnerable. We are vulnerable to error, to challenge, and to being or seeming foolish, over-committed, or out of control. All of these feelings require that we open ourselves to change, to being affected by our relationships, to be changed by the workshop, seminar, program, and the message of our work, and our surroundings. Becoming focused on and centered within the participants in our lives and the groups we influence, teach, and learn from, is a resolution to this vulnerability.

NOTE

The states called "foolish" and "out of control" are more normal than not. Our history, our science, institutions, forms, failures, and sometimes even our successes all tell us that "foolish" and "out of control" are not only normal, they constitute the majority experience of most people much of the time. It is interesting to note that this reality is rarely admitted by the people who are actually involved in the experience at the time it is happening, nonetheless. Other people, however, rarely miss it. This is the stuff of which human folly is made.

"You do not need to worry about making people think you are foolish. They will do that without any help from you.

Jeff Justice

When doing work with Improvisation and feelings, we need to be able to laugh at, and with, ourselves. This is part of the reason Improvisation works. Improvisation events help us become comfortable with a reality that life and culture are not ours to command completely. Life and culture are ours to experience, to become part of, perhaps to influence, and from which we may learn and, maybe, teach.

The Wonderful World of Confusion

We are often distressed by confusion. Our highly structured lives and systems are a tribute to our dislike of disorder and confusion. In contrast, it is true that embracing level of confusion and facing the unknown confidently is among the requirements of deep learning, of clear reflection, of personal change, and of creativity. Disorder requires reorganization. Reorganization leads to developing new perspective, invention, innovation, insight reevaluation, introspection and, ultimately, to learning and change in your behavior.

Confusion is a relative of fear and it too can lead to immobilization. It can also lead to hostility or aggressiveness, to calcification of our ideas, to holding onto old forms, to repetition of erroneous patterns, to disorientation, and even to a general reinforcement of the negative. Confusion can be pretty nasty stuff.

In order to avoid confusion, many people do a number of interesting things: refuse to participate in the moment, fail to listen, listen selectively, interpret selectively (understanding only that which agrees with their current ways of thinking), devalue selectively (the presenter, the information, the experience), forget, forget selectively, and avoid being present in the moment in a variety of creative ways. A thing I tend personally to do in the face of confusion is to argue, either overtly or covertly. We may also discount ourselves, or the other participants, or life in general.

The Art of Being Confused

Improvisation's way of dealing with confusion is to accept it, then to relax into it and allow it to be part of the natural process of organization and reorganization. We must learn to distinguish the confusion that comes from reaching into the real change and learning from confusion caused by errors in timing and focus.

As Improvisation Professionals and leaders, it is good to learn and understand how we feel and respond when we are personally confused. A good way to do this is to do things that will give us practice in the art of being confused. A primary reason that travel broadens us is that it provides practice in confusion and its resolution. Attending places of worship that are not our own, or public gatherings that are outside our norms can also provide such broadening practice. Improvisation is also a good source of practice in being confused.

An Exercise in Timing

Develop a list of things you could do to place yourself into confusion without placing yourself in physical danger. Perhaps walking around with your eyes closed in a safe place, perhaps with a guide. Attend a meeting of an opposing political party. Attend a function with an age group that is twenty-five years older or younger than you are. Attend a children's movie on Saturday morning by yourself, or with a new friend. Find a big field and spin around and around in circles until you are dizzy and can hardly stand up. Call a stranger on the phone and generate a conversation about life. Create a "confusion challenge" of your own.

Practice and training are done to improve timing, as well as strength and a number of other attributes of excellence. Usually our experiences with confusion come in the middle of a crisis, just when we feel that we need our wits about us. Usually we face the issues of confusion at critical moments when family, friends, business, time, and money are at stake. It is better to become good at handling confusion in practice settings. This is a subtle attribute of work with Improvisation.

Emergency Training in Managing Confusion

My background includes mountain search and rescue, and rock climbing training as well as suicide intervention and crisis counseling, welfare crisis intervention, martial arts training, first aid, water safety, CPR training, and U.S. Naval Line Officer training, which included a live, shipboard-fire, fighting school.

Each of these experiences required dealing with serious consequences and serious states of confusion, my own and that of others. In order to deal effectively with the various aspects of emergency work, it is necessary to experience higher and higher levels of stress and confusion, along with increasing numbers of choices. The success comes not from surviving the confusion. It comes by encompassing it and thriving on it and understanding it as a source of reorganized information.

Confusion, by its nature, comes from there being too many choices, or no apparent choices, at moments of crisis. When there are too many choices, time spent "practicing" confusion teaches surveying, analysis, prioritizing, selection, and commitment to a course of action. If there are no choices, practice teaches patience, personal control, inventiveness, and creativity.

When groups engage in the human phenomenon of confusion, the lessons often take forms of cooperation, teamwork, interdependence, rapid problem solving, "crew response", resource management, open communication, sharing, and basic connectedness.

Improvisation includes and requires practice in the art of being confused. Confusion is a good thing unless we are operating at high speeds, or far above the ground. Fear of confusion can inhibit learning and teaching. Failure to approach and embrace confusion can render learning and change ineffective.

Confusion requires a disorganization in our control mechanisms which allows us to begin the process of moving from the known, which is not working at the moment, into the unknown. This action is the basis of learning.

A Feeling Called Blending

Blending is more than just mixing together, more than becoming "one" with something outside other. Blending results in synergy, that circumstance in which the whole is greater than the sum of its parts. Blending requires that the teacher or trainer do more than merely accept his or her own confusion. We must actively present our open confusion as the realm in which the greatest possibility of blending lies. It also requires that the trainer request, accept, feel, and thus blend with the participants' confusion.

As with all Improvisation ideas, blending is so simple as to be complex. Blending creates a bonding. Objects mixed together can usually be easily sifted or separated. Bonding is the product of blending.

Improvisation Chef

In cooking we use the term blending to describe components being brought together under the influence of an outside agency. Under the influence of milk and heat, we find that flour and sugar blend nicely to create pastas and pastries. This is a lot like the process of working with people!

Sometimes people want someone to come in and change their culture, or solve long festering problems by devoting a few hours to the process. This is a bit like wanting bread to appear by mere mixing and stirring, without allowing for blending, kneading, rising, and cooking. Kneading is a blending activity. The whole process takes some time.

Rising and cooking are biochemical. Blending does not usually have the harshness of chemical reactions nor the permanence of biochemical changes. Blending is softer and gentler. It is more interactive and less sudden. Rather than creating a release of energy, there is a gathering of energy, a creation of potential energy. If you have never kneaded bread with your own hands, I recommend that you do so at the next opportunity. Bread baked by your own hand is better than well....

Sand Castles

Something creates a kind of magic that appears when everyone is suddenly on the same wave length; we begin walking together, as individuals, and then as a gathering, and miracles seem to happen. Considering sand castles helps us understand what seems to allow this to happen.

An interesting thing about sand is that clean, dry, pure silicon crystals (sand bits) are free and loose particles. Dry sand slips through the fingers. Each particle is disconnected from all others, beholden to none. These same sand particles can be heated to high temperature and melted into uniform crystalline structures we call glass, wherein the unique character of each particle is lost to the whole form. Wild sand, however, the kind found in nature, has odd shapes including tiny shells, shell particles, and fine dust.

The dust is a key component in a simple yet powerful process. When aided by the agency of water the sand crystals and particles and dust all complement and enhance one another. A temporary working relationship is created just as in Improvisation. The wet dust becomes a temporary mortar, a binding that gives the possibility of structure for the sand particle. With this fine and simple structure we can create sand castles. Also we must also continue to add water or the sand castle will turn again to bits of dust.

People can be like crystals of sand. We can be hard and jagged and separate and isolated, and irritating. We also may be melted into unrecognizable forms with our individuality as invisible as glass. We can also be brought together for higher purposes that do not destroy our individuality, yet create more than the single person can create alone. We too can be blended into sand castles. We too must be replenished with a magic binding.

When working with Improvisation, the binding materials – the liquid that brings and holds people together, the magic that blends includes consciousness, attention to detail care-fullness, laughter, kindness, self-awareness, and ultimately nothing less than love in its most wondrous forms.

Love, Luv, Love

> "Perhaps Love is like a resting place, a shelter from a storm. It exists to give you comfort. It is there to keep you warm."
>
> **John Denver**

Ai is the Japanese word that expresses the feeling that there is a real bonding between people. The word is pronounced "eye". It forms the first part of the word *Aikido*. *Ai*, can be translated as harmony, balance, compatibility and reflection, relationship, and by some as (dare I say it?) love. The words *ai*, and love invoke the powers of mutual respect and awareness. *Ai* suggests honoring, encouraging, allowing, and encompassing difference. There is a gentleness as well as a firmness in *ai*. *Ai* speaks of overview at the same time as it speaks of detail.

Ai describes the harmony found in the relationship of the fingers to the thumb while making a fist, or the cooperation of clasping two hands with intertwined fingers. It includes grasping, clinging, and letting go. It may note holding of hands by couples or the holding of hands by people in a circle. *Ai* expresses itself in forms clapping hands, snapping fingers, beating drums, or bodies with hands, and with arms weaving and intertwining in the complexities of dance.

Ai, as harmony, balance, love, acts like water with wild sand. It is a unifying influence that allows for blending between humans while encouraging our very distinct individuality, and uniqueness.

Blending as an Applied Improvisation Professional

Practice in the blending of Improvisation activities establishes connections between people. These connections stay in place for a long time in an Improvisational environment; an organization that promotes the philosophies and practices of Improvisation.

In training and classroom settings, I tell participants that the most common teaching format describes one teacher with some number of students. Improv sees the gathering as having all the people in the room functioning as teachers as well as students. If I am truly to be a student, I must allow myself to be altered and affected by all my teachers. The more students, the more teachers, the greater the probability of real change, of real learning. Teaching by example, teaching participants to teach. As a student I model students to become one who learns. As an Applied Improvisation educator, I must do both.

NOTE

One thing required of teaching by example is real participation in the games being used. Improvisation structures are powerful as agents of change that the leader or teacher may be seen as a manipulator unless there is personal participation.

Leading and Leadership

There is a fundamental difference between leading and leadership. The ideas of leadership tend to identify someone who is in charge, who holds responsibility, one who makes decisions, and one who tells us where to go and what to do next. Overly strong leadership can actually inhibit learning and change. A teacher who seems to know too much can actually destroy a participant's motivation to learn. This does not mean that we should abdicate leadership, only that we must put it in a more effective perspective.

To Lead

From the Old English, *lithan*, meaning to go. Leading is such a complex thing. All skills of the effective Applied Improvisation Professional are grounded in leading. All the skills of management, supervision, de-elopement, production, organization, reorganization, communication, learning, and commerce are grounded in leading.

"To" go. This suggests that we must go where we ask our participants to go. Having been there before is not enough; even when we have been there time after time, we must go there again with new sets of people, and with new perspective.

Go where? Too often we think that this means only that we must go to the end of the trail, at which point the job will be done. This can be true, and goals are great for tracking and seeking benchmarks, for correcting and motivating, and for getting the job done. However, with Improvisation there is no end point. There is no final goal. There is only a process that grows as the participants grow. It is truly limitless in the extent to which it can be explored. It is more than a skill. It is more than a craft. It is an art that can be taken to the level of spiritual practice. Perfection or an end point are not within its aims. Leading, like Improvisation, is an exploration, and an experience that can be enhanced by a personal training system such as *Aikido*, meditation, tennis, or volunteer work.

Improvisation moves us into a state of mind in which we learn by doing. Being active in the use of Improvisation ideas and processes time and time again, and we must lead our participants by our personal example. As with other aspects of Improvisation, leading has a mental component, an emotional component, a physical component, and a spiritual component.

Mental Leading

Mental leading requires proactive composing of one's own mind. This usually takes some kind of disciplined practice, such as breathing, focused reading, prayer, exercise, stretching, mental gymnastics, listening to music, or meditation.

Mental leading requires creating an air of possibility. It is knowing that the work can be done and that the goals can be reached. Your position must be based in reality and honesty and must be continually reevaluated.

Mental leading really has the most to do with language based communication skills. I recommend that you read *Language in Thought and Action* by S. I. Hayakawa, and *Impro, Improvisation and the Theatre* by Keith Johnstone for developing these skills. Listed in the Bibliography.

Mental leading also has to do with time and place, and preparation. Chapter nine, "Language Is a Funny Thing", has further exploration in the realm of being on time and in time.

Emotional Leading

Emotional leading also requires preparation and disciplined practice. The preparation and discipline may be the same in both cases. Any physical or training practice may be enhanced by giving it a focus. Five minutes of making music, meditating, or running, or devoted to each aspect of blending and leading can result in 30 minutes of productive work. A problem in emotional leading is in identifying our own emotions. We must have a command of the field in order to lead. Just naming the emotions gives us some power over them. As you may have noted in the earlier exercise, naming your own emotions may be more difficult than one might expect. In an Improvisation exercise called *Emotional Symphony*, players call out the names of emotions and mimic sounds that might accompany them. At first I would line up six or eight people and ask them to name some emotions. It fascinated to discover that people began to run out of names for emotions when the group reached seven or eight of the basic of fear, hate, love, anger, lust, and joy.

My father was convinced that there were only thirty-two human emotions. He never gave me a list, yet it is probable that I had accepted the limit of his thinking. I could not imagine the limitation of people who could think of only eight or twelve ways to describe feelings. Then a participant arrived with a list of one hundred names of human emotions. Later I discovered a chart in the office of a psychologist that presented an array of nearly two hundred names for the ways we feel. I have since found a brainstorming program that very kindly, capriciously, whimsically, idiosyncratically, eccentrically, and humorously presented just over 2,700 descriptions of emotional states.

Whatever emotions we are feeling as we face participants in an Improvisation session, it is good to be aware of as many names and descriptions, variations, and subtleties as possible. The next exercise will help you in finding your own list of possibilities.

Your Own List of Emotions

Develop a list of all the emotions you can name. Do this in a single sitting and note the number you can generate from your own, unaided vocabulary. Keep the list and add to it over time. It is very good to work with the list before and after sessions in which you use your Improvisation skills and techniques. Check how many emotions have been evoked or used each time. Also take note of the levels of emotional intensity experienced. If you come up with few emotions or few highs or lows, the depth of your work may need more attention. Do the same after work that achieves breakthrough, insight, or enlightenment, or in sessions in which you have experienced stress, difficulty, or failure.

Try to come up with thirty-two names of emotions to start. Note that "OK" or "fine" are not names of emotions. If you have such words on your list, replace them with words that describe some real "feeling" that happens when the words "fine" and "OK" come to your mind. Hunger may be an emotion; hungry is not. Begin to observe yourself and your activities in relation to your list of emotions. Use a highlighter to note the emotions you most often experience or express easily.

Note the emotions with which you are least familiar for later personal work. Over time, explore internally for feelings described by the emotions with which you are not familiar. If you cannot access the feeling of unfamiliar emotions, try imagining what kind of situation might generate such a feeling in yourself or in others.

When you use feedback forms or evaluations in your group work, place your list of names of "emotions" on the evaluation form. Ask for distinctive names of emotions. Ask the participants for the number of these emotions that they have experienced. Ask about the intensity of various emotions. The exercise will help you and your organization to become increasingly aware of emotions, and where the effect of emotions, or lack of them, is impacting your work.

Freedom of emotional expression enhances learning, and supports retention; it also works to encourage deep changes in behavior. Emotional content that is excessive, disconnected, erratic, random, unnoticed, co-dependent ignored, or suppressed, can also stop development as well as twisting it beyond recognition. Improvisation will touch on the emotions of the participants. Effective teaching that includes the development of emotional content requires that we continuously lead the way in the exploration, and it is a good idea to look over our personal growth before, during, and after our organizational and presentational work.

Physical Leading

Physical leading goes beyond merely telling people what to do. It is another compound, complex concept. At its most basic level, it seems to work best when it requires that we put our own body on the line; that we have significant engagement in the plan at hand.

Sometimes this can be as simple as asking the gathering to stand up and sit down together. Physical leading often means giving up crutches such as podiums and notes. Sometimes it means taking a physical hand in helping to move the furniture around or serving refreshments. It has a great deal to do with being present, on time, in time, engaged in current time, and fully in your own physical body. When working with children, I find that I must often ask them to stay inside their own bodies. With adults I must do the same thing, yet more subtly and more gently.

Physical leading requires the use of our own laughter. Sometimes physical leading requires feeling and sharing more of our own true emotions. Emotional control may indicate strength in some circles, yet it is emotional comfort that creates a leader. As a matter of fact, failure to lead by example can easily teach the participants to withhold the emotional component of their own work.

Leading in the physical arena requires open sharing of our own weaknesses, errors, limits, mistakes, and personal evolution. Children learn a great deal from the sharing of the foibles and mistakes of their elders. Adults do the same, yet tend not to admit it. Adults usually have trouble sharing our weaknesses with others. This results in lost resources for everyone.

We really do respect people who have learned from their own mistakes, so it becomes necessary to present ourselves as being experienced, having accomplished enough to have made mistakes, and being smart enough to have learned something from them.

People want to know about people who have had real experiences and have overcome struggles. In leading with Improvisation, we learn about our own struggles so that others may use them.

Aikido

Aikido is a Japanese martial art developed entirely on the premise of using only defensive techniques to overcome overly active aggression, or what is often called an attack. There is no hitting nor kicking, hurting, or harming in *Aikido*. The art of *Aikido* is founded on the principle that violence begets violence, and therefore violence cannot be effectively managed by the use of violence. Having practiced, taught, studied, and lived this art for nearly 40 years, I am still learning to comprehend its depth.

Aikido is the practice and study of a wide range of physical and emotional techniques and principles. The mind is trained to be focused on, and to function from, the center of balance of the physical body, in motion. The center, or *hara*, will be explored in greater detail below.

The *hara* is considered to be the center of the will: the will to be, to do, to influence, and to create. The center of the being is connected to the center of everything. Discovering and understanding our own "center" is important in developing the heart of leading and leadership.

It takes effort in consciousness, practice, and discipline to locate our center and then more of the same to learn to move with and from that point. In any gathering there is also a center of balance of the group as a whole. It is independent yet interconnected with the centeredness of the organizational leadership and the individuals themselves. Centered leading and leading from the center are important ingredients in effective Applied Improvisation.

Relaxation as a Technique

Anything that must be done regularly and repetitively, or must be done over a long period of time, must be accomplished in states of relaxation that are balanced with activity. Relaxation and active tension, balanced in the body of an active leader, inspires confidence. Relaxation, or tension alone, in the same body, can inspire confusion, inattention, tension, fear, or even anger.

Complete relaxation requires consciousness, practice, and discipline.

In any exercise it is good to relax as completely as we can in between moments of muscle and body tension. While we are learning new movements, we may be fairly tense or awkward. This is partially because we are using our mind to do the learning. As we begin to let our body take over the learning and the practicing, our mind can become engaged in helping to relax the rest of the body.

I first learned the exercise that follows nearly forty years ago, and am still working to perfect it. It is a simple physical exercise that may come to you more or less easily. Twenty minutes, or a lifetime, spent learning this exercise will be worth your while.

The instructions are purposefully not accompanied by an illustration. It is important that you take the time to work through the process. Ask a friend to talk you through it if you wish. Once you are able to do the exercise a few times, the instructions will seem very clear and they will disappear. The remaining clarity is what we seek.

One Step, Two Steps

The steps begin with standing. There is a nearly perfect sweet balancing spot, the *hara*, which we can discover by standing with your feet a little more than shoulder width apart. Adjust your posture so that you are standing tall and easy in your body, hands hanging loosely, yet lively at your sides. Shift your weight back and forth between your feet. Do this to find that perfect, easy width and balance for your feet.

Once you have found that width, try to balance your weight evenly on both feet and evenly on both the balls, and heels of both feet. Do this for a while. Play with it. Dance with it, without moving your feet. Explore your whole body in your mind as you do this.

Once you are able to be comfortably balanced on both feet, begin shifting your weight back and forth from foot to foot. Keep readjusting your balance so that the weight stays equally on both feet and balanced on each foot as they find new places. Be aware of feelings in your body as you do this. Become aware of your arms. Keep them loose enough to swing slightly as you move.

Try moving your feet to new positions for a while: further apart, closer together, one a bit in front of the other. If you have fully explored this range of balance, and if you do not have other movement practice or training, this much may be enough for one session. If you are having fun. Move on.

One Step

- From your standing position, keep one foot gently and lightly in place.Shift and keep your weight evenly distributed as you step forward, then backward again and again with the other foot. Switch feet

112

and do the same with your feet in the opposite position.

- Then pivot. With your feet about shoulder distance, one in front of one another, keep one foot in place. Step forward again and again as you pivot around the foot held in place. Switch feet and go in the other direction for a while. Play with this and keeping your balance and your weight evenly distributed.
- Pivot backward. Switch feet and repeat the movement in the other direction. Remember to keep breathing.
- If you feel any dizziness, slow down and rest if needed. Notice whether you feel energy or tension anywhere in your body. You may feel tension in the back of your neck, tightness at the top of your head, or a constriction high in your chest. Breathe as though you are breathing into the locations of the feelings you notice.
- Each time you can invoke the connection between your feelings and their locations in your body, your ability to relax will grow stronger and gentler.
- This may be enough unless you are having too much fun.

Two Steps

Stand with your left foot pointing forward about a foot ahead of your right. Your right foot should be slightly, comfortably turned out, away from the direction in which your left foot is pointed.

- Keep your left foot in place. Step forward with your right foot.
- Slowly turn your hips to the left, letting your feet turn as well, until you are facing the opposite direction. At this point, your left foot will be forward. Your right foot turned slightly, gently outward.
- Then step backward with your left foot, allowing your right foot to adjust to pointing in the new forward.
- You are now standing with your right foot in front of your left, and facing the opposite direction. See that your right toes are pointed forward and your left toes comfortably away to the left.
- You will reverse the process and go back to where you began.
- Step forward with your left foot.
- Without letting your right foot stick to the floor, turn your hips to the right until you are facing the opposite direction. At the same time allow your feet to turn so they will face the same direction.
- Step back with your right foot.
- When you have successfully moved from the original position and back again, you have completed one whole set of Two Steps.
- You should be standing in your original position, facing the same way

as you started with your left foot forward. If you are not exactly in this position, take a short break and try the exercise again from the beginning.

- Once you have done it successfully, try two stepping for a few moments to make sure you have the hang of it. Learning to do just this much may be enough for a whole session.

NOTE

If you are still having trouble doing this exercise try contacting a local *Aikido* dojo and ask if you can come in and have someone teach you how to do this. The people at the dojo may know it as the two steps, *irimi-tenkan*, or as *udefuri-undo*. You can find an *Aikido Dojo*, practice hall, through The *Aikido* Association of America in Chicago, The United States *Aikido* Federation in New York City, or *Aikikai* Foundation in Tokyo Japan for international locations.[26]

Once you have mastered the Two Steps, giving twenty minutes a day to the exercise can have a positive influence on your physical, emotional, mental, spiritual, and organizational well-being.

If you are going to teach this exercise to others, it is necessary to practice advanced two stepping, as described below. It is important that you consciously consider the manner in which you personally went through it when you first tried. The more difficult it was to accomplish, the more it was an indication that you were not operating through your center of balance. Knowing this about yourself can give you valuable information for working with others doing the exercise.

Advanced Two Stepping

Keep trying until you can do the original exercise with ease. Remember that I am still learning after nearly 40 years. Try again to learn whether you have a sense of where the major weight or motion tends to reside in your body. It may be in your shoulders or forehead, your knees or hips. It may be in your hands, feet, jaw, or chest.

When you are doing Two Steps fairly easily, you can begin to move more quickly. As you move faster, you may find yourself leaning backward as you take the backward step. If you experience this, you can begin to shift

---

[26]My recommendation in your home town is to be certain that you are contacting an *Aikido* dojo and not a martial arts organization that advertises *Aikido* as one of a number of arts.

114

your weight forward at exactly the same moment that you step backward. This will compensate for the centrifugal force and the momentum going in the opposite direction. As we begin this compensation movement, we are liable to find ourselves tilting to the front. As soon as you become aware of this happening, begin to shift your weight toward your center of balance. Play with this.

If you have been successful taking these two steps at a faster and faster pace, you may notice that your hands and arms can have a lot of effect on how the movement works. If your arms are just flying around, they can pull you off balance. The higher the speed, the more this is true. If you are holding your hands and arms stiffly, they will cause your body to stiffen and will inhibit the speed at which you can turn. Begin to relax and you can gain gentle, supple control of your hands and arms as you turn.

At this point it may be good to think of this as spinning playfully around with the goal of being the ability to stop fully balanced and completely centered, relaxed; weight held equally by both feet, and your whole body all at once, breathing easily, filled with love, light, laughter, and joy.

Try to start the turn with your hands directly in front of you, fingers in relaxed tension, arms relaxed and slightly bent. The palms are facing each other a few inches apart. Your hands should be extended a few inches away from your body at about the level of your navel. Starting with your left foot in front of your right. If you are relaxed, your right hand may be slightly ahead of the left. Take your next Two Steps.

As you make the turns, bring your left hand close to the front and center of your body, cupped with the palm upward. Lay your right hand into the cup of your left hand with the fingers pointed in the opposite direction. As you face the opposite direction, extend your hands in front of you again. Now your right foot will be forward and, if you are relaxed, your right hand may be a bit in front of the left.

If after effort and practice, this does not make sense, then contact an *Aikido* dojo for guidance. It is not unusual for people to need some assistance in accomplishing the exercise at this level. If you can work it out for yourself, there will be hidden benefits. The more you practice the easier it becomes. There is no end point. It is a lifetime exploration.

This exercise will bring you into a closer working relationship with your center of balance. Being in your center of balance will enable you to be much more aware of the balances involved in your work and play. Working from your center of balance is very helpful for inspired Improvisational work.

Once you have mastered this movement, you may find that it is an excellent activity to teach to small groups. It has been my experience that vast amounts of development can be accomplished in a minimum amount of time by teaching this simple task. Do it with minimum talk at first and add words later. Do not plan the actual presentation. Lead the exploration through the presentation.

Spiritual Leading

The use of Improvisation to its fullest brings us again to an invisible aspect to life. Improvisation can entice individuals to look more deeply into internal, invisible aspects of their lives and personal motivations, which will lead to the extraordinary invisible powers of laughter. Laughter is a healing mechanism. Laughter brings people together and helps them to overcome differences. Laughter offers perspective. These are the very things of which the spirit is made.

The leadership of the spirit comes not from the way in which we do things, nor from the way in which we talk about things. It comes from the way in which we walk in the world. In Improvisation we walk facing the invisible, looking into the realm of sprit. This is also the direction of the source of creativity.

We all must approach and learn of the spiritual world from our own personal perspectives. Improvisation works and has value as merely a methodology and technique. Extraordinary benefits, however, come from deeper exploration. Much like deciding to investigate the deeper aspect of Two Steps, we will be served well to seek the depth of the invisible, the realm of the spirit. We must put its lessons into practice, and then perhaps, in a lifetime of joyous pursuit, we may learn to master a spiritual approach to Improvisational Leading.

Finding your feelings and feeling your way are methods of living what has been best called the examined life. Doing this will require you to become aware of the feelings and emotions of others, as well as becoming aware of your own feelings and emotions. When you engage Improvisation, you will find yourself faced with such real tools as the power of love, and the depth of blending. You will learn to delight in the responsibilities of physical and emotional leading, and the wonders of the spirit of Improvisation.

We can also use Improvisation as a tool without considering any of this. We may use the games, exercise the exercises, gain the benefits, walk the paths, create the creativity, and benefit from the results without doing anything more than participating and playing according to enough of the suggested considerations, the tips, maxims, rules, guidelines to help it work and be fun. The depth and power are part of the process. If we really work with it, our consciousness will be altered. In order to develop the process and take advantage of the power of Improvisation, it is also good to review and notice the power of language, as seen in the next chapter.

CHAPTER NINE

Language Is a Funny Thing

Language is a primary means by which we engage one another in conversation, literature, poetry, information, directions, education, song, mathematics, prayers, curses, invectives, and *Babble*. Language is both "funny ha, ha" and "funny peculiar." Language can be the most important of things, and the least important of things. Words have many meanings and endless connotations, yet any single word is merely a symbol squiggled on a page, or a wave vibrated through the air. At the same time, a wrong word can leave an eternal scar. A right word can help us transcend time itself.

Language can become the least meaningful in verbal form. The messages sent by your body can overshadow the meanings of the words. Body language can modify, enhance, expand, or deny the message of your words. Body language can send messages that are either parallel or at right angles to the original intent. Effective Improvisation Management suggests that we engage in extraordinary attention to the details involved in all aspects of the use of language.

A Look at Language

The human vocal system is capable of hundreds of small sounds. Standard American English has forty-seven specific sound units called phonemes that have been cataloged and identified in the International Phonetic Alphabet.[27] The human body is capable of thousands of subtle movements. The small "signals" of the human body have not been fully cataloged, although some researchers calculate that as much as seventy-five percent of our message is carried by our body language.

English language dictionaries define about two million entries. There are many agreed upon meanings of body signals with considerations that widely diverging cultures may have great differences: a wave, a shrug, the irritated ping of a foot. There are definitions of physical signals used in various industries: airport guide signs, TV and movies, the military, among others. There is an agreed upon international sign language for people with hearing difficulties. There is, however, no general dictionary of the language of the body. It is, so far; too personal and too vast to encompass. A wink of the eye may say nearly anything.

We cannot objectively observe our own body language in action. We can rarely really know exactly what is being communicated by the language of our own body, if only because the meaning resides completely in a usually non-verbal interpretation.

As Improvisational Executives we must become extraordinarily aware of what is being said by the entire individual, and the body of the gathering. This skill develops with awareness of our own bodies.

Improvisation operates at amazing speeds, activating very deep feelings. Without an understanding of the depth and nature of the language of the body, we can find ourselves behind the curve of comprehension. Without engaging in an understanding of the languages of the body, we may create resistance and ill will within a gathering. Being completely present with and aware of body language opens many doors to using Improvisation as a business tool.

---

[27] E. C. Glenn, and S. Forman, *Your Voice and Articulation*, Englewood Cliffs, NJ: Prentice Hall, 1989. For an excellent overview of the components of the human voice and language.

Presence

At least 15 percent of our communication will be transmitted by our personal presence. One form of presence is known as stage presence, the ability to fill a room with our energy and to give our being to be felt by all.

This has to do with energy, and the ability to be completely, and passionately involved in what we are doing.

This form of presence can be most apparent in our relaxed confidence. It is reflected in the brightness in our eyes, the lightness of our step, and the ways in which we reach out to the people around us. Everyone knows someone who commands attention by simply entering a room, without fanfare nor introduction. This is sometimes called "star quality" at higher public levels. When working at a business level, some skill in this out-going presence is a basic skill.

Another form of presence I have spoken of before is being present in the moment; that is, the act of being totally and completely in the current moment, with *these* feelings, in *these* surroundings, doing this thing, focused on these people, thinking about this event and these words, without reference to any other time or place. The most powerful presence comes from being so completely in the present moment that there is simply nowhere else to be.

Let's take a moment to add up the amount of communication "stuff" that is used up before we utter a single word. Seventy-five percent body language, and fifteen percent presence comes to ninety percent. I maintain that an additional five percent of available communication energy is wrapped up with the language we speak, the syntax of our first language, and the semantics of our meaning.

Five percent remain for cognition, energy, process, or whatever it takes to carry the message you have in your mind. Remember the message is the "last, most important" element in our communication, even though we tend to spend much of our energy and focus on this five percent. If you will offer only as little as half of your attention and energy to the ninety-five percent of what happens before the words begin, the chances of your success in Improvisation can be increased a thousand fold.

General Semantics

A specialty field in the study of communication is called General Semantics; the study of the meaning of meaning. It considers such questions as "How and why do words have meaning?" and "How do we know what meaning is made of?" If something means something it has meaning, right? What do I mean by that? "I mean, what does the meaning of meaning mean?"

This academic pursuit has origins in the work of Count Alfred Korzybski, as articulated in his exceptional work entitled *Science and Sanity: An Introduction to Non-Aristotelian and General Semantics*, published in 1933. A more accessible book in the same field is by S. I. Hayakawa, *Language in Thought and Action*, first published in 1939.

General Semantics searches deeply into the exciting and extraordinary miracle that words and actions can, indeed, communicate thoughts and ideas, that one human being can actually formulate an idea and another can receive that idea through language. The truth is that we do not fully understand how this happens. That a language can be learned and spoken and written is a foundation of civilization. While whales and elephants may be able to communicate with one another over long distances, they cannot, we assume, learn the languages of one another, or of humans. That human language can be reproduced, recorded, broadcast, electronically transferred, and maybe even psychically transmitted surpasses the miraculous.

Levels of Abstraction and Stasis

Very important elements of the study of General Semantics are the theories of *abstraction* and *stasis*. The organizing principle of stasis is that all language-based communication deals with abstract thought.

All that language can do is to provide names, or descriptions for things, and processes, and relationships. The names are abstractions; they are not the things themselves. The word for a chair is not the chair itself. The word for a thought is not the thought itself. Words are only an imaginary and agreed upon depiction of the item or the concept. They function as a map that helps us understand the real thing. However, as Count Korzybski said, "The map is not the territory". Personal abstractions are "maps" attached to words that may make our communication even more complex.

Consider the following levels of abstraction as we explore the word and idea that we call a chair, a simple thing to sit on. The furniture dealer may "abstract" the chair to the level of representing his inventory, or his personal income. These are certainly some steps away from the original chair. To a craftsperson the chair may represent an abstraction of her self-image. To an engineer the chair may suggest a structural principle, or design pattern, and to an atomic physicist the very same chair may be seen as a combination of atoms and subatomic particles. To a son or daughter a chair may be abstracted to the level of a memory of an ancestor, Grandma's heirloom. To a freezing person the chair may be a source of wood heat. To a person of the spirit the very same chair may be representative of a higher being, a God who is responsible for the existence of the chair.

Each of these "meanings" indicates that a different level of abstraction has been attached to the original item. The meanings assigned are all at different imaginary steps away from the real chair, this specific chair, the particular set of atoms and molecules that make up this real chair at this real time, which is absolutely unique in all the universe.

If one person sees the chair as a four-legged thing on which to sit and the other sees it as a piece of furniture on which to sit, there is still a slightly different level of abstraction, yet they are not so far apart that there will be confusion or conflict. When people are speaking of the same chair at the same level of abstraction, or at a level of abstraction that is close enough for communication to work, it is said that they have achieved "stasis." If people are speaking of the same chair, and one of them is talking about a source of heat and the other is talking about a treasured memory, the levels of abstraction are distant, with disturbing misunderstanding. In this circumstance the participants have not achieved stasis.

If a child leans back in a chair as an exercise in learning balance, it can conflict terribly with a teacher who abstracts the action to the level of disrespect for public property. With an understanding of "stasis", we can hope to manage our differences; we can actively seek the same or similar levels of abstraction in the matters about which we communicate.

Through this brief description of stasis, we can see how complicated things can become when we are sharing about something as simple as a chair. Imagine what happens as we engage in more subtle and complex matters, things such as emotion, time and space, politics, religion, philosophy, and the unknown. Try talking about love, hate, truth, and beauty without achieving stasis and it may turn out to be explosive.

The realities of communication, and the theories of Improvisation speak to the need for understanding, and arriving at a state of lovely balance by the simple engagement in Improvisation games. This engagement operates at pre-verbal levels. We begin with the commitment to being in time and on time, in the current moment. Because we force ourselves into the time frame of the present, many of the problems of stasis failure are never encountered. Because we are actually inventing meaning and agreeing on our levels of abstraction as we work and play together, we automatically either come to stasis, or we create situation comedy, if not trouble.

Situation comedy is the embodiment of stasis failure. In the television program "I Love Lucy", almost every difficulty arose from the fact that Lucy was working on some fear, jealousy, or insecurity and Ricky was operating on some ruse, or at face value. Improvisation executives will do well to study stasis and to seek stasis.

On Time, and In Time

Language is so complex that its fine points operate at speeds faster than jet travel. It actually operates at the speed of sound. It takes extreme concentration and attention to avoid errors, and even total concentration can fail. To engage concentration it is necessary to be on time and in time. Improvisation suggests that you commit to a real discipline being on time and in time. One of the less abstract meanings of this idea is that the Applied Improvisation Professional must be on location, and in the location of the gathering before your assigned and advertised time.

It is my experience that unless we are present a minimum of half an hour before the beginning of an event, we may be "on time", yet not ever quite "in time." Fifteen minutes may be enough time only if we have worked in that location earlier on the same day. If you have not, my recommendation is that you arrive a minimum of half an hour prior to the time of group activity.

Being in time and on time requires forethought, desire, planning, focus, discipline, and effort. When I am unfamiliar with a location, my practice is to arrive ninety minutes to two hours prior to the start time. When working in a strange city, my preference is to arrive a day before. In Improvisation, though there is no time spent in rehearsal, preparation is still a major part of the Improvisation formula.

The truth is that we, as professionals, are able to work in any setting as an accomplished improviser, I adapt immediately to any circumstance. As a professional Improviser. I know that the seating and setting can turn a walk in the park into an uphill battle.

I have had the experience of sending a floor plan to site planners only to arrive to find the setting completely wrong, not just incorrect, yet looking as though it were designed specifically to facilitate difficulty and failure. I have also experienced the delight of setting up a room the night before for an early meeting only to find that some kind soul has rearranged it by meeting time.

Proactive Presence

Even if we are actively involved in a specific discipline designed to help keep us in current time, it is important that we seriously engage in some activity to bring ourselves into the space of the event and the moment of the gathering. Being on time as described above will result in being in time as well. If we are time lagged, it is extremely important that we engage actively in some practice that will help us achieve and stay in the present moment. If you are a "morning person" working in the afternoon, you must give yourself some discipline that will bring you to the "there and then".

You will find that ten minutes of quiet time can do wonders for your presence. Prayer or meditation is an active practice that can bring us into this moment. A quiet walk, breathing exercises, a wide variety of physical exercises, singing a specific song, and clapping your hands to a set rhythm will all provide help in bringing you to this most important Improvisation rule. Several exercises in this book can be used to enhance your presence in the moment simply by focusing on being present as you do the exercise.

Surroundings

This discussion is still really about language. I make certain that I have time to wander around a larger activity location. Some of this helps me be familiar with simple logistics and housekeeping. It is good to know where the restrooms and ATMs are. It is even better to know what the restrooms look like and how the water in the building tastes. This is very important in your own business location. It is even more important when your business has multiple locations and you are gathering people in a location where you do not normally work.

It is good to be familiar with some of the particular day's experience that may have an effect on participants. I have been known to walk in a circle around a building and to wander around aimlessly just to see what the participants see as they arrive. In hotels, convention centers, corporate headquarters, and business meeting facilities, I gain early access to the meeting space, ride the elevators, and check out food, water, coffee, and other amenities. I find my way into adjacent areas, audiovisual booths, back rooms, and service access areas, it gives me information regarding secondary surroundings. Go in the side door. Take local transportation. Walk around the block. Do anything you can to experience the surroundings that will touch you and your participants. In your own organization, it is good to look over familiar locations periodically with new eyes just to see what you have never seen before.

When working in a strange city, it is always good to be familiar with recent news and weather, with sports events, and with local politics. Listen to the radio, take a look at a local television station, and read the headlines, and Google the site.

If we are aware of the circumstances that can affect our participants' sense of the present, we have a much stronger chance of leading them into and keeping them in the present moment with us. The more we know about where they are at the beginning, the more able we will be to go along with them to where we all need to be.

Playing with Words

Humans have a natural tendency to play with words. This can be both fun and frustrating. An informal game we all play at some time or another is to say one thing when we mean another. When working with Improvisation, what we are saying out loud and what we are feeling inside needs to be as close to the same as possible. If our words to the people with whom we are working are "Hello, I'm glad to be here", and inside, we are asking "What am I doing here?" the inside message will be transmitted behind and underneath everything we have to say.

The people around us often know how we really are, no matter how good we are at keeping our thoughts and feelings inside. My second Improvisation idea is that we must strive to become honest with our self. My third Improvisation idea is that we must learn to be honest with at least one other person. So, even when we are really good at keeping our internal language to ourselves, we are struggling against basic rules, if it differs from the external.

Avoiding the Pun

My son, since the age of three, has been delighted by the fact that words can have more than one meaning. As he has grown, he has both loved and hated the fact that many words can sound the same and have different meanings or sound the same and then have the same or similar meanings and different sounds.

While my love for the pun is deep and long, my delight is heightened by more expansive terms such as "word play', and with the French for double entendre, or triple entendre.

The word "pun" first appeared during the 17th Century. Its roots are in the idea of quibbling over a fine point. The pun is a limited form of word play. Except in the form called *Word Montage*, the pun has little value in working with Improvisation, and can actually be detrimental to its goals and purposes.

The best way I can explain the problem of the pun is to have you imagine that there is a "pun gremlin." When the use puns appear, a pun gremlin also appears, and encourages an infectious trend whereby one pun results in another and another, often leading to a pun battle.

Pun battles, considered by themselves, can be fast, fun, and furious. The pun path can lead from duels to wholesale wars of words. It can also break down into a deep silliness and mind debilitating searching for the next sally. The problem with the pun in an Improvisation situation is that there is different neural circuitry involved in the process. The search for the pun requires a survey of old patterns based in verbal language processing.

While the use of the pun can encourage wonderful language creativity, it is not, in and of itself, creative in the sense of creating new things. It is a little like using old Lego® pieces to invent new structures, and it can be destructive to the processes of Improvisation.

The pun event is also generally based in competition. In learning and organizational settings, competition is generally counterproductive to Improvisation processes. Personal, internal competition is something else, yet when working with Applied Improvisation it is best that competition be avoided.[28]

Listening to Our Language

Creative word play includes more than the simple use of puns. There are the complexities of semantics and General Semantics to consider as well as the interplay of cultural and linguistic differences in language.

Semantics refers to the idea that words may have many meanings and a variety of connotations. These meanings can change across regions, cultures, subcultures, and age groups and over time and space. There are many parts of the world in which the English language is spoken, yet can barely be understood by others who speak the "same" language. Other generally recognized issues of language appear when we run into words that anger or vilify particular individuals or groups. These may be known as "buzz words", as "politically incorrect" words, or simply as mean, thoughtless words.

There are sets of words that cannot be used in polite society without negative consequence, and hosts of words that can mark a person as a member of or as an outsider of a particular social group.

Deeper than this is the fact that individuals associate meanings that are personal to many words. Such meanings may activate memories and emotions and may even generate endocrine system responses. Further, the activation of certain responses in one person can be transmitted to others in the group. Sometimes these reactions are transmitted via body language that may be visible to the observant and prepared presenter or executive. Sometimes reactions are transmitted via pheromones even before body language is apparent. A single word can activate human response. The presence of laughter in the forms of Improvised Creativity can overcome, or at least ameliorate, the negative effects of the power of words. It can also enhance all levels of communication.

Considerations of language, and body language, and of General Semantics, and of stasis all lead us again to the power of being in and on time. To help our language-based communication to be better for all, we can manage the factors and effects of personal presence and our connotative surroundings. This leads us again to the notion that "information is the last, most important element in a communication".

The mind is like a home; it must be opened in order to be used to its fullest extent. New materials must be introduced gently and consciously.

---

[28] Keith Johnstone invented an Improvisation competition form called Theatre Sports® and David Shepherd created Improv Olympics®, and there have been a number of games and structures in Improvisational Comedy Theatre that have found great fun in having teams compete with one another, yet never within any team.

Old patterns must be changed carefully and with respect. Fear must be allowed to surface and be addressed. The body and its languages must be engaged. Every available element of language must be considered and attended to. Then will come the gifts, joys, long lasting effects, and miracles of the use of Improvisation as a tool in all aspects of real life. With a grounding in some of these mechanics, we can begin to use our words, to play with our words, and to discover that deep within the desire to communicate, wholesome laughter leads the way.

CHAPTER TEN

Wholesome Laughter Leads the Way

Knowing how to use laughter is as important as any other necessary, human skill. Communication, made safe by the joyful development of wholesome laughter environments, is at the center of creativity. Improvisation is an important subdivision of the study of laughter. Easy and effective use of laughter requires practice. Exercise your skills of laughter to keep them strong and to make them limber. We can train ourselves in the ways of laughter and practice its use. The existence of laughter is a gift; treat it with respect and awe.

"There are three things which are real: God, human folly, and laughter. Since the first two pass our comprehension, we must do what we can with the third."

Aubrey Menen[29]

The laughter that surrounds us provides some true points of evaluation of the quality of our lives and work. The measurements of laughter are abstract. The precise rules and graphs of laughter's tracks are not perfectly understood; a bit like gravity. Still there are useful things we know about laughter that allow us to see our world under brighter lights.

Using brighter light is a technical matter. The manipulation of light energy, electromagnetic play, is at the foundation of our advanced technology. From the computer to relative quantum biochemical probabilities, we work with light.

If the computer is the box
where Schrodinger placed his cat,
then our computer mouse will
bring us 'round the circle.
Laughter is a quality of light.
Light laughter is a healing thing.
Laughter lightly bears gifts of perspective.
Quality laughter guards against and heals
the roughened edges of stress.
Loving, hearty, laughing, lightly,
guarding, healing colleagues are a bliss.
Natural laughter is a blessing as a human skill.
Hearty laughter has a host of healthy benefits.
Light, real, healing, hearty, quality,
relaxing, energizing, guarding
laughter is a gentle teacher.
Happily laughing students
are easy to learn from.
True and fair laughter
supports living things.
Honest laughter lifts our minds.
Light, real, healing, hearty, quality,
relaxing, energizing, guarding,
teaching, happily learning,
true and fair, supporting, honest
laughter lifts our spirits.

---

[29] Aubrey Menen, *Rama Retold*, p. 231, 1954. In the first edition of Improvisation, Inc. this was erroneously attributed this quote to Elizabeth Neeld. Apologies to all.

Appropriate and soft laughter among us can encourage easy and productive communication, especially when the business at hand is both serious and difficult. A basic measure of excellence in organizational development is visible when communication is easy and productive, especially when matters are both serious and difficult. Helping organizational communication to become easy and productive and to stay that way takes practice.

Training and practice in the presence of good, light laughter become more efficient and most pleasant. Training with laughter is a skill and study of its own. It begins with taking notice of some values and disciplines of laughter.

Some Values of Laughter

It is said that happy, healthy children laugh out loud up to hundreds of times in a day. It has also been calculated that normal, healthy adults laugh as few as ten or twenty times in a day. For a creative environment, this is not enough. For some, laughter once a day is as much as can be hoped for. For many, the lack of laughter accompanies loss of vitality and health.

As adults we really do need to practice the art of laughing to keep it alive and well. We can discipline ourselves to generate laughter as part of our daily lives. This effort is good for our health, good for our souls, and good for our general states of mind. It is good for our children and all our loved ones. It is necessary for our work as Improvisational Leaders.

A Few Simple Disciplines

A first simple discipline in developing laughter is to actively seek things to laugh about, and to look for people with whom we can laugh. Perhaps a survey of your life is in order. Over the course of a few days, keep notes to count the frequency of your own laughter. Notice how this process works for you. The days you record do not have to be consecutive. Keep a small pad handy to keep a simple tally; it can be very telling. Keep tabs on the categories you discover.

Try the following:
- Tally a mark each time you are aware of hearing laughter in your surroundings. Make one list for home, one for business, another for social settings.
- Tally a mark each time you hear laughter from your spouse, parent, child, or associate.
- Tally a mark each time you notice a silly sign.
- Tally a mark each time you smiled at someone and said thanks.
- Tally a mark each time someone smiles and says thanks to you.

129

- Take special notice of the time you spend not keeping track.

Set a goal of adding five incidents of laughter to your day. Then set a goal of adding five incidents to each category each day. Seek cartoons, jokes, audiotapes, or videotapes, or merely look around and find new things that can help you laugh. Once you have started to laugh five more times each day, begin adding five more incidents at random to days or to categories. Then add more categories until you begin to lose count. If you already laugh more often than you can count, and if that laughter is wholesome and delightful, then figure out for yourself how you could double your laughter a couple of days out of a week. Perhaps this will support the points at which you can add laughter to the days of others.

Laughter Workouts

There are a number of ways of establishing a wholesome laughter environment. One is by simply committing yourself to laughing out loud for no reason other than to generate laughter. Do this ten times per day. If this is uncomfortable for you, then find or manufacture new reasons to laugh ten more times each day. If this is difficult, try for five each and build on that.

Laughter Workout Equipment

If you are going to train yourself in laughter awareness, you may want some work-out equipment. This includes humor books and tapes of all sorts. YouTube has wonderful resources of comedians and comedy history. There are also many cartoon books that deal in really good, clean fun and frivolity. I like some of the larger cartoon books that are available in most bookstores. My personal preferences run to *Calvin and Hobbes*, *Peanuts*, *The Far Side*, *Pogo*, and *Sylvia*. These works offer a depth and breadth of primarily clean humor that is above the average.

I encourage you to find any available source of wholesome humor. Personal laughter is personal. Laugh at anything that tickles you. Find anything that will help you enter into the realm of habitual, wholesome laughter. I also recommend against material that explores too deeply or too intensely the negative side of laughter. This is no indictment of negative humor, nor of humor about negative things. Rather it refers to the fact that negative humor does not work as efficiently for the development of a wholesome daily laughter environment. It has other purposes both in healing, and in destructive endeavors. It is probably also good to avoid strictly topical humor about business, politics, and religion while building a daily laughter environment. Most political cartoons fall into this category. These excellent areas of a mirthful universe are better explored with a firm foundation of positive, wholesome daily laughter already in place.

If your taste goes to the macabre, the old "Addams Family" cartoons are worth a look. I also enjoy the "Doonesbury" cartoons, although they tend to a level of seriousness that is, for me, close to borderline in regard to building a living laughter habit. "Garfield" sometimes sits on a negative edge, as "Dilbert" definitely does. Most of the daily newspaper cartoons are not as negative as they are insipid or pointless. They may not offer the best laughter equipment.

My cartoon references are probably fairly out of date yet there is much laughter to be found even going back to "Archy and Mehitabel".

There are many audiotapes and videotapes filled with great laughter material. Almost any of the tapes, audio or video, are better for your laughing soul than almost any daily newscast. Be aware that many recorded stand-up comics are completely based in dirty humor. Again, laugh! Yes, laugh. And note the source of the laughter and go for a higher standard. There are a wide variety of books of humor, joke books, and books of humorous stories.

A fellow humorist, Jeff Justice, recommends that we keep a humor file. This file may be a manila folder in which we can keep funny pictures, cartoons, and stories that come by us in the course of each day. If you will keep such a file and commit to putting material into the file each day, you will begin seeing sources of laughter that might otherwise pass your notice. These are training tools that can help build a wholesome laughter environment.

The Kindness of Strangers

Engaging strangers in light conversation can seem a little more difficult, yet it is also very effective in the pursuit of a wholesome laughter environment. Random comments made out loud in public can garner random responses and can open conversations, create contact, or maybe merely gather a smile. This practice is not about telling jokes nor "going for laughs."

Fishing for light conversation is to be done with great kindness, gentleness, and light fun. All comments should be spontaneous and random. It is very easy to offer such comments out loud in grocery or movie lines or on elevators. There is very little risk involved, and it can be quite fun.

To encourage conversational contact with a stranger while standing in a line, look around and notice things going on around you. Then simply speak out loud about what you have observed in the direction of someone you do not know who is standing near you. If this is difficult, take a friend along to stand nearby who can pretend to be the object of remarks. Challenge your friend to try doing the same. If there are several people in line no one will know to whom your comments are made. At first, comments do not need to be focused on humor or laughter. They do need to be positive and should require no reply. Quick complements are always nice. If you keep trying, eventually you will begin to find comments that create laughter. Keep trying, even after you have stumbled onto a few funny lines that you have tried and no one even notices. Keep training. Keep watching humorous tapes and reading books, and looking around yourself for the humor that is natural to life.

Elevator Laughter

On elevators it is best to have at least three other people present when offering random comments out loud, otherwise you may frighten someone. A particular business elevator was in my life for a number of years. The elevator had a voice that says things such as, "First floor, going up" and "Tenth floor, going down". Often, when I was on the elevator with a few others, in response to the elevator I would say, "One day I expect it to say, 'First floor, going sideways.'" I always got some laughter. Once in a while someone moved a little farther away from me.

On another business elevator there were always people entering on various floors so when someone asked "What floor?" or "Where to" my response would be something like "Bermuda, please," and there would always be laughter. This did not require that there be several riders in the elevator. Eventually when I asked for Bermuda another rider chimed in with, "Saturday, please".[30] Before long there were a few others, I had never seen, who began to use the shtick.

Elsewhere

During meetings, workshop sessions, or gatherings of any kind, use some of your break time to practice making random observational comments, out loud. Use the same techniques as you use in grocery store lines. There is a higher level of risk in this exercise because there may be colleagues present. Find anything you can to say about a painting, or talk to a coffee pot in imaginary conversation. Complement a tie or a necklace, or a smile, or a room decoration, or the time of year. Do this out loud. It is not necessary to become a "jokester". This discipline is also fun and pays great dividends. A discreet healing laughter, focused comment to a person near you, or merely out loud to no one in particular, can create a mirthful moment and a satisfying human event. Play with this idea. Make it your own.

If you are too shy or too nervous to engage in these sorts of activities, simply work more slowly with yourself. Start with tapes or cartoons and

---

[30] When I started doing this my request was for Majorca until one young woman looked at the buttons, became distressed, and pleaded, "What's that?" Thereafter I kept my comments simple.

build up to it. These small practices will add humor to your life and laughter to your days. They can also help you to build a repertoire of stories of human contact if you keep a laughter journal.

Active participation in laughter discipline, as a necessary and healthy part of life, is important to the successful development of an Applied Improvisation practice. We can lead the way by the manner in which we live, not merely by the words we choose to deliver.

Some Improv Humor Suggestions

These are my own guidelines for Improvisational humor. I have discovered that they apply to Improvisational work at all levels. They also apply to other humor venues as well. They are especially functional when working with family, business, academia, and community. Following these guidelines can help to create the atmosphere of safety in which Improvisation and creativity can work best. The use of these suggestions helps the mind to seek the highest and most creative expressions. The use of these ideas will help to keep improvising participants in current time. All this is done to encourage healthy playfulness.

Laughter Heals

Invoke laughter, yet do not seek it. Seeking laughter for its own sake is the work of the comedian. Invoking laughter by developing a receptive environment is the work of the Improviser. Laughter is a healing force in the human world. The means by which we create laughter cannot be separated from the laughter itself. If we laugh to the delight and innocence of others, we cause an increase in joy. If we laugh at the expense of others, we cause a decrease in joy. Educating ourselves about the nature and value of laughter heals as well.

It Is Good to Poke Fun at Ourselves

You have the right, and sometimes the obligation, to poke fun of yourself. There is strength and confidence in the ability to point to your own errors and unique ways. The practice of seeking humor at your own expense develops your authority as well as your humanity.

Beware of Making Fun of Others

To poke fun at others is usually dangerous, and can be offensive. If we feel you must do so, your target must be members of a group easily identified as our own group, or members of a group that is clearly superior to our own. Men may usually roast men yet not of women, nor women men.

Young people can safely taunt one another, yet doing the same with their elders. Elders who make fun of themselves can be delightful yet when they make sport of youngsters they can create distance and reinforce generational separateness.

If we mock another who is in a superior category to our own, we may risk being eaten (figuratively, if not in reality). This may also be necessary, in spite of the consequence. If we ridicule another who is in some category that is weaker than ours we may be seen as a bully or worse. If we cannot easily and immediately discern these distinctions such as these, never make fun of anyone other than yours and yourself.

Keep It Clean

"Dirty" humor has absolutely no place in an Applied Improvisation setting, remembering that all humor can be good fun in the correct surroundings. With the exception being exceptionally clever, or very new - a rare thing - dirty humor is adolescent at best.

This category includes blue humor, toilet humor, sex jokes, innuendo, double entendre, scatological humor and anything that might be considered unacceptable by the group as it is composed. This also includes racist, sexist, ageist, feminist, masculinist, and anything-else-ist humor. Should you encounter a group in which dirty humor is acceptable, do not go there yourself. Your Improvisation will suffer if you do.

Keep It Gentle

Avoid humor based on gender, religion, sexuality, terrible disease catastrophic events, aircraft accidents, Nazism, recent deaths, and politics in general. It is probably a good idea to avoid humor based on any of the most awful news of any day.

Our Bodies are Truly not all that Funny

Generally avoiding humor based on bodies and their functions is the best practice. This includes reference to nose hair, ear wax, fingernail and toenail clippings, belly button lint, body hair, body parts, body size, body shape, body sounds, body odors, and all private body realities.

Use Your Own Stuff

Do not use another person's words as your own. Especially avoid humorous lines from movies, the Internet, television, and radio. Others saw the same shows and they will know the source of your wit.

Sweet and Easy Carries the Day

Be considerate, thoughtful, playful, careful, kind, fun, delighted, joyous, filled with light, personal, grateful, interested, other-centered, open, relaxed, sensible, and as sweet and easy as you can be.

Will, Not Wit

The very best humor comes from true observation of the moment. It does not come from wit. The best laughter often comes from honest atttempt, regardless of the results. "Laugh, and the World Laughs with You."

Seek laughter as a part, as a discipline of life. Seek creation of wholesome laughter environments. Laugh. Laugh some more. Keep laughing.

Laughter as a Measurement Device

This is as technical as subjective laughter measurement gets. If we can gain useful feedback using laughter, we can gain some control over the effectiveness of all communication environments. The measures of laughter are abstract and approximate, just as some measures of subatomic particle activity are abstract and approximate.

First Measure: Types of Laughter

There are qualities in laughter that we can identify. My search for definitions produced an initial exploration.

To Laugh: vi
1. a: to show mirth, joy, or scorn with a smile or
chuckle, or explosive sound.
b: to find amusement or pleasure in something.
c. to become amused or derisive.
2. a: to produce the sound or appearance of laughter.
b: to be of a kind that inspires joy.

Laugh: n
1. the act of laughing.
2. a: cause for derision or merriment.
b: an expression of scorn or mockery.

LOL: Internet chat language meaning to laugh out loud.

Laughter: The sound of laughing.

I was not satisfied with these definitions. There was nothing in the

135

dictionary that spoke about side-splitting, face-hurting, falling-down, sustained explosions of joy and delight. This kind of laughter had been so much a part of my family experience. I extended my search to a thesaurus and came up with more words.

Snicker: To laugh in a covert or partly suppressed way.

Chuckle: To make a continuous gentle sound like suppressed mirth.

Titter: A loud, high-pitched chuckle.

Giggle: To laugh with repeated short catches of the breath.

Guffaw: A loud or boisterous burst of laughter.

Something still seemed missing. I was still bothered by the words like "suppressed", "gentle", "short catches", and "bursts". I think of my fine son at eleven-years-old screaming with laughter, "Stop, Daddy! Stop, tickling Daddy, stop! I can't take it anymore. My tummy hurts." I remember my mother laughing with me until we both found it hard to breathe, tears streaming down our faces, each word more funny than the last, until any sound or reaction would increase the nearly painful ecstasy. I looked again. Where were the definitions my son would recognize to describe our experience? Where were the words to paint the picture of me and my mom?

Joy: The emotion evoked by well-being, success, or good fortune or by the prospect of possessing what one desires.

Rejoice: To feel joy or great delight.

Exultation: Leaping for joy.

RAWLOF: Internet language for "rolling around with laughter, on the floor".

When considering terminology for measurement with laughter, we may also consider and observe other forms and sources of definitions including joke laughter, embarrassed laughter, smut laughter, insider laughter, pun and word play laughter, intellectual laughter, job laughter, ironic and sarcastic laughter, surreal laughter, pain laughter, and more.

Enough of dictionary limitations. Let us scale new heights and seek new levels of laughter, delight, glee, general merriment, silliness, sympathy, joviality, jocularity, clowning about, and making funny fun. Add to the list. We can find many more distinctions as we observe this wonderful human signaling device called laughter.

For now, let us dub laughter as follows:

Improvisational Laughter: "Uncontrollable and sustained tittering, giggling, guffawing, and otherwise exploding with joy in rejoicing exultation until the sides hurt and tears stream and all of existence is filled with the delight of life, and light, and love."

By seeking such distinctions, we may learn about our own humor and laughter. We may use these observations as measurements of the levels and kinds of laughter being generated by our communication and relationship practices. If you are laughing (becoming amused or bemused) twenty times a day, increase your practice. Try chuckling five times and tittering twice. Maybe you can rejoice at least once. If the laughter in your organization does not come easily, or if it comes from negative or weak sources, it is a sign of problems that must be dealt with. The minimum required engagement is acknowledgement of the fact.

Second Measure: The Frequency of Laughter

Professional comedians and humorous speakers are generally seeking laughter each five to seven seconds. If the intervals are longer, there is a chance that the audience is losing interest. If you are doing Improvisation work and laughter is occurring seldom or only at predictable intervals, it is a measurement signal that your participants are not involved enough. They need to be more physically and mentally active.

During the Improvisation games, there should be some laughing at important junctures and completions. There should be some chuckling, tittering, and giggling when groups first get together. When people are working in general icebreaking sets, there should be light laughter and general merriment.

At the points of completion, there should be some laughing out loud and maybe a little guffawing. This can be even more true when groups are working in circles. There may be some bursts of laughter when whole processes are completed.

There should be periodic laughter mixed with periods of quiet discussion during longer processes. The frequency of laughter needs to be viewed in terms of type and the quality of the laughter as well. A good mixture of appropriately timed laughter of the highest possible kind is like the sound of a smoothly working internal combustion engine. You can hear it purr, or you can tweak it to make it purr more easily.

Third Measure: The Quality of the Laughter

Deep, resonate rolls of laughter may be the sign of a bonding in the gathering. The very power of the sound breaks down barriers that are unseen. This kind of laughter really means that everyone is working and the source is all who are present.

Hearty general laughter usually indicates that some common core of understanding has been touched or has been brought to the surface. This is one of the reasons that the guidelines of humor are so important. The things that are common to our core are both positive and negative. When we build laughter bridges, we can explore problems and we can leverage our resources.

Light, clear, general laughter usually means that you have said a thing and has touched the fancy of the crowd. It is a sign that wit is noted by the gathering. You are being appreciated.

Innocent Laughter is a Symptom of Health and Wholeness.

Thin, high-pitched, disjointed laughter generally indicates nervousness or stress. It can be a sign that people are not connected somehow. It may be possible to detect the location of the disconnection by listening carefully.

Missed laughter, laughter with bad timing, or laughter at items that are not funny often means that something or someone is out of time and space. It may mean that there is an unnoticed imbalance in the event or the gathering.

Private laughter by a small or isolated group means they may not be in tune with the larger purpose.

No laughter at all is usually not a good sign.

General Measure: Where and When

We must be especially aware when the negative qualities of laughter are present and when the quality of laughter changes. It may be related to the introduction of new material or activities. Is it related to the nature of the information? Is it related to the makeup of the gathering? Are you wearing socks of two different colors? Note the locations of the laughter in the gathering. Negative qualities of laughter are rarely general. Negative laughter among a small set of participants may indicate unfamiliarity with members of a subset. Negative laughter quality can indicate an insular subset.

The quality of laughter as a measurement device is unique to every group. You will have to listen and identify clues each time you are together. Careful focus and study can develop this into a useful tool.

Getting Laughter is not the Object

Generating laughs is not the object using Improvisation tools. Going for laughs can actually inhibit the creative spirit of Improvisation. Building a wholesome environment of laughter is a complex process that requires self-analysis, group analysis, organization, training, and measurement in order to work. There is a distinction between "getting laughs" and "generating laughter" in a laughing environment. The first are events; the latter is a process.

Laughter Feedback

We have learned that things happen when we take small, successful, incremental steps toward our visions. We are lead to flashes of insight, to understanding, and to cognitive leaps. This also works when using laughter as feedback for the Applied Improvisation Professional.

As we use Improvisation Techniques in our work, we will become more and more sensitive to the details of our communication and relationships with our participants.

If our steps are the right size, if they are successful, and
incremental, there will be various kinds of positive
laughter. If our goals and processes are driven
by relationships, there will be good laughter.
When we learn from our errors, there will be
bittersweet laughter.
If the examples and setups of our work are wholesome,
thoughtful, and clear, there will be wholesome laughter.
When we have flashes of insight, there is inspiring laughter.
When we all laugh at ourselves, there is knowing laughter.
When understanding occurs, there is amazing laughter.
When we take the cognitive leap, the lights come on,
there is magnificent laughter.

If we are strong and clear and disciplined, even in agonizing reappraisal, we can find laughter. Improvisation leads the way and shines the light of laughter on the path of laughter.

Laughing at Ourselves

The ability to laugh at our self is a gift to ourselves and to others. In Improvisation it is a gift to all who work or play with us. Laughing at our self is also essential to making great connections with people.

A Story

I spoke to the professional development organization of a very large utility company. The evening dinner setting was outdoors by the pool at a fine hotel. I was to motivate and inspire the gathering. People were finishing dinner as I began to speak. There were some people not yet with me, I searched for the words and gathered the energy that would allow the connection to become complete.

Suddenly I felt something drop onto the top of my head. The people became silent and perfectly attendant. There was neither branch nor tree anywhere near, and the deep blue summer sky was cloudless. On my pant leg was the remains of the bird poop that had bounced off the top of my head. The gathering had become wonderfully focused.

It would have been easy to have become flustered by a rude interruption. Being in the Improvisation state of Impro, I grabbed a napkin, wiped the remains from my head, and said that I hoped it was not a comment on my message. There was a gentle, respectful laugh. I was a professional. Later, a jet airliner flew above us. When I ducked and covered my head, the crowd cheered. To this day I thank that bird. It brought us closer together. It made my serious message more real, more human, and more memorable. It demonstrated that I could laugh at myself.

We Lead by Encouraging Laughter

The power of laughter begins with you; you the leader. We need to learn to laugh out loud for no reason at all. Your example of laughter can lead your participants to their own laughter. Our own laughter can lead us to the most effective tempos, rhythms, and incremental steps while arriving at our own vision.

A Test

Can you laugh out loud for no reason at all?
Can you sustain laughter for one full
minute with no reason at all?
Can you sustain laughter for five minutes?
Can you sustain laughter for ten minutes?
Can you laugh and laugh until your eyes water
and you want to yell, "Stop, stop,
I can't take it anymore.
My sides hurt"?

If the answer is "no" to any of the above, you can decide that this approach is just too silly, or you can work on your own to learn to be able to say "yes" to all the questions. You may even use Improvisational skills to accomplish this.

Considering wholesome laughter, leads the way to a lifetime study. Laughter is an art and craft, and it can open the doors to our own creativity. The basic ideas of Improvisation need to be approached with laughter; when we enter the realm of feelings and emotions, laughter will bring the healing and perspective necessary to search more deeply. Everyone knows that wholesome laughter is infectious, that it brings people to us and creates connections.

Laughter will lead us through our patterns and the difficulties we encounter as we challenge the patterns that do not work. Although laughter can be caused by a memory, by the vision of a future event, or by the imagination, the laughter itself is an event of the current moment. Learning the use of laughter is a discipline of its own that will lead you to the most creative application of Improvisation Management, beginning with the size and design of creativity.

PART THREE

Applied Improvisation Methods

CHAPTER ELEVEN

The Size and Design of Creativity

The numbers of people with whom we work and the ways we gather people into sets within our gatherings are very important. How we gather people and how we assign people to sets will have a great impact on our use of Improvisation in all settings. The information presented here is based on professional observation. The ideas apply to general realities of most gatherings of human beings. The realities of the size and design of the gatherings of an organization can be studied as factors within Improvisational activities. Understanding the kinds of things that can happen when there are changes in group size can give us terrific tools for "tweaking" our organizational development skills in the search for excellence and efficiency.

NOTE

My favorite setting for Improvisation Work is an open space where people can move around freely, perhaps with seating available around a periphery. When there is an audience bound by theater or classroom style seating, or is bound by dining tables, some of these numbers do not have the same impact, though there is still value in the information.

Size refers to the overall numbers participating in a group, as well as to subdivisions used to manage larger groups. Shape refers to the spatial configurations of the environment in which your work takes place. It also refers to the physical proxemics among the participants, including such things as the crowding of the space, the setup of the chairs and tables, whether people are sitting, standing, or moving, or whether they can gather in circles or move their chairs around.

Size and design also encompass the general physical location and environment in which we are working. This includes the building and facilities, the traffic and parking, the weather and weather portents, the city or the town, and the major local business, sports, and news events of the day.

In training settings, we must take care not to place participants in physical situations that are too far beyond their levels of comfort and ability. At the same time, challenging comfort and ability is good and necessary in order to promote creativity and change.

Human Set Design

"Human set design" is my term for the way we put people together as we work and play, especially in creative settings. My observations come from many years' experience with organizations and gatherings. About one third of the observation has been in Improvisation work. The remainder has occurred in businesses, schools, day care centers, universities, government offices, the military, hospitals, volunteer and non-profit organizations, teams, clubs, crowds, mobs, parties, and martial arts classes.

This chapter contains a lot of numbers. Prepare yourself for this. If you need to, take a break before proceeding.

Nearly Natural Sets

In general, there are natural groups of gatherings among people, including the numbers: one, two, three, four, seven, fourteen, twenty-one, twenty-eight, thirty-five, forty-two, forty-nine, ninety-eight, 245, and 499.

These numbers begin by building toward seven, then are multiples of seven. Seven has factors of four and three.

Certain communication changes, and changes in group dynamics can be observed when sets of people go from one of these numbers to another. When such changes are noticed and planned for, they can be managed and used to our advantage. Failure to notice these changes can result in many problems.

Primary Human Sets

The more sensitive we become to these ideas, the more observant we will become within our groups. The more we observe, the more we become sensitive to dynamics that can and do shift with changes in the "primary human sets". One, two, and three are all unique operating units. In terms of this view of group dynamics, units of four, five, or six all operate just as were four.

The next operating units are larger groups, first of seven each: seven through thirteen, fourteen through twenty, twenty-one through twenty-seven, twenty-eight through thirty-four, thirty-five through forty-one, forty-two through forty-eight. In each, the general group dynamic changes so that the differences between seven and 13 are about the same, 14 the same as 20, and so on. At forty-nine the dynamics and logistic requirements of a gathering change again. Groups of 49 to 99 are about the same.

The point of all this is that believing that the dynamics of two, which is company, is the same as three, a crowd, is an error that can have disastrous results in communication. The same is true if we are thinking that the addition of one, taking the crowd from 13 - 14 can have the same level of change, multiplied by the increased numbers involved. This is true at 20 - 21, 27 - 28, and so on.

Larger groups have issues with seating, comfort, logistics, sound, safety, entrance and egress, lines of sight, media factors, and the possibility of additional staff having large numbers who may or may not obviously interact. There are still aspects of set design at work. The larger groups are generally 100 - 250, 250 - 500, 500 - 1,000, and larger than 1,000. The larger the numbers, the more the changes tend to have to do with logistics rather than with individual dynamics.

The addition of only one or two in a group of 99 may not be noticeable. An addition of three or seven or 14, will have increasingly apparent impact. Adding 10 or more to a group of 100 or more can have quite noticeable effects.

At each of the junctures listed above, changes may be seen in all areas including: group dynamics, in learning efficiencies, in learning deficiencies, interpersonal relationships, personnel management, environmental imper-

145

atives, personal development, quality of training, and Improvisation results.

Small Sets

Generally, shifts are more easily noticed when there are fewer people involved. Our reactions may vary, yet the fact that there are differences is obvious.

In smaller sets it is possible to remove the person of the teacher or consultant from the number being considered. It seems to be a matter of professional guidance. In an exceptional psychological analysis session, a strong professional can generate action and observe almost private interaction between two people. My experience has been that with six or more participants my presence always counts in the number consideration. Careful observation can give clear information about how we should count ourselves. This will be discussed a bit more below.

Larger Sets

In terms of communication, group dynamics, interpersonal complexities, and Improvisational management, the sets of seven, eight, nine, ten, eleven, twelve, or thirteen function much the same. This means that working with seven is very much like working with thirteen. Adding another person changes the set to fourteen, which is more like working with twenty. There are clear differences between working with nine or with twenty, and I maintain that similar differences occur between working with thirteen and working with fourteen, although this shift is much harder to see. Always remember that a small difference in numbers can find us working with a change in the environment that may not make sense without considering this theory.

Human Design Mind Sets

Certain stages of learning and development are common to human beings. My work with people has led me to be aware that developmental events often take place at ages that match the "human design set" numbers. At seven we usually accomplish the final transition from toddler to child. At fourteen we enter full-blown adolescence. (Unusual life experience and the onset of puberty may skew these numbers.) At twenty-one we become adults, whether or not we are grown up. I think the ages of twenty-eight, thirty-five, forty-two, and forty-nine, and fifty also provide benchmark events in normal human development.

It is interesting to note that a gathering or organization can go through the same stages of development. An organization can go through

146

the changes in minutes, hours, days, weeks, or months as well as years. The organization, like an individual, can skip around, miss steps, and double back as well.

It is also interesting to note that the combination of the creative experience, Improvisation, the factors of group dynamics and the nature of people and organizations in general, can force people to recreate, re-enact, or finally complete any numbers of the stages of personal development. When we are with people in creative and active settings, we can find ourselves working with adults who exhibit the attributes of children, or of adolescents going through various stages, or who suddenly find their own young adulthood, or fears and exhilarations of aging.

The Toddler

One toddler is a job to challenge a village. Two is a stretch, three is a task, and from four to six is a trial. Seven to thirteen requires professional management skills and, in most civilized locations, education and licensing. Fourteen to twenty toddlers require a team and a system, twenty-one to twenty-seven toddlers require an organization, and twenty-eight or more toddlers or children of almost any age may require an entire school.

The Adolescent

My experience, is that with a fourteenth participant in a set (whether by dint of age or psychology), a herd like consciousness appears and must be dealt with. This is a generalization yet, as with many stereotypes, is worthy of note. If the change from thirteen to fourteen is not noticed, a group can become a single unit capable of extraordinary resistance, ignorance, stupor, or hostility. If recognized and managed, this same unit can be capable of the most extraordinary demonstration, growth, wonder, and creativity. One adult with good skills, maturity, patience, and luck can keep up with and manage thirteen adolescents. Add one more adolescent and there must either be more adults available or extraordinary methods must be used to maintain positive outcomes. Often this becomes a control method with military style or "X" style management. A successful single adult faced with fourteen or more adolescents will often recruit one or more of the adolescents to act as a pseudo adult in order to manage with light and delight.

The Resistant Mind-Set

When people do not wish to be together, when we do not understand what is going on, or disagree with the purposes of the gathering, or when there are hostilities, inanities, or insanities afoot, careful set design can become very important. Under such conditions, manipulating set design is sometimes one of the few things we can do to create change.

You can tell if there is a need for work with set design management by listening, feeling, and observing very carefully. When using Improvisation techniques one can always tell that set design management (or set serendipity) is working. There will be a great deal of animation and laughter as various groups find themselves completing steps and processes. If things are not working as you would have them, try changing your set design to gather people together in terms of the numbers discussed above.

Issues of sets and set design do not always surface. When people are truly comfortable and have been together a long time, the problems of group size have sometimes been handled at deeper levels. More often they have been adjusted to, settled into, bypassed, or suppressed. If this is the case, we may see attendant limitations to the creativity and effectiveness of our organization and efforts.

How to Use this Information

The first thing to do with this information is to think about it and observe the sets that are active in your organization or gathering. A survey of the numbers can be very important. How many people are in the office, the support center, the company, the division, the location, on the factory floor, at the gathering, in the breakouts, in the subsets? I have seen many small businesses and groups that simply could not grow past a certain point. This point is usually at or around a natural set number. The next consideration is size of subsets.

Size of Subsets

When using Improvisation formats, you may find that two-person activities, when there are observers, tend to be more risky and require a higher degree of ability or self-confidence on the part of the participants. If you divide the gathering into smaller groups, where pairs may work together and there are fewer observers, it may reduce risk. Subdividing the whole gathering into sets of two will also relieve pressure of having "watchers" and can reduce the sense of risk. However, reducing the set to two in intimate settings, where there is no feeling of others present, can increase the sense of risk.

Working with people in circles may reduce some of the risk factors and can help to create a space of safety for many participants. For other groups and purposes, a circle may lead to too much intimacy or confrontation. The number of people who may be accommodated in a circle varies. Circles with six or fewer people often seem too intimate to work well unless the guidance is inspired. I have worked successfully in circles with up to forty-eight people. At forty-nine the dynamics change and circles tend to become difficult or inefficient.

Just how Big is Small?

Some of us are more comfortable and most interactive in a small group. Many prefer medium-size groups, and others find the greatest personal comfort in larger groups. The expectations of a gathering may also influence our comfort levels. A prepared public speech may be comfortably presented to a "small" group. Yet, just how big is small? Having to present impromptu remarks before an influential group of ten may make ten seem like a very large number.

A particularly shy speech student of mine was convinced that three was a large audience. I once spoke to a very small gathering with only one hundred people present. The definition of small, medium, and large is in the eyes of the beholder.

Traditionally, the number in a "small" group has been defined as somewhere between four and twelve, maybe fifteen, depending on the author, the time, and the location. Two is defined as a dyad, three as a triad, and one as a lonely number.

Among those who know, or claim to know, a "medium-sized" group may have as few as seven and as many as thirty. Some experts insist that a group is "large" when it reaches twenty, or thirty, or fifty, or whatever meets an individual's personal perception of "lots of people". Often, "large" is defined as more than one hundred. There are cultures whose entire system of numbers counts only, "One, two, three, and many".

The nature of an event also has an effect. Perhaps three is a crowd. A group waiting for a store to open may be considered small or large with twenty or thirty, depending on the size of the store. In a big theater, fifty to one hundred may be a small group. A concert attendance of 250 to 500 may be small.

The size and design of a space may have a dramatic effect on perception of size. An elevator can turn ten people into quite a large crowd. In high school our team made it to the regional football finals. We played in the Rose Bowl in Pasadena, California, with a seating capacity of more than 92,000. There were more than three thousand people from the two schools attending the game, the largest gathering in the history of both schools. However, almost everyone had a seat on the fifty-yard line on both sides of the field, and the rest of the stadium was empty.

We each have preferences, perceptions, comforts, and definitions in regard to the size of gatherings. As Improv Executives, our personal feelings, perceptions, and definitions need to be managed in favor of functional realities of the group.

Group Size and Behavioral Change

If a human being does not feel "safe" in terms of the size and design of the set in which he or she is working, it is unlikely that significant behavioral change will take place, or that information will be retained. Feelings of safety may not reach one's consciousness. They may stay at the emotional level. Panic is a standard feature of human reaction when certain numbers in a crowd, or certain numbers in a confined space are perceived.

Just remember that a set of three or four can be intimidating to some and a set of fifty can be safe to another. A set of seven may be liberating to one, in the same way that a set of twenty-one may be confining to another.

Self-Evaluation

Doing a self-evaluation in this area will be of value to you as an Improvisation Professional. Answer the following questions for yourself, and then remember your answers as you plan and review your gatherings.

- What is the most comfortable number in your preferred set?
- How do you define small, medium, or large in a gathering?
- Do you prefer small, medium, or large gatherings?
- What types of circumstances or situations cause a change in your feelings?
- What size group best supports you in changing your behavior?
- Does the size of the group affect your own learning retention?

Take Control of Set Size

When we are consulted about overall group size, there is a tendency to jump to generalizations. If you have control of the numbers of people you will be working with, try to gather participants into the most effective natural sets, and make adjustments as needed.

Set and size design can be a powerful tool for creating structure and safety, or for generating disturbance and the need for change. Sometimes merely paying attention to patterns precipitates change. Just as a certain degree of safety is necessary to promote change and learning, a certain amount of disruption or disturbance may also be necessary.

If random, haphazard, unconscious, or thoughtless set design happens to work, there will have been luck, or grace at work. Perhaps set design was not an issue, or the success may have been a result of what I call design chaos, or design serendipity. It is also possible that nothing really happened at all.

If you do not have influence over the number of participants, it is imperative that you be aware of set dynamics and influences, though it is always best to take control of the subsets that you use in working with Improvisation. Real success can build on our awareness of these factors.

Set Gatherings

With larger sets, the subsets will fall into some of the patterns noted here. People will "settle" and gather into sets that are most comfortable for their personal feelings of "how big is really small". Often they will settle for whatever is the setting such as imposed by round hotel tables.

The most powerful and healthy set is a unity of the whole. If you are working with six people, a set of six is the most powerful and dynamic. A set of six is, however, extremely complex. It can be six sets of one, two sets of three, three sets of two, sets of one and five, or sets of two and four, Moreover, it can change with fluidity between these various sets, at will, and as a result of reaction to change and challenge, learning, and creativity. You do not have to micromanage the numbers. You must, however, be aware of the process that is going on and how it can affect you and your participants.

Odd Sets

When we have a gathering that is not consistent with the realities of human set dynamics and with primary numbers, very interesting things can happen, and we must simply fall back on unfettered Improvisation.

Remainders

Unless the numbers in the general gathering or the subsets are evenly divided by smaller numbers (two, three, four, seven), there will be remainders. Remainders can greatly affect the interaction of a group, creating disconnected individuals. Disconnected individuals can operate in the same fashion as free radicals in a living organism. They can cause general breakdown and deterioration of the greater system. If we can identify people who are remainders, we may pull them from the groups and have them work as "observers" who may wander from group to group without participating. They can also help us manage the set design, and the position of the observer can be used for learning and developing creativity.

Sets within Sets

When there are ten people present, a group may operate as a unity of the whole by luck, magic, or excellence in professionalism. They may also be manifest in sets of seven and three, which actually works well. When ten devolves into three sets of three with one left out, there is often a set breakdown. The unmanaged set of ten may shift into sets of four and four and two, which can be very difficult to deal with if we are trying to reach a group goal. This same breakdown can be good to gather ideas to report back to the gathering of the whole. Another example of an unmanageable ten is five and five, which can also be two sets of three and two, which can result in cliques, conflict, dissonance, and inefficiency.

It can be very useful to identify the ebb and flow of smaller sets within gatherings of 13 or fewer. With more people it is very difficult to see the relationship changes and shifts as the power of smaller numbers tend to be diluted by the larger numbers. This is somewhat in the fashion of trying to be a lone individual, or couple in a rushing crowd.

Shifting Individuals

Specific individuals are not particularly hardwired members of a particular set. Rather, individuals can move and shift among various sets as circumstances change and responses vary. Sometimes, individuals or groups will roam about trying to find or create a comfortable natural set. This can result in a loss of focus and energy. Sometimes two or more people may function as a single unit in a set. The process is a little like the action of atoms and electrons, which attract and attach and detach from one another in the processes of molecular change and development. This process can look like chaos or resistance, or it can look like crystal structure.

NOTES

The gatherings in a set may function at physical, mental, emotional, and spiritual levels.

Please do not fall into the trap of believing these numbers have power themselves. Use them as a lens.

Simply understand that changes in the numbers of people result in changes in the ways in which people learn and function with one another. Attendance to the points of change as described by this theory can give us valuable information about how to manage any gathering.

Member or Moderator?

If we do not understand our positions as a member of the group, or as a facilitator, a moderator, or an observer standing outside the group, we may be the locus of a set change, and perhaps the cause of confusion and resistance.

With a set of seven we are facilitating, that is a set a seven, plus a facilitator, This can be a very strong group as a unity of the whole set of seven.

152

If we unconsciously become a member of the set, then there are eight in the set. I do not enjoy working with sets of eight. Eight is a number that is hard to bring to a unity of the whole, and it can break down into too many sets of small, insular units.

There are actually fourteen combinations of the primary sets when there are eight humans together, and the only combinations that have natural strengths are the whole set of eight, which is difficult to maintain, the set of 2 + 2 + 2 + 2, which is not particularly functional as teams, and the set of 4 + 4, which can function fairly well. Yet if you are one of the eight, it can keep you effectively absent from more than half of your group. It is interesting to note that most hotel and convention center dinner tables are set for eight.

It may be necessary for us to become a set member to keep the numbers in line as we go through some group progressions. It may be necessary for us to identify and utilize people who are knowledgeable about these theories as roaming units whose function is to adjust and guide sets into more functional numbers.

Set Progressions

As an Improvisation Facilitator it works best when you are in charge of set progressions. You need to fashion decisions about how the group will be gathered and what numbers will be included in the subsets. You are in charge of the progressions, including the pace of change and the way in which numbers are added to or subtracted from sets at any given time. You may also decide to let the group come up with its own sets. This should be a conscious decision. If you do so, one of your goals should be observation, analysis, and deep debriefing of the group regarding the process.

Critical Situations

We must consider an evaluation of the existence of a "critical situation" whenever we consider set design management. In critical situations it is generally best to start small, and grow slowly. Begin with dividing your group into sets of two or three and build from there.

Critical situations occur: when hard new information or change is coming, when we do not know the gathering well, if there are a lot of people who are strangers to one another, if there is tension or fear in the organization, if there is hostility in the setting, if people do not want to be there, or if previous programs have been seen as a waste of time. Add to this list as you will.

When making major shifts in matters being explored, small set changes are generally better than large set changes. Changing set size too often can also cause unnecessary discomfort. When new material is being introduced, unconscious set changes can disrupt the process. I have seen a group of twenty-eight making extraordinary progress that was destroyed by suddenly breaking the group into sets of seven at the wrong time. A necessary interim step may have been two sets of fourteen.

Some Thoughts about Subsets

- The unity of the whole is an ideal, most efficient set.
- Subsets should be created with the objective of achieving or supporting the unity of the whole.
- It is generally best to grow a group upward toward the largest sets.
- When experiencing successful participation, it is usually good to build upward slowly.
- When introducing chaos, it is generally good to move to smaller sets.
- When experiencing chaos or resistance, it is generally good to move toward smaller sets.
- Sets of three are stable.
- Sets of three are good for mixing strangers.
- Sets of three can create cliques.
- Sets of two are good for creating bonds or for building safety.
- Sets of one can create alienation.
- A mob is composed of fear-bonded sets of one. It is not a unity of the whole.
- Sets of seven are very powerful and flexible structures.
- Sets of eight tend to be unstable. Unstable may not be a bad thing.
- Sets of eleven, thirteen, seventeen, and nineteen are often unstable or unruly, as they do not factor into strong primary sets.
- Add or subtract people or energies, or frames to create primary sets and subsets.
- It is sometimes better to disassemble sets and reassemble them at higher numbers rather than to simply add sets together.
- Groups of twelve are natural to our culture and our minds, yet if they break into subsets of four there can be good flexibility with little stability. If they break into subsets of three, there can be great stability though less flexibility.
- When sets are added together, the existing internal subsets can tend to maintain their integrity. Thus, unless you are doing something to help it to work otherwise, a set of seven operating as 3 + 4, when added to another set of 3 + 4 will very often end up as a two sets of three and two sets of four, rather than two sets of seven or one set of fourteen.
- Add to this list as you become increasingly aware of these ideas.

Summary of Human Set Design Basics

Once you become aware of the patterns and dynamics of human set design, you will begin to gain a natural feeling for the changes that occur as numbers shift. The numbers and benchmarks described so far are useful for preplanning and excellent for post-analysis. It is complicated and sometimes a bit difficult to work and manipulate set design factors as you are actively engaged in the process of working with people. It is easier to observe and adjust as needed. It is also very easy to become caught up in them and to put this theory between yourself and those with whom you work. This theory provides only a formula with which to work.

Sociologists and mathematicians may quarrel with the numbers used. Others may argue about the numbers identified as "primary". Your interpretation and use of these numbers will be greatly influenced by your personal background. You may wish to change the numbers to fit your unique system. What does not work for you does not work. Regardless of the exact numbers used, the basic truths of human set design can be of value when you must help people to learn and to change their behavior as a response to the information that you have to impart. Use your experience and imagination. Notice what happens.

Try not to become entangled in the numbers. Do study the ideas and watch for the signs of "set design breakdown". Try not to manipulate or work your groups according to any formula. Your work will be more functional when presented in the direction of guidance rather than management. Do consider a reevaluation of the set design before you give up on a gathering, or give up on yourself, or give up on the ideas you are working with. Try using these sets when gathering people together for Improvisation games and exercises.

Any time there is a change in the set numbers, the next activity is best kept simple, or stable, and nonthreatening. Sufficient time must be allowed for the individuals to settle into new set patterns. When the process is working well, it is a sign that the set design is working. When this happens it is time to reinforce and verify the success by making the next activity slightly deeper, more relevant, more serious, or riskier.

As you learn to become aware of the sets in which people function best, you will achieve success and you will learn an incredible amount about each group, the individuals, the organization, and the next steps to take. This is a truth that operates beyond the specific focus of the gathering.

The larger the group, the more carefully and consciously we need to create and guide the set design. Excellent and creative set design can lead to extraordinary success with gatherings of "many" in your company or your event.

Joyful use of human set design can develop useful management controls when working with hundreds or even with thousands of people. Creative set design is an important concept in working with Applied Improvisation.

Parts of the Whole

One of the most powerful, effective, loving, loved, and satisfied people I have ever known was Vernon S. Cox, director of The Marin Center for Independent Living, who was made quadriplegic by polio at the age of eleven. With a limited set of physical tools, this man gave more and experienced more than most people. His heart and mind and the work of his life have influenced my thinking at every turn.[31]

Ability to function with parts missing or not working is an attribute of groups of people. A remarkable amount of good work and good product can be created by small numbers, even within a dysfunctional or debilitated organization. We sometimes become satisfied by the work generated by small groups within the whole. Unfortunately, as smaller and smaller numbers take command, greater and greater numbers can become isolated and disenfranchised.

If we do not move in a direction that creates a unity of the whole we can be in danger of creating its opposite, the mob, an extreme case of "critical mass" in a human group. Contrary to common perception, a mob is created when the entire gathering breaks down into separate individuals "apparently" moving in the same direction. The gathering resembles a unity of the whole, yet is actually its exact opposite, a large group that has deteriorated into sets of one bound by fear and anger, subject to being swayed by almost anything. Someone may yell, "Break down the doors!", or there may be some other inflammatory call to arms. Still, the people do not turn to one another and discuss the process.

A Short Play about Something that Never Happened

[The stage is filled with groups in a milling crowd]
   [A shout from off stage.]:

"Break down the doors!"
First Mob Participant (Yells): "We got it about the doors, shall we break the windows as well?"
Vice from off-stage: (Confused): "I don't know. We'll look into it and get back to you."
First Mob Participant (Shouting above the crowd): "Hey, you people!

---

[31] *Happy Vernday Birthcox: Revolution, Evolution, and an Uncommon Commune – 1970*, Robert Lowe, RLJ Publications, Atlanta, GA USA, 2015.

Yes! You over there!"

Member of Second Mob Group (Irritated): "Yeah, what?"

First Mob Participant: "Are we breaking windows too?"

Member of Second Mob Group: "I don't know. Wait a minute."

First Mob Participant: Please hurry. We've a mob to run here."

Member of Second Mob Group (To member of third mob group): "Say, are we breaking furniture or just doors and   windows?"

Member of Third Mob Group (Surprised at the naiveté): "Sure! Why not?"

Member of Second Mob Group (To all participants): "Hey everybody! Furniture too."

Second Mob Participant (Gratefully): "Thanks. Say, do we use rocks or are bricks all right as well?"

A mob comes from a fatal breakdown of sets. The gathering of the whole group becomes disconnected, frightened, lonely, hurting, sad, mad individuals. Each one has foregone personal control. When one has been a leader for a long time, we will have had to deal with a mob in one way or another. They usually do not break down the doors and lynch the innocent. Any one person who is not part of the process at hand is a potential member of a mob.

Repair Procedures

Much of the work in Improvisation and communication requires creating and developing connections. When connections are weak or not fully developed, it is usually necessary to make repairs. Many of these repairs are a matter of size and design of the gathering. We do not have to understand all the reasons why repair is needed. We may never know exactly what happened. In the early stages of working with an organization or a gathering, the participants do not even need to know that a repair is being done. In the early stages it is usually not very effective to stop the process, analyze the situation, and conduct repairs in public.

Small Changes

The first procedure in bringing about repairs is to introduce small physical or structural changes. In a group something as simple as a stand-and-stretch break may restore the balance, timing, or comprehension level and thus allow for willingness to move forward. It may also restore connections among the people. An extra-long break may be too much for this process. Many groups of people express their need for a break in the form of set shifting, resistance, confusion, noise, distraction, fear, and similar mechanics. A proactive change in the set design may be needed.

If a set design change does not create a shift, it is likely that there is some deeper problem and a second set design change may not work either. It is just as easy to become caught up in our repair design as in our original organizational or information design. It can compound errors and create complex problems.

A shift in the physical location of the executive or manager, consultant, presenter or trainer may be needed. A simple shift to the side of a room may do. A change in the physical distances between individuals or particular groups of participants may be a clear enough structural change to repair small problems. It is possible to begin repair of a group by working from the back of the room or by having the participants re-arrange their chairs.

In a business setting, this sort of repair procedure may be accomplished by small changes in the locations of extraneous furniture and space focus elements where people are working. Simple space focus elements may be pictures, water coolers, copy machines, or free-standing tables or chairs. If making such a change is complicated or time consuming, it no longer qualifies as a simple structural change.

A change in the format of work being done may be effective as well. In presentational style, changing from lecture to interaction, to feedback, to a game, a physical activity, or to some sort of information processing can start repair processes. In the organization, similar repair may be brought about by small changes in patterns of communication, such as changing the times of, or the locations of regular meetings or changing the memo format or locations of bulletin boards. Try to find small changes that can be made in Internet or local network communication systems. Use your imagination and creativity to come up with small structural changes that can help shift the organization at times of need.

You may discuss this idea with the participants and use Improvisation exercises to encourage the organization to come up with creative, simple structural changes that may repair problems.

Levels of Operation

Levels of operation refers to the complex interplay of the following elements:

- Complexity or intensity of the material
- The seriousness of the matters at hand
- The degree of participation by the participants
- The pace of change
- Competence of the leadership
- Confidence of the leadership

- Confidence in the leadership
- The sense of safety among the participants
- The set design factors of the gathering

Many more elements can be added to this list, depending on your unique situation.

Change in any of these elements results in a step up in the level of operation. Such changes can be increases or decreases in intensity or additions or subtraction of elements. Changes in set design or small changes in structure often accompany changes in the levels of operation.

Share the Problems

Another repair element may require sharing that there is a problem. Sometimes simply noting that it is there seems to be a lack of connection will open up connections. Similarly, telling the organization or group that we are observing resistance may actually release the resistance and things will work well from then on. Keep in mind that my fourth Improvisation idea is that one must put work out for public view. Be careful not to present this information as criticism or blame, merely as an observation. You may need to accept responsibility for the problem noted, *whether it is your fault or not*. Also remember to acknowledge that resistance in an organization touches on resistance in every individual at some level.

Sometimes just asking the people what they are feeling or thinking about the process will clarify something that was confusing, or may allow for release of fears so that balance can be restored and connections re-established. If asking such a question produces energetic, open discussion, there may be a processing problem in need of work.

Sometimes simply sharing with the gathering that you, the leader, executive, trainer, consultant, or presenter, are feeling disconnected, or experiencing your own resistance or lack of balance or confusion (or whatever you are really feeling at that point) accomplishes the repair.

The Pit Stop

If you are experiencing serious problems related to connectedness, you may need to stop everything and take a "pit stop". This may take the form of a general group discussion of the work being done or of the feelings being brought up. If this is necessary, you should work in facilitation mode and operate from a different perspective than the one used for repair procedures. Your primary goal will be to create "ownership of the process" by the participants. (This is always an excellent goal.)

Often participants simply do not see the purpose of working with the program or game at hand. There may be fear surrounding the way people are thinking and reacting in relation to their working or learning environment. There may be difficulties between cohorts. There may have been changes in levels of operation that have not been noted or attended to. If any of these are true, it is probably time for a pit stop.

Another use for a pit stop involves creative use of set design. Breaking into small groups for facilitated discussion and mini "self-help" teaching sets may accomplish repairs. Sometimes a pit stop is a longer break. Sometimes a written process, a two-person debriefing, or a discussion process will work wonders.

Letting Go Again

Another repair procedure calls for letting go. Sometimes the Improvisation Mystery operates at extraordinary speed. You may have accomplished more than you think. It is possible that the deep work has been completed before the process is complete. It is at this juncture that you must let go of the goal or the plan as originally conceived.

Occasionally the Improvisation process itself has been used at an inefficient time and the original goal of accomplishing that process must be released. Another possibility is that a weak process was selected to begin with. In any of these instances, it may be necessary to "abandon ship" and to go on to another process. Let the Improvisation determine the next process. Go back to a basic game.

Letting go is sometimes difficult. We must first admit that there is some problem we did not anticipate or a plan that did not work out. We must then present ourselves and the problem to our organization in our most weak and vulnerable state. We must then release in public our plans, our goals, and our thought processes.

Among the things that are more difficult than admitting an error is dealing with the consequences when we have made errors and we do not admit and repair them. When we have seen the error and do not correct it, it is worse than if we did not notice it at its inception or in development.

The size and design of creativity is a discussion of critical detail. Details really count in all we do. Paying close attention to people is very much a matter of attention to detail. Creativity itself requires close attention to detail. In formal research settings, the perception of your relationship and role in the search for truth is called reflexivity. The role you play, and your knowledge of that role, in relationship to your working sets of people, to your gatherings, and to your business can be the determining factors of success. Active participation in making repairs will serve our purposes. Giving full consideration and awareness to these details will reap nice results. With the explorations to this point in mind, we can now begin the fascinating Improvisation adventure of working with others as we consider the opening exercises in the next chapter.

CHAPTER TWELVE

Opening Exercises

The great Chinese philosophical work, the *I Ching*, or *Book of Changes*,[32] cautions us, saying: "Difficulty at the beginning works supreme success". It tells us further that "Times of growth are beset with difficulties. They resemble first birth. Difficulties arise from the very profusion of all that is struggling to attain form". Working with Improvisation Techniques requires great care at the be-ginning, because of the profusion of all that will be

---

[32] *I Ching or Book of Changes*, Richard Wilhelm Translation, Rendered into English by Cary F. Baynes, New York, NY: Princeton University Press, 1950. P 16.

struggling to attain form. Preliminary steps are needed to bring the organization or the gathering into Improvisation, or up to optimum Improvisation participation levels.

Your own confidence in the process will create a great deal of difference. Plan to start slowly and with easily accomplished work. Attend to set design. You have done good work and study to bring yourself into the present moment, and now you must help those participating with you to help them into their present moments. You need to help them attain the desire to participate.

There are many ways to begin. We may have folks do some simple, physical, and active things. We may, as suggested in Chapter Six, request that they stand up and turn around twice in one direction and three times in the other. Another good and simple action is to ask the people with whom we are working to all shake hands with someone who is two or three people away. Easy, simply demonstrated action, which generates 100 percent participation, can create great stirs of activity and begin to build desire to play.

If the whole assemblage is not moving easily and quickly, it may help if you tell the gathering what you are doing. It is also good to demonstrate the actions you are going to ask people to take. Do not simply describe the action. If it cannot be easily demonstrated, the action is probably too complex for beginnings.

Formats designed to analyze the gathering as well as to engage people in physical activity are particularly useful. Such exercises can help us learn how readily our participants may accept Improvisation characterized as games.

Paper Chase Exercise

The exercise that follows requires a supply of 8" x 11" sheets of paper. Plan on three to five sheets for each participant. You may use the distribution of paper as an exercise itself. The exercise may take ten to twenty minutes, depending on the amount of detail engaged in. Distribute the paper. Colored paper can be fun when slowly introduced into the exercise.

Starting the Exercise

- Wad a single sheet of paper into a ball, throw it into the air, and let it drop at your feet in front of you.
- To the participants say exactly, "Take a piece of paper and do the same thing." Note how many of them follow your lead exactly. Note how many do something else such as catch the paper, toss it to someone else, let it land behind themselves, or to one side.
- Ask them to pick up the paper ball. Be aware of how they do it. If need-

ed redistribute the paper balls so that everyone has one again.

- Without saying anything, begin to toss the ball into the air, catching it with one hand.
- Switch the paper ball to the other hand, toss it and catch it with the same hand. Be silent and keep doing this until everyone is doing the same thing. This step may take some time and patience.
- Toss the paper ball from one hand to the other until everyone follows along. Prompt only if necessary and note if you have to do so.
- Toss the ball to another participant.
- Begin to increase the number of paper balls being handled by the group. Do not give instructions regarding the increase. Let the participants figure it out.
- Make and juggle two, then three paper balls. It is fine if you cannot juggle three at once. This is not about juggling nor accomplishment; it is about opening doors to creativity with simple activity,   participation analysis, audience bonding, having fun, playing, and taking small, successful, incremental steps toward a goal.
- Invent other things you may do with the paper balls. Let the Improvisation inspire other things to do with them. Help the participants become inspired to invent other things that can be done with them.
- By the time you reach the juggling phase, you may note those who are beginning to "drop out" of the activity. Some may quit participating because they are not willing to go any faster or any further, others because they have reached some internal limit. You will learn a great deal about how quickly we can move a group. Others may begin to "over-participate" or fixate on accomplishing the task as they currently understand it. Others may enter into competition (either as winners or as losers). Take close notice who is doing what.
- At the end of the game have the gathering clean up the paper as quickly as possible. Tell them you will time the clean-up activity. You may tell them that if they deposit all the paper into a container within sixty seconds there will be a twenty-minute break following the activity. If it takes longer, there will be a ten-minute break.
- Ask if anyone is willing to recycle the used paper. Let the Improvisation spirit invoke new ways to deal with the paper.
- If you play this game with simplicity and gusto, you will have fun and your participants will have fun. You will gain a wealth of information about the people with whom you are working and you will have established a sense of play and of activating the cooperative process.

Scavenger Hunt

The Scavenger Hunt is another model of a simple active, mind-opening

163

exercise. You will need a list of fourteen to twenty-one items that this group should be able to find easily in the immediate location in which you are working, for example, a paper clip, a pencil, a quarter, and a notebook.

Very quickly form in groups of three, four, seven, or fourteen, depending on the overall size of the group and the imperatives of the location.

Tell everyone that each "team" will start by finding seven items. The first group to find all seven is to yell out, as a group, "We have them." Then a spokesperson must name the collected items out loud.

Stop the process when the first group finds the items. Ask the winning group to select and join another group, doubling the size of that group.

Ask all the groups to join with other groups and then call out three more items to be found for a total of ten.

When a group yells that they have found ten, call four more items, until a team calls out that all fourteen have been found. Then add four more.

When a group has called out that they have found the eighteen items, name three more. At this point twenty-one items are being searched for.

Depending on the number of people with whom you are playing, you may ask the groups to team up with other groups at each increase in the number of items to be found. With skill you will achieve a great degree of controlled chaos, which produces surprising results.

While desired, it is not necessary for all groups to be successful. Careful observation and conscious attention to the dynamics of the participant groups is required. As Yogi Berra said, "You can observe a lot by watching".

A vital Improvisation skill has to do with moving at precisely the pace of change that the gathering can handle. The pace is most effective when it is just a step or two beyond the perceived limit of the gathering. Moving too slowly can be as problematic as moving too quickly. If you have moved at the pace that works well for this organization, there will be a flurry of activity, participation, self-organization, reorganization, and production. Also, a number of small, successful, incremental, steps toward following guidance, and altering behavior will have been taken.

An Invitation to *Babble*

Babble will be discussed at length in Chapter Fourteen. I have found *Babble* to be valuable and applicable with virtually every group and every level of mastery. I have used this precise methodology with a success rate nearing 100 percent. I use the following script or template for introducing *Babble* into the mind.

Instructions

This exercise will take a small amount of time. Spending five minutes with it produces a very nice insight. You may easily give yourself ten or fifteen minutes to do this exercise yourself, alone. If you do it with another person it may take twice as long. With a larger group you can present this exercise and a variety of variations successfully for up to a half an hour of real exercise.

Begin Here Using this as a Script

"I shall ask you to take some action. I will ask that you follow some easy instructions and do some simple things. I am going to ask you to do some things you may not have done recently or before.

"Will you do a favor with me? I want you to make real, out-loud sounds with me." Make the sounds out loud.

[Pause]

"*Babble* a sound out loud. Verbalize a couple of nonsense sounds, something such as 'Bla bla bla. Blal Bla! Bia bla, bla. Bla, Blal'. Come up with some more sounds of your own." [You can extend the time you spend here. You can also explore this process many times with many groups and gain new insight each time.]

"Next try making some nonsense sounds as though you were angry. Try to do more than just growling. Make the noises sound like words: 'COLOSIL GOP DAGIBIL WAT!!!'" [You can extend the time you spend here. You can revisit this exercise many times.]

"Can you produce *Babble* that sounds like language? Can you communicate in that language? Can you place emotion into your communication? Take some time and play, out loud, with your new languages."

[Read the following sentence out loud.] "Ble-galing profo-dalop mandel fluflu- flu." [Try it again with more volume. Say it with determination. With humility, with delight, with grave understanding, with comfort.]

"Use your *Babble* language to talk about your sadness. Then tell about being happy, confused, delighted."

It may be a good idea to do this exercise for yourself a few times and to read Chapter Fourteen, *Babble*, before you demonstrate and ask others to do this work. You may encounter some resistance the first time you ask others to *Babble* in public. If you encounter resistance, you will find that it probably is a reflection of your own resistance, and if you relax and move at a pace appropriate to the gathering and Improv ideas, the resistance can be turned into creative energy. It takes personal trust and self-confidence to support this process as an introduction. The more love you can include in the process, the better. The game itself, if done playfully, helps create the trust and confidence needed.

You should start the next procedures after you have been successful in leading the group of participants in making fairly loud and enthusiastic *Babble* responses.

Another quick *Babble* form can ask you and your gathering to mingle with gathering to mingle one another and to introduce themselves to three or four different people using only *Babble* sounds. Closely monitor the reactions and responses of the participants. You may be able to identify resistant or enthusiastic individuals, or pockets of resistance or enthusiasm at this point. You can easily do this, with variations, for 10 to 20 minutes.

To prepare for *Babble* you may want to lead others through the process called "Exercise in the Present Moment", detailed in Chapter Two, "Open the Doors to your Creativity". Learn to conduct that exercise in your own words and with your own timing. The exercise works best without the use of notes. Conducting the exercise to maximum effect may require practice with a tape recorder until you have the sequences under your control.

Meta-dynamics: The Life of the Group

Just as there are group dynamics, there are group perceptions of realities, which may override your purposes in organizing, leading, motivating, or training any specific set of people. There can be feelings that "the more things change, the more they stay the same". There can be perceptions that "the decision makers do not really want to change". There may be expectations that "they" are at it again. There may be a legend that "this change or reorganization system will go the way of all things". There may be perception that "learning new resources is a form of disloyalty to the older ways".

There may be the presence of a sense of malarkey. These are a few of what I call "meta-dynamics". If these feelings are present in the group at large and we are not aware of them, or we do not deal with them, our program may be in danger.

In organizations it is necessary to be aware of the absence or intermittent attendance of leaders, decision makers, executives, managers, supervisors, or others who are key players. In professional and academic settings, corporate or organizational culture identifies, and creates many "meta-dynamic" behaviors. Improvisation is operating at multiple levels and the meta-dynamics of the participants can become visible by the manner in which the people engage in the activities.

Note any who are not participating in the program even if they are present. Note whether the absence is due to distractions or to state of mind. Willingness to allow such distractions may tell you a great deal about the "meta-dynamics" of the organization with which you are dealing. It may give you clues to glitches in your organizational communication.

The Improvisation process is so powerful that people find it very difficult to resist, if it is done in the right spirit, using the guidelines and suggestions intelligently. People will see changes in themselves and in others. For some that will be proof that change is possible. For others it will reinforce their natural desire to learn and grow. For some it will generate a kind of meta-dynamic distraction syndrome. For a few it may bring up strong struggles. For some it can reveal deep and great resistance. For these and other reasons, it must be engaged in with love and respect for all.

All Resistance is not all Futile.

Resistance on the part of some individuals some of the time is not a bad thing. Resistance by all the people some of the time is not a bad thing. Electrical systems do not work well without the use of appropriate or intermittent resistors.

Some resistance often precedes "breakthrough" experience. I have heard it said that some metals become extremely hard prior to the onset of metal fatigue. They become harder than normal. Such metals then become brittle and can shatter with a light impact. People can exhibit similar behavior in creative developmental and learning environments.

Watch for the hardening effect within yourself and among the people around you. Whether resistance and hardening appear in the group as a whole or in only one individual, it works best to become very patient. The individual may be expressing a group mind. There may be human fatigue and the need for tender love and care. This is a core Improvisation event. The Improv is, after all, an agent of change.

Opening exercises prepare the path for the people in your organization. The paths of Applied Improvisation will lead them through all the learning, self-analysis, discovery and challenge of patterns, and feelings and emotions that you have experienced to the point of experiencing Improvisation as a Gestalt. Going through such experiences together increases their effect. The beginnings are the most critical times. You will want to move both as slowly as and as quickly as the gathering needs. You will want to adhere very closely to Improv ideas and to pay close attention to keeping to fundamentals (your own as well as those suggested here and elsewhere). How you lead creates how others will follow. You may wish to engage in creative use of human set design factors. Carefully listen to the people with whom you are working so that you can be aware of the meta-dynamics of the organization. This will serve you and those who are important to you.

Having discussed getting started, explored Improvisation fundamentals and opening exercises, we are ready to explore basic Improv exercises (games, formats, structures, processes, simulations, and activities.)

PART FOUR

Basic Structures

CHAPTER THIRTEEN

Word for Word

Word for Word is a classic Improvisation form that is nothing less than a miraculous communication tool. In nearly forty years of exploration, I have yet to find the limits of the use of this game, first encountered here as a method for opening the mind in Chapter One.

NOTE

Each Improv exercise, form, structure or game, by any name, is a true holographic matrix within which the entire field of Applied Improvisation can be experienced.

This structure was originally developed as a performance piece and is easily converted to presentational and training purposes. In its most basic form, three participants stand shoulder to shoulder facing the rest of the gathering. If you have an open space it can be good to form groups of three whom you ask to face one another. You ask the gathering to help you come up with a name of a personality from the past, or from fiction. Playful people may call for Christopher Columbus, Elvis, or The Road Runner. More serious people may ask for the "CEO" or the "auditor".

The participants answer questions as though they are a single person, each limited to a single word at a time. The first goal is for the group of participants to compose a complete sentence.

NOTE

As your skill and practice advance, you may work this process with larger and larger sets, and with various sizes of sub sets. I have played this game with up to five hundred people in various set sizes.

Another goal is to challenge the teams to come up with their sentences quickly and smoothly, so that the answers sound like the normal speech of a single person. Humor comes from the mere accomplishment of either task. There is a bonus in the fact that the cooperative effort often results in funny and insightful responses.

Benefits include cooperation, creating and engaging in relationships, being true to the process, going for broke without hope nor fear of the goal, and putting it out there. Seeking laughter is not necessary. The format brings the laughter with it when it is played in the spirit of Improvisation. Here's an example:

"Mr. Columbus, what was the greatest challenge you faced in reaching the New World?"

First person: "There"
Next person: "were"
Third person: "too"
First: "many"
Second: "waves"
Third: "in"
First: "the"
Second: "ocean."
Third: "period!"
First: "Big"
Second : "Ones."

The next person in line begins the answer to another question, and the process continues. This structure works well in gatherings up to 270; that is ninety sets of three each with no observers. The numbers of participants in the subsets is easy to escalate along the primary number sets up to some rather large groups. It is lovely to witness a circle of 27 people who are creating cogent compound, complex sentences using one word at a time. This can go on very successfully for five to 10 minutes for each set of people who try it.

If sentences are not working or people are stuck, or breaking down into conversation and discussion, or sentences are going on forever, you may intercede. You may offer coaching comments out loud to the whole group, or you may provide side comments to sets or individuals. It is often good to aim coaching comments in the direction of someone who was doing very well in order to have maximum effect on others who may not be doing as well. Give credit to this person for good work.

About seven rounds for each "character" is about the maximum that this process can support before it loses some charm.

Playing with *Word for Word*

Before You Begin

People learn best by doing. It is usually an error to spend too much time talking through a processes. Too many instructions at the beginning of an event can be lost on us. How many people read the entire manual before opening the new computer or a new software program? Imagine a new car buyer:

IMAGINE

"No, I don't want to take my new car with me today. I' would like a few days to read the manual thoroughly first. Here is my down payment. Please call a cab. I'll be back next week."

Too many instructions, steps that are too big, and big chunks of information can spawn resistance. As we work with smaller steps, there is much to be gained in careful observation and analysis of the responses to our instructions. Observing people who have received short, quick instructions that are not too detailed can give you large amounts of feedback. You can then use the feedback to guide everyone into the next steps.

A lot of people, because of training, individual personalities, their public personas, or their public and private responsibilities, do not wish to take action until they are assured of success. Sometimes they must be convinced that they know what they are supposed to do before they take action. Small, successful, incremental steps work wonders.

Introducing the "Game" Idea

Word for Word begins its usefulness as a tool for analysis of the participants, and participation dynamics. It is also an introduction mechanism useful for taking people through small, successful, incremental steps toward a goal.

For some adults a thing called a "game" is not to be taken seriously. With some gatherings you may wish to name the exercise in terms your particular group can best accept. "Communication exercise" is good. "Interactive process" may work. "Communication simulation" might be all right.

NOTE

It is important that we do not use the term "role play" along with Improvisation. Role play is a distinct practice of its own. Improvisation is not role play, and the use of the term can cause assumptions and confusion.

If there is concern on the part of the participants, talk with them about sensitivity to the word "game". If you must refer to the game as an "overt, intentional, interactive, intra/inter-human, interpersonal, introspective, co-developmental, programmable analog, analytic, virtual communication matrix for future needs fulfillment", do so. You may diffuse resistance and receive joy in some laughter by then saying something such as, "A game is still a game".

Forming Sets to Play

Word for Word is excellent for working in small circles. It is good with sets of two. Primary sets are good grouping sizes. Smaller sets can sometimes help people to be more comfortable. Building to larger sets can help develop interaction as well as confidence and communication skills among the participants. I prefer standing circles for this, although they are not necessary. Sitting around a table can work, though a table can also become a barrier that inhibits free communication of the body, mind, and spirit.

Tell the participants that the goal is for the group to answer a question by making a simple complete sentence with each participant contributing a single word at a time. It is not unusual for some people not to understand this instruction. You may need to repeat the instruction and to do some demonstration work with a single group as an example.

Sometimes, however, you may decide to experiment to see if the group will try to develop a sentence without being told to do so. If they create a sentence on their own, you may compliment them on how quickly they are moving. If they do not, you may congratulate them on their participation and then tell them that next they are to try to complete a simple sentence.

You may demonstrate with something like, "What do you think of the weather today?" then point to each person around the circle as you speak, "I...think... it...is...very...hot... today." Laugh and point and say, "Of course they may come up with, "The...day...cold...what...beautiful...huh."'

Let the Game Begin

- Formulate a simple question about something that has absolutely no risk to it. You may use the season or the current surroundings ("How do you like the meeting facility?") Keep the subject matter neutral. It is even best to avoid questions about sports, politics, and religion.
- Select the person to start the process, with a group in a circle, in a line, or in small sets. You may merely point to someone and indicate whether the answer will move to the right or to the left. You may ask for a volunteer, select a "volunteer", or have a volunteer select a volunteer. Do not spend much time getting started.
- Ask each question clearly and loudly, "What do you think of the weather today?" and repeat the question at /east once or twice.
- Say "go!"
- Say things like, "OK, that's a perfect example of the next step." Or
- "We all must {speak up, speak clearly", "Try not to think too hard", etc.}. "Now, let's try it again."
- Let the process unfold itself.
- Success should be rewarded by great encouragement.
- Difficulty or failure should be praised for participation and effort.
- Laughter should be encouraged.

If Any Exercise Is Not Working

- If your "level of operation" is simple and the process is not working, engage in a quick personal evaluation and continue playing.
- Attend to problems regarding connections.
- Toss in small changes in the structure of your work. Have participants answer going in the opposite direction, have participants change places, have small groups re-mix their positions.
- Investigate and help the release of patterns. Break up cliques.
- Explore changes in the elements affecting the levels of operation.
- Engage in the management of fear. (See Chapter 7.)
- Be sure that instructions are being given at a pace selected by the peo-

ple involved.

- Encourage exploration into more serious matters followed by things less serious, followed by things more serious.
- Promote and manage emotional responses in the work.
- Identify and help people who are blocking the process. A typical blocking response is resistance followed by confusion or non-participation, or the reverse.
- Identify and help people who are helping too much.
- Identify and help people who need too much help.
- Give instructions quickly, and prompt quick action and a lot of it.
- Encourage more playfulness.
- Attend to language quirks.
- Encourage more laughter.
- Check for set design problems, including dropouts and position shifters.
- Do more. Play more.

If Someone Is Blocking

If anyone appears to be stuck, unable to utter a word, or holding his breath, simply say "breathe." Have everyone take a breath and try again. It sometimes works best to have someone repeat the group's words up to that person's turn. If others in the group try to provide words, say things such as, "Thank you. Let's try having her come up with his own word." Say, "Breathe." Repeat the words to that point again. Start over if you must. You may have to prompt the blocked participant, saying things such as, "Make any sound; any sort of, uh, sound, to it" or "Say any word. Say 'word.'" Be light and in laughter as you do this.

If an individual simply cannot or will not participate at this level, reorganize that set or all the sets and begin again with the lagging participant as an observer. There is no such thing as failure in this exercise. The process itself is rife with feedback. Observe the feedback and try something new until there is forward movement. The only way you can keep this process from working is by ignoring the feedback.

Among my favorite experiences was watching a group of teenagers in a theater arts program handle Word for Word the very first time with minimum instruction. I started them out as a group of eighteen. (I know, I said that this is too many adolescents for one person. Exceptions prove rules.) I gave them a deep and serious question on the first try. (I know, I said to start small and simple.) They immediately came up with a compound complex sentence that not only made sense, it had a great deal of wisdom in it as well.

With a group of businessmen meeting in an oak paneled boardroom

A lesson was learned. They were men of substance, experience, creativity, and training. They were embarking on a two-year, multi-million-dollar project. No one was shy. I offered clear and simple instructions for Word for Word. It took nearly half an hour before they were able to come up with their first clear, simple sentence. It altered their thinking about teamwork as they realized what was happening.

This game, with continued practice, and use of solid Improvisation ideas, can help address many hard questions easily and creatively.

Guiding Discussion

After the group has had success in answering some more difficult questions, it is good to have a guided discussion about the *Word for Word* process. First, ask the people involved what they think made the exercise work. You may hear answers such as "teamwork", "cooperation", "listening", or "participating. Encourage a lot of responses. Add to their suggestions. This is only my partial list.

Behaviors That Help *Word for Word*

- Everyone participates. If anyone does not add a word, the whole process can falter and stop, unless saved by an Improv.
- No one over participates. (We know the over participators. Some of them never stop talking.)
- Everyone listens to every word being said.
- Everyone remembers the words that have been spoken.
- Everyone considers what has been as said before his or her own turn.
- Everyone thinks about where the sentence might be going.
- Everyone works as a member of the team.
- Everyone also expresses his or her own individual power. It is their very own word.

If any one of these elements is missing, the game will not work at its full potential. Your list, and the one you share with your participants, may be different.

I find it helpful to present a serious question at this point. What would our world be like if we were assured at all times that these behaviors would be present whenever we spoke to another person: equal participation, listening, remembering, consideration of what has gone before, consideration of what can follow, working as a team and as an individual responsibility at the same time?

Look at your own communication habits and think about how often you engage in all these behaviors when others are speaking with you. What would your world be like if the people you live with, and love and work with, could always be assured that you would engage in these behaviors all the time?

Variations

The basic form as previously described is played with each player supplying one word at a time, speaking in order, and in a pattern. A variation is to use two words each. After doing two words successfully, have the players use three words each. Do not use more than three words as it changes the dynamics of the process and turns it into another game called Group Story telling.

Another variation is to change the order in which the players contribute their words: Have each player point to the next person to speak. In a circle or in a crowd, encourage the participants to point to others randomly. Help them to avoid pointing to the person next to them so that the form does not turn into going around in a circle again. Encourage the players not to pick the same person each time they point to the next speaker.

Another variation allows each player the personal discretion to choose one, two, three up to seven or so words at each turn. Encourage the individuals to avoid the tendency to fall into a pattern of using a particular number of words.

Working with Pairs

Many applications can be started by having people play *Word for Word* in sets of two. When working with pairs it is a good idea to have the two face one another. Prompt them into saying their words faster and faster each time through. This exercise is especially powerful for bridging gaps and forging bonds between individuals. When people are in conflict, this process can also be used to help them to communicate at a basic level. It can allow them to say things that they could not say to one another otherwise. It may allow people to speak cooperatively who could not, or would not under other circumstances.

Working with Large Groups

Working with this format in larger groups requires making the demonstrations bigger and less complex. Also, the use of a public address system is usually required. In a large group we are working more for energy shift and awakening than for achieving specific, detailed results. The amount of interaction and laughter that can be generated in a large group is immense and can be the basis of fundamental change in the organization.

Building Sets

Word for Word is wonderful for creating a set of the whole. Start with two, then three, then four, seven, fourteen, twenty-one, and twenty-eight. A very connected set of the whole can be achieved very quickly. Your goal is a quick and smooth transition for a large number of people.

Debriefing

It is good to facilitate a group through a debriefing whenever there has been a significant event, or the completion of an Improvisation Structure. With groups of seven to fourteen, instruct the participants to talk among themselves about what they have been experiencing. More than fourteen in a group is workable, yet requires more skill.

Walk around and listen to some of the conversations. If the talk is general and social, you may need to attend to more of the special needs of the group prior to continuing. If the conversation is more about the process of the exercise, you are on the right track and you can go on to more complex work.

We may decide that we have accomplished as much as we can with the gathering at hand. If we can achieve this, we will at least have a good number of things to say to the group about Improvisation and its use and effect in creating a group mind. Conclude with a summary of the benefits of listening and cooperating with the basic ideas.

We can associate the activity with general purposes of the gathering, and with Improvisation as a philosophy in which any single event can be applied to any circumstance, question, problem, or particular goal.

Applications

Celebrations of Beginnings and Endings

Word for Word can be a good opener for gathering, seminars, presentations, and projects. It can be used to open a demonstration, or for entertainment at the culmination of a gathering.

In training and educational settings, we may try using personalities from the organization rather than historical or fictional figures. Used this way, the game is a good focusing device, attention getter, and ice breaker. Historical figures from the participants' field of business are also good choices. Other examples include founders, inventors, lecturers, researchers, discoverers, innovators, and retired persons in the field.

Inanimate and abstract things can be made more real, formidable, and more human with this matrix. The new computer, the new filing system, funding realities, the new desks, regulation changes, or the latest reorganization, for example, can all be made animate and asked to "speak."

The competition, the other department, the outside consultant, the new kid on the block, all can be subjects of spontaneous creativity while helping the gathering or organization come to terms with sensitive issues. A special feature of the structure used this way is that the answers are not the product of any single mind.

Discovery of Direction and Focus

Use *Word for Word* to answer the simple questions, 'What is our purpose here today?" and "What would we like to accomplish?" The form is a good tool for directing a meeting, class, or training session. To use *Word for Word* in this fashion requires that the gathering be grounded in the use and rules so playfulness with the instructions works nicely.

A good question is, "What would I like to learn or receive from this event?" This use of *Word for Word* requires the question to be considered by the individuals while calling on the group mind for an answer.

A common business complaint is that many meetings have no clear focus or direction. These types of questions, answered by the group with *Word for Word*, can give a meeting a focus and direction that could otherwise take a long time to achieve.

Review of Accomplishment

Word for Word is useful for finding out what has been accomplished. Questions may be framed in many forms: "Today we have come to the conclusion that. . ." With today's work we can now. . .", "Our next step is to. . .", or "This work tells us that. . . ." If meaningful answers do not arise in this process, the process devolves into silliness or silence, it may be a good idea to take a really good look at the event to see whether anything actually was accomplished.

Problem Solving

Frame the questions in the form of the problem to be solved and play the game. For this to work the participants must be grounded in the use and rules of the game. You may have to play with it a little before applying it to the serious aspects of problem solving. The first lighthearted or even silly disjointed answers will clear people's minds and help to pave the way to the group's more committed and serious work.

The more a group is willing to go around the circle with new attempts at answers, the deeper and more real the answers can become. Given some time and commitment to the process, the group can often find serious solutions and serious action steps. Allow for instances of silliness and confusion interspersed with good sense and wisdom.

When a problem solving or strategic planning meeting comes to a minor problem or plateau *Word for Word* can re-energize the group and refocus the work at hand. When side issues come up, the game can be used to resolve them and help the group to find its way back on track.

Simple Learning and Reinforcement

Word for Word is a good format for helping people work with information learned from other explorations. Imagine any topic. Begin the process by framing a content question such as: "The merger was undertaken because...", "The County budget hearings will challenge us primarily by...", "The new Windows requires the operator to...", "The new compensation system will allow us to...", "New education mandates will...", "OSHA requires new employees to...", "The marketing function is characterized primarily by...."

There may be silly answers and even individuals who have no clue. However, if the process is adhered to, the results can be considerable as the players begin to develop creative answers as a group.

Word for Word is an exercise and practical communication tool with unlimited possibilities and variations. It is easy to begin and can be developed into complex forms very quickly. It has fun and creative elements that can be used to teach Improvisation ideas. The game can help develop awareness of Improvisation fundamentals and can provide a forum for valuable practices in working together.

CHAPTER FOURTEEN

Babble

We first encountered this wonder in Chapter Twelve as an opening exercise. *Babble* is a challenging sport capable of deep impact when applied to real-time situations. It is a primary developer of pre-verbal human communication skills. If used in basic form with reasonable goals, it works very well as a starter process. I have used it as a basic game hundreds of times with extraordinary success. Some people consider this ultimately to be an advanced exercise.

In traditional Improvisation the use of meaningless language is usually called gibberish. A classic form is called Poet Interpretation. One participant offers gibberish noises in such a manner as to suggest a poem. Another player "translates" the poem into English (or whatever is the common language of the gathering).

In non-theatrical crowds I prefer to use the term "*Babble*". It is easier to convince people to "*Babble*" than it is to convince them to "gibber". At a deeper level, Western culture has an ancient interest in the city of Babel, and an archetypal relationship with Babel and its meaning in reference to the failed climb to heaven.

Before You Begin

This form sometimes seems innocent and silly on the surface. Do not be fooled by the simplicity. The work being accomplished goes to an extraordinarily deep level in the human psyche. There are elements of meaning and connectedness that are not visible while the game and process are being explored. However, they can become apparent over time.

It is the very most fun, and the most effective to approach *Babble* with great care and exceptional sensitivity. Also, special care focused on management of the set design will allow you to do the best work, especially in terms of being aware of the elements of risk. A small step for you could be a large step for the people with whom you are working.

The elements of risk and the challenges to our sense of meaning and purpose can shake an individual, or the gathering, to the point of distress or disorientation. In these instances, many people shut down rather than act out. If this happens, you may experience it as resistance or perhaps as a negative evaluation at the end of a program.

The specific guide for teaching *Babble* depends entirely on the nature of the gathering. In some cases, it may be necessary to use more explanation in the introduction. In other cases, it is necessary to weave the explanations into the activity as it progresses.

You may need to use demonstrations more in one case, and less in another. You may find it helpful to call on allies in the gathering in order to move the group along, or to move very slowly in one case and very quickly in another.

NOTE

This form is ideal for an introduction to Improvisation at a business level. *Babble* can give us a significant evaluation of the people, the organization, and its culture if we are not sure of the creative capacity of the audience.

I have often found it best to use *Word for Word* as my primary introduction to Improvisation. *Word for Word* followed by *Babble* can accomplish a great deal.

181

Introduction

If we are truly on time and in time, introducing and using *Babble* will go quickly. If you are not on time and in time, there is a very good chance that the audience will resist or block the process.

This exercise has an extraordinary range of uses. As an icebreaker, it can be demonstrated and used in a few minutes with only yourself and one other willing participant. If your purpose is to illustrate an idea of communication, it may be introduced and demonstrated in as little as twenty minutes. As a team-building exercise, it may be used for an hour or more. As a deep form of group dynamics development, it can cover a three-hour block of time. You can play this game many times with the same group. There are always deeper levels to which this structure can take a group.

Let the Fun Begin

- Introduce the crowd to the basics by proposing the idea that we often tend to speak in "*Babble*." This idea will be discussed in detail below.
- Demonstrate the most basic "*Babble*" by saying, "Bla, bla bla. Bla! Bla! Bla bla, bla. Bla. Bla." Ask the participants to do the same as a group.
- Each step requires that you be aware of the real participation level of the group. If they do not respond at the highest and most enthusiastic level possible, then we must become more playful, encouraging them more, demonstrate some more. You may say such things as, "This usually requires that your lips move" or "'*Babble*' is often accompanied by sound."
- Ask them, as a group, to "*Babble*" as though they are angry. Wait for a response. Demonstrate as needed. You must become a measuring device, a sort of sound meter. If the meter does not go into the red zone, you may need to cheerlead and encourage them even more.
- *Babble* your own anger more energetically, more loudly. Bring them to a fevered pitch, in small, incremental steps.
- Ask the crowd to *Babble* as though they are sad. If you developed the anger response to full advantage, you should not need to encourage anything here.
- Ask them to give their babble sounds more like a language, avoiding any language they actually know.
- Ask them to *Babble* as though they are confused. Asking them to sound out their confusion is necessary.

Interpretation Formats

If you are familiar and comfortable with poetry forms, you may use the poem interpretation format. Prompt the participants to call out possible poem topics or titles. Then have one person speak in *Babble* sounds to convey the feeling and cadence. The other player will "translate" it into a poem. A translation may be done in free verse, which does not have to rhyme.

If you or the audience are not comfortable with poetry, it is possible to substitute a variety of topics for the interpretation. You might try "Supervisor Interpretation", "Politician Interp", "Boss Interp", "Volunteer Interp", "Regulatory Agency Interp", "IT Person Interp", or Board of Directors Interp". Also, virtually any process or system can be used as the material for the interpretation: "executive management", "quality control", "atomic theory", or "math 101".

Communication Lesson: Part One

Do not announce the name of the exercise until later, as directed below. You may introduce and use this game as a communication lesson. This process can take half an hour. This step is not necessary to the introductory use of *Babble*, though it is a powerful lesson in creativity and can be used to take the process to deeper levels.

- Begin by asking the audience the following questions about languages. The precise words in these instructions have been developed in response to a lot of feedback. You may feel free to adapt this process to your own style and words. Be careful to keep the idea very clear and simple.
- Ask, "What is the language spoken by the largest number of people on earth?" Depending on the crowd, people will usually say Chinese, English, Spanish, French, and German. Depending on the gathering, you may be faced with blank stares.
- Prompt people to answer out loud. Continue prompting even if someone gets the right answer immediately.
- Often an audience will hear someone say "Chinese" and everyone will stop giving responses, assuming that the answer is correct. If this happens, compliment them with some comment such as, "I like a knowledgeable group. Someone got the answer so no one else needs to say anything". Continue to prompt them anyway. You will generate some more answers.
- If someone gives the precisely correct answer, which is Mandarin Chinese, ask what language is next on the list.
- Prompt with gestures-hands open, arms out, palms turned upward, fingers wiggling back toward yourself you as though you are beckoning them.

- As you receive responses, give the crowd positive feedback, saying "Good" "Yes", and "More".
- After you have received three or four answers, compliment interesting and unexpected responses.
- If you have not received any particularly creative answers, you may note that some creative individuals in other groups have answered "body language" and "Esperanto". There was one particularly sweet person who said, "The language of love."
- Whether it is called out or not, mention that "body language" is a good answer, and note that body language can be as specific to a particular culture or country as is verbal language. Notice whether heads are nodding at this point.
- Now give a short talk about the answer in your own words.

NOTE

The language with the largest number of native speakers on our planet is Mandarin Chinese with just under one billion. Next comes Spanish with around 400 million. English has about 360 million native speakers and another three hundred and fifty million outside English speaking countries. Its use is probably the most widely distributed across the planet. As much as 80% of the language used in computers is English, and the majority of mail in the world is addressed in English.

The most understood language next comes from combining Hindi as spoken, and Urdu as written at about 350 million. Arabic, Portuguese, Bengali, Russian, Japanese, and Punjabi follows.

The Hebrew language, since 1948 the resurrected national language of Israel, may be as widely distributed across the planet as English. There are approximately fourteen million speakers.

These figures will be out of date within a minimum of five year or less.

This conversation can generate a great deal of discussion and may need to be managed to avoid getting off track.

- Following your discussion of languages say something like, "I believe, however, that there is a language that everyone uses at some time or another. That language is *Babble*." There is often a laugh at this point.
- "How many of you have had someone *Babble* at you recently?" You will normally prompt some hands in the air.
- Prompt for more. "You know how this happens. You watch their lips move and sounds come out and you have no idea what they are saying."
- Then you may say, "How about being really honest. How many here

have spoken *Babble* to someone else in the last couple of weeks?" I have
- noticed that this question almost always elicits general agreement and enthusiasm. Encourage this.
- As you explore these issues, move back and forth between humor and seriousness. Encourage participants to go into details and to tell stories.

Communication Lesson: Part Two

- To go more deeply into the communication lesson, you may ask participants to consider situations in which people in the organization, department, or household have been at odds with one another.
- Ask them to remember whether there were heated discussions about any issue.
- Encourage them to share their own stories with the general group.
- Ask if anyone had seen two people standing "toe-to-toe" in a major disagreement and noticed that the two were really saying the same thing.
- At this point I tell a story about communication without the use of language. You are free to share this story if you are willing to give credit to the source. It will be much more powerful, however, if you can find a story of your own to share.
- Better still will be to search your current world for some similar revelation about the ways in which people communicate with one another beyond the bounds of language.

A STORY

Once, in a great city plaza, I watched a very sweet human event. Springtime blooming trees scattered color about. Two unrelated people happened to be watching, as a mother bird swooped down to a limb, and pushed a fledgling back into the nest.

They then turned toward one another and each noticed that the other had been watching the same event. They turned toward the tree and then back to each other, and together they laughed and laughed.

What was lovely was that he was at least eighty years old. He was Asian and probably did not speak English. She was seven or eight, Euro-Caucasian, and probably did not speak his language.

They had little in common, not age, culture, nationality, gender, language, nor family, nor anything except their humanity. There communication, however, was elegant.

185

Guiding Discussion

A truth is that we are all, always, speaking *Babble*. Whatever we say, there must be some translation in order to arrive at understanding. We must decide that there is something of value to say. We must decide whether a particular truth has meaning to us. We must decide whether we know what the speaker is talking about. We must confabulate all this in order to translate everything to come to common meaning.

I sometimes do a demonstration by acting out babbling as a toddler who needs something and does not have the words for it. I then turn away from the imaginary child and back at the audience and back at the child as though I am an adult responding to the child and say, in a disgusted voice, "I'm sorry! You just come back when you can express yourself more clearly." We can gain much by watching the audience response.

Offer the point that we should respond to our co-workers and our loved ones, indeed to everyone, in the same way we need to respond to children, and to those who do not speak our language clearly, that is, with the understanding that we must participate in the translation. Reinforce the idea that we must take the time to allow for translation.

We need to understand that what we mean and what we say are often very different. We can understand that what we say and what others hear are often not the same. This is not because we are inattentive, or stubborn, or expressing bad listeners. It is simply because at some level we are all always speaking some sort of *Babble* and we must translate in order to create sense.

Striving for 100 Percent Participation

If you are working with three, or six, or thirteen, strive for 100 percent participation. I you are working with twenty-seven people, *strive* for 100 percent participation. If you are working with any number between one and a thousand, strive for 100 percent participation. If you cannot *strive* for 100 percent participation, then limit your goals and revise your horizons.

You may introduce the idea of *Babble* and you may take the first step, or even finish the game, with less than 100 percent participation; however, it is very difficult to progress to higher levels without continuous striving.

Achieving 100 percent participation is possible. This does not mean that we can maintain 100 percent focus, and attention all the time. If we are truly influencing people they will tend to wander away and into their own thoughts when we reach inside them deeply enough. Our goals and purposes need to be deeply involved with gaining and regaining participation, again regaining, and regaining again,. *Babble* is uniquely suited for encouraging this.

This work touches on deep levels of human experience and communi cation. If we demonstrate angry *Babble* from our minds, and not from our souls, it will be unreal to the participants and they will follow our un-real lead. They will be just as unreal as we want. If we *Babble* from our hearts, people will tend to follow.

If we do not have a good understanding of our own internal emotional states, they can sway us from our time center in this realm of Improvisational exercise. Anger or sadness can easily come out too strongly in our own demonstrations. (These tend to be among the most repressed emotions.) The effect may be that you will back away from the reality and the audience will follow your lead, each in the direction of their own repressive notions.

Holding *Babble* Conversations

To develop confidence in the use of Babble, we may help the participants to *Babble* with one another at the level of conversation. This works wonderfully with larger gatherings.

- Start by demonstrating a *Babble* conversation with one person. Make eye contact with an audience member and *Babble* noises that sound like a question. Expect and encourage an answer in *Babble*.
- Repeat the *Babble* sounds until you receive an answer in *Babble*. Answer in *Babble* and engage the willing member in a conversation.
- After this you may ask the general gathering of participants to move about randomly and *Babble* with one another. The best forum for this process is an open arrangement, where the participants can stand up and move around.
- Ask the audience members to find someone they do not know well by engaging in a *Babble* conversation.

This exercise can be extended into any general workplace to create a break, and a shift in the day's energy. If people are not moving about or if there is less than a great deal of noise and energy, we may need to backtrack and repair before moving on. We may increase the energy and participation by asking our participants to engage in communicating a frustrating or serious, touchy or difficult, reality or fact with their *Babble* partners.

Translating Introductions

This is a *Babble* translation process. You will need to demonstrate this.
It works best with sets of seven to thirteen. It is good, sometimes, to identify volunteer group leaders in the gathering.

- Tell the participants that a volunteer or a person selected by the vol unteer will start the process.

- The person who begins will introduce himself or herself to the audience in *Babble*. The *Babble* can be as basic as "Bla, bla-bla, bla", or it can be as sophisticated as to sound like a real language. Always take care to insure sure that the participants do not use a real language.
- The person to the left of the beginning participant "translates" the introduction into the primary language of your gathering for the rest of the group.
- Then the first translator introduces herself in *Babble* and the person to her left translates, and so on around the circle.
- Show the people how to *Babble* in short phrases and demonstrate for the translators how best to translate in short phrases.
- An advanced step will be to have people around the circle ask questions. This can be done with any language/*Babble* translator combination.

NOTE

A problem encountered with this form is that one group may move more quickly than another. Adjust your instructions to help people who have finished in order to keep them engaged in the event. You may have people in the quicker sets play another *Babble* round with a more complex instruction, or to play *Word for Word*, or to discuss some of the thoughts and feelings they have been experiencing while others are completing earlier tasks.

Debriefing

Whenever you finish using an Improv exercise, it is good to ask the gathering for feedback about how the process worked, what has been learned, how the learning may be applied, and about their feelings. We may start by asking whether people found meaning in what they heard. Ask for examples. Prompt with such questions as, 'Tell us about something that happened in your group." "Did anyone experience feeling silly when you were babbling?" Was it harder to *Babble* or harder to translate? Share your own experiences of using this exercise.

A STORY

When I first began using this format I was known as "the comedy teacher" and I imagined that the people expected me to be funny. For me it was pretty easy to generate laughter with the *Babble*. I could act a little foolish and put a lot of energy into it and people would laugh. When I became good at making my *Bab-*

ble sound like real languages the audiences and participants loved it.

When I had to translate, however, it was often not funny. I think this was true because I was trying to make it funny, breaking the first Improv rule, working outside the present moment by trying to achieve a particular end. Worse still was that the participants who were not trying to make something happen would say whatever came to their minds, and the results were most often very funny.

I became convinced that it was more difficult to translate than to *Babble*. As I used the form more with business and professional audiences, I began to notice that a lot of people were more uncomfortable with the *Babble* part. It became apparent when a participant came up to me and said, "If you *make* me *Babble* again I am leaving."

I have surveyed many audiences and it turns out that about 45 percent of us find the *Babble* tougher, about 45 percent find translation more difficult. Without exploring feedback, I would never have known about the discomfort of the persons babbling.

Applications

Babble can be used as a simple basic introduction to Improv forms, ideas, fundamentals, and structures. It can also be used as an advanced tool for deep exploration of ideas or emotions, problems, systems, and relationships. The variations have not been fully explored. As you work with this format, you will become more familiar and more comfortable. You will find that you can combine or include *Babble* with *Word for Word*, *Four-Square Matrix*, *Story Telling*, and with many of the advanced exercises described in Chapter Seventeen. The more you use the game, the more you will discover applications of your own.

CHAPTER FIFTEEN

Four-Square Matrix

In all organizational development matters, this exercise can be adapted to virtually any setting and circumstance. Attention needs to be focused on area labels, the relationships, the setup, and logistics. Interspersed there will be considerations of the subject matters being explored. Except for area labels, the other elements of this exercise have applications in most of the games discussed in Advanced Exercises, Chapter Seventeen.

Before You Begin

Divide the exploration space into four distinct areas by making a large plus sign (+) on the floor. This can be done with the imagination. It can be done with participants in standing circles so that multiple sets can be operating at one time. Select up to four participants to stand into each area. Assign "area labels" to each. It is good to start with simple things such as emotions or environmental factors: heavy gravity, no gravity, cold, hot, sticky, or fluid.

As the participants become more confident, the range of area labels can be expanded. Use titles or relationships of the players to provide focus. For example, we can use a business or organizational focus (executive, management, sales, line), or community of interest (local people, regional people, developers, global people), or family focus (father, son, sister, brother). We may use generally related professions (computer analyst, graphic artist, web master, architect), unrelated professions (carpenter, musician, accountant, politician), or community organizers.

As skill with the structure increases, area labels can become the people in the gathering with their own positions in relationships at work, in the community, in the environment, or in the family. Be cautious with this. Be certain that the people are ready for high energy, and deep exploration, as this form can bring up powerful feelings, or can uncover hidden or unknown conflicts.

Set Up

This form can be presented in such fashions as: a problem to be solved (new system will be a week late, iPads have arrived before the new cell phones), a conflict to resolve (environment versus development, conflicting areas of responsibility); or things to do (prepare for a meeting, plan a future event). As an introduction, or in teaching people how to play, the situations can be unusual or bizarre (lost on an ice cream cone, captured by army ants).

Let the Joy Begin

There are a multitude of ways to play in the matrix. You may have individuals discuss an issue as they move through the squares together. Try one person in each square. Have each one talk about an issue or problem from the viewpoint of the area label where they are standing. Then have the group shift one space clockwise until each person has spoken a few times from each position. Have one individual discuss a specific issue while walking through, allowing herself to be guided by the labeled areas keeping the subject the same.

You may rearrange the directions in which the participants will move through the squares. A simple way to use the matrix is to have people talk about a challenge as they move between the spaces, changing to the position of each area label as they move. Encourage the participants to keep moving from area to area. They may walk in a circle or move randomly from area to area. The simple necessity of speaking from four different viewpoints often brings enlightenment and understanding.

It is possible to have a large number of sets of four, operating at once. Participants may be seated at tables, standing, grouped in the corners of a room, or gathered into more general areas that you have designated. In each area, ask the people to talk among themselves from the perspective of the area label. After a reasonable period, ask them to rotate to another area and to continue conversations from the perspective of the new area label. Everyone must have a chance to be in each of the four squares at least once. It is best to have the people move rather than to move the area labels.

More than six to eight changes will tend to exhaust the range of conversation in most large groups. The wrap-up can be done in smaller discussion groups, through large group discussion, or as part of the debriefing following the exercise. The logistics, as with all Improvisation parameters, are subject to change and invention.

After people are familiar with the Matrix, have them create their own area labels, setups, issues and movement patterns.

Playing with Larger Groups

It is possible to have a fairly large number of sets of four operating at once. It is not difficult to have five hundred people in 125 sets in a ballroom.

Participants may be seated at small, square tables, standing, grouped in the corners of a room, or gathered into more general areas that you have designated. In each area ask the people to talk among themselves from the perspective of the area label. After a reasonable period, ask them to rotate to another area and to continue conversations from the perspective of the new area label. Everyone must have a chance to be in each of the four squares at least once. It is best to have the people move rather than to move the area labels.

More than six changes will tend to exhaust the range of conversation of most large groups. The wrap up can be done in smaller discussion groups, through large group discussion, or as part of the process following the game. The logistics, as with all Improv parameters, are subject to change and invention.

Investigating Area Labels in Depth

Great creativity can come from the thoughtful use of area labels. Emotions work well for entertaining, ice-breaking, teaching the basic format, and for playing before beginning to discuss serious matters.

When using emotions as area labels. It is good to let the participants call out the emotions. You pick out a strong, clear, simple, direct emotion, then repeat the process asking for a contrasting emotion. Do this twice more, each time asking for an emotion that is in contrast with the last one. This can take just a few minutes.

If participants are not comfortable with their own emotions, they may have difficulty calling out emotions. In this case it may be a good idea to have a set of emotions in mind when you begin. Such basic emotions as happy, sad, angry, and confused can be used early in the process. As competence, creativity, and enthusiasm set in, be prepared to use emotions of heightened intensity, such as ecstatic, mournful, enraged, or disoriented. If you feel you must provide the emotions for the participants, it is important that you understand why you believe the participants cannot do this without your help.

Assigning Relationships to Participants

We may also assign relationships between the people who are working in the exercise. The relationships among the people who wander through the labeled areas can create a great deal of fun and can lead to much insight by the participants.

If we wish to explore a particular relationship that exists in the organization, we may place two people with a real relationship into the four-square matrix with area labels attached. Have the participants talk about a selected topic as they move through the squares. Remember the rules of complexity and simplicity when you try this.

If a relationship is strained, it may be good to have two alternate strong people play the roles while those in the real relationship observe. If there is a particularly strained or difficult relationship, it may be necessary to set up an allegorical, or symbolic relationship for this work.

In this fashion, relationships may be described as "big as or as small", "strong or weak", "tall or short", "plus or minus", "old or new", and "true or false".

When using this exercise to work through relationships, the area labels work best when carefully considered. Environmental conditions provide an excellent working grid: hot, cold, dry, moist, heavy gravity, light gravity, windy, and rainy are effective. Light, sight, and sound can provide effective changes. Area label names may include bright, dim, grainy, high-contrast, invisible fuzzy, loud, low-volume, and unclear. The rule of complexity and simplicity is at work again. The more complex and sensitive the relationships, the more simple and less serious must be the labels. The more complex the relationships, the simpler or safer must be the space.

The instruction is to not move toward a completion, nor toward a particular, or correct, or ideal or even toward a possible solution. The instruction is simply to try to move in the direction of solution.

Using the Setup to Advantage

We can also use the setup as a problem that helps participants move toward solutions. Seeking a solution is more powerful as a process than as a thing. If solution seeking is viewed as a thing, we may find ourselves creating one after another without facing underlying problems.

It is usually best to guide participants to the ability to develop their own setup. This provides an opportunity for them to frame their own concerns and to analyze their own situation in Improv terms of, "Our problem. Our solution".

The Form of the Setup

- It may be based on any of the ways in which we work with one another.
- The setup may be about communication; the ways we actually talk with one another. It may be organizational; based on the rules, formats, and forms we use.
- The setup may be educational, analytical, playful, directive, freeform, focused, or specifically not focused.
- It may be social. If the setup is based on the way we act with one another, a good problem choice would be a social problem, something that has to do with getting to know and to trust one another. Examples include adjusting to new members of a group, dealing with differing perceptions or differences in emotional commitment, to ideas and organization. There are opportunities to explore deeper issues and levels if you wish: violence, racism, misogyny, system failures.
- The setup may focus the group's ability to receive and respond to directions. Here the setup is organizational and goal oriented. It might be good to use difficulties regarding resources. Examples might include a problem of having more deserving people than there are bonus days available, or perhaps only one person can go to a conference.
- The setup itself is designed also to be a tool for learning the game.
- The setup should be simple, non-threatening, seasonal, or environmental, constructed with fun, and dedicated to two ideas.

The first idea is that one of our old friends at the beginning, "small, successful, incremental steps toward change", will lead to wonderful leaps toward behavioral change.

The next idea is that a primary function of the Improvisation exercises is to give the executive, or facilitator, feedback about the group as it is functioning here and now.

Selecting Subject Matters for the Matrix

You may use any subject matter in this format. The deeper and more thoughtful the discussion and subject matter, the deeper and more meaningful will be the Improv experience. It must only have to do with the truth and with reality.

Truth in Improvisation[33]

There is a stage in life, and during Improvisation, in which people must learn to say true things among peers, superiors, and others. This can be a very subtle event and a process that can be practiced before entering into deeper, more serious life matters.

When dealing at the level of truth, it can be good to pose classical human problems. We may use the matrix to explore such things as angels on the head of a pin. Our organization, and communication can benefit from some well spent time dealing first with such as, "The chicken or the egg?", "If I hurry I can't get it right; if I go slowly I can't get it done." "What is the smallest particle of matter?", "How do I balance work and family?"

Hybrids of the Matrix

It is valuable to learn to mix area labels creatively first with the setup and then to mix these together with the relationships and subject matter. This can lead to extraordinary results.

Examples

An entrepreneur, an arbitrageur, an impressionist painter, and "a sincere sense of wonder" move through areas labeled "the investor", "accelerated time", "solutions", and "contradictions."

A blue sky, a graphics program, an ad campaign discuss a problem of inventory control, while wandering though areas labeled "why not?", "been there", "Yes, and . . .", and "windswept".

A cow, an ear of corn, a dietary supplement, and a fine Swiss chocolate

---

[33] Thanks to Charna Halpern for my sub-conscious use of this phrase, so close to her title of *Truth in Comedy.*

argue through areas labeled "food", "hunger", "starvation", and "eating disorder". For a stretch, try omnivore, vegetarian, vegan, and breatharian.

Life Matters and the Matrix

We can use terms that express current issues in our organization or gathering. Start slowly, build processes and create relationships of trust and safety. Start with general issues, move through regional to local issues, to specific organizational issues, as described below:

- If the issue is creativity, you may practice active creativity by playing with area labels such as "clarity", "tools", "permission", or "denial." The participants could be "right" and "wrong". The discussion could be about "possibility."
- If the issue is quality of communication among the people in the communication loop, play with area labels such as 'appreciation', 'honesty', 'good sense', and 'kindness'. The participants could be "internal" and "external". The discussion could be about courtesy.
- If you are dealing with issues about groups, networks, and individuals, the area labels may be "groups", "networks", "individuals", and "observers", The participants can be the same. The discussion can be "complexity", "emotion", or "technique".
- We may use the structure itself to help discover new and creative ways to use it. In training and academic settings, begin deeper explorations with philosophical issues, move to general considerations, then specific details, then to the problem at hand.
- In organizational development events, start with positive elements and matters of small initial risk. This will allow the participants to establish safe communication links within the problem areas.
- Listen carefully for feedback so you may best help the group leadership to develop on its own.

Listen for the kind of laughter that is going on and engage in it. Be willing to interpret, facilitate, and to give up power when exploring at these levels.

Thoughts about Using *Four-Square Matrix*

With this structure we are creating a virtual, programmable, living matrix, which is an emotional, virtually logical, interactive, analog human computer. It is composed of a long list of details, with many elements being addressed at the same time, with strong integration of the various possibilities, and it requires a lot of playfulness.

We can use this process wherever we wish. We may have different area labels among different sets of "four squares". We can have overlapping squares of four. We might have them spin together as pinwheels to create a virtual communication dance around a real issue. It is possible to have the results of interactions turn into new discreet squares. You can use more than four squares. You may use colors or work tools as area labels; you may add music to the process, and dance through this wonderful matrix.

Advanced Applications

Deeper exploration can be achieved by using communication postures for area labels, such as "must always say no", "must always be right", "must always block new ideas", "must always praise every idea", "must always see the bright ways say yes". You may wish to add to this list based on what you know about the people with whom you are working. It can be good to include postures that exist as well as postures to be desired within the group.

You may want to use real people from the participants' business, organization, or industry. It is usually safest to start with general titles and positions, however, if you are strong, and centered, you may use the names of real people, if they are also strong and centered.

Area labels can describe fields of responsibility, such as management, accounting, line workers, volunteers, board members, and investors. Try using terms for consumers, developers, R&D, sales staff, and marketers. In an educational setting, area labels such as teachers, students, parents, and administrators work well.

Use your imagination and your creativity in developing area labels and follow the rules of complexity and simplicity: The more complex the area labels, the more simple must be the goals. The more complex the relationships, the more simple must be the labels.

When the matrix has been learned and the communication needs of the gathering are being cared for, it can be used to explore deeper levels of real problems in business and learning.

For example, identify the areas as "strategic", "tactical", "logistical", and "personal". Identify the relationships of the participants. Create a list of participants who may have an interest in the organization or the problem (such as engineer, cost accountant, executive, foreman, lead worker, competitor, consumer, government agency or bureau). Play with people moving through these labels while discussing serious and specific questions of business.

Sometimes you will need to act as a facilitator and direct the gathering or organization through a whole exercise. Sometimes you will need only to prime the pump. *There will always be more power if the group can take its own lead.* The Improv works better when the leadership and the participants are operating from a perspective of "Our Problem-Our Solution".

Playing in general, and playing with the Four-Square Matrix specifically can help you deal with other, perhaps more common perspectives such as:

- "Your problem, you fix it!"
- "Your problem, I'll fix it!"
- "What problem? I see no problem!"
- "'They' are the problem; there is no solution."
- "Life is the problem. What would we do with a solution anyway?"
- "This is my shop, and we have no problems in my shop!"
- "Oh, that problem. Are we going to solve that problem again?"
- "We do not discuss family problems outside the family."
- "This is his or her problem. Why should I have to fix it?"
- "Our problem is as old as earth. Solving this problem could mean our end."
- "The problem's solution is more money, time, energy, etc."
- "Life is hard. Overcome."

Developing Insight

Some people are moved in this process by the simple fact that they have trouble changing their viewpoints. Others gain insight by watching people express themselves from unexpected viewpoints. Interacting with others from different perspectives can bring clarity to one's own views.

In a safe environment most people are willing to consider opinions and positions of others as they wend their way through the problem. Many people who are further up the ladder will share the experience of having been in positions down the ladder. Doing this in a semi-public forum adds a large amount of power to the process. When done in the spirit and form of Improvisation, the exercise rises to a level very much like reality.

When we are analyzing systems, we need to know the most about the people in the systems. The Four-Square Matrix process allows us to observe the people in relationships and in revealing interactions. We can see communication weaknesses, conflicts in style, and aspects of blocking. We can also see how smooth the people can be, how creative they are, and what potential is there.

Training Values of the *Four-Square Matrix*

Students of any curriculum can benefit from the Four-Square Matrix. The areas may be labeled as eras of history, the most important individuals, the most important rules, the first steps, or laws of physics. Have the 1920s, the 1930s, the 1940s, and the 1950s become the locus of discussion and feedback about hiring practices or employee benefits, or answer questions about new IT realities and moving through a variety of perspectives. Use Microsoft, Apple, Facebook, Twitter, LinkedIn, or Instagram, as platforms to discuss the Internet.

Try having a rotating discussion of the system being considered. The participants or the area labels can be "the hard disc", "the monitor", "the keyboard/mouse", "Wi-Fi", and "the operating system". Try a look at the stock market, rotating people through the perspectives of "the Securities and Exchange Commission", "the investment banker", "the CEO", and "shareholder". Explore and reveal the medical realities from the perspectives of the patient, the nursing staff, the physician, hospital administration, the family, the lawyers, the insurance providers, the laws, and bioethics perspectives.

The *Four Square Matrix* provides a review of what people know, or don't know, at a given point in time. The evaluation for the participants can be established quickly enough, safely enough, and with enough laughter to provide a high level of motivation for further study and learning. Having to publicly present the facts, issues, or events moves information out of the realm of *Four-Square Matrix* is another great overall Introduction to the whole field of Applied Improvisation, and it still has very complex forms that are unexplored. Use the form to teach the form; use the exercise to explore the depths of your organizational development needs, or to work at deep levels of relationships among the people who are important to you.

PART FIVE

Advanced Improvisation Techniques

CHAPTER SIXTEEN

Storytelling with Improvisation

During the writing of *Improvisation, Inc.*, two important works with valuable information about storytelling were not available. Keith Johnstone, *Impro for Storytellers*, London, UK: Faber and Faber Limited, 1999, and Kat Koppett, *Training to Imagine: Practical Improvisational Theatre Techniques for Trainers and Managers to Enhance Creativity, Leadership, and Learning.* Second Ed., Sterling, VA: Stylus Publishing, 2013 (First published in 2001).

Storytelling is a fundamental skill in all public speaking. It would be great if we all had the craft to charm others merely by telling a story. Most people actually do have some of this craft. All it really takes is a comfortable

201

moment in a safe atmosphere, someone to listen, and a person who is willing to talk about some real and interesting event.

The craft of the classic storyteller is taught in other books. Improvisation storytelling is a different kind of thing. There are, however, common
practices. Helping people to tell their stories is an important skill of the
Applied Improvisation professional. Stories teach us about one another.
Helping people tell their stories easily and clearly requires the creation of
an atmosphere of safety, openness, laughter, and playfulness.

People enjoy telling stories when it works. Even the terribly shy can
enjoy the attention of being a storyteller when a gathering is huddled
around and listening intently. A problem occurs when the storyteller for-
gets about the story and begins to think about himself or herself or becomes too aware of an audience. This is an example of being out of time,
and not centered in the moment.

The tricks in general storytelling are in selecting and saving good, applicable stories, learning to tell the stories well, and staying in the present
moment while telling them. The most loved stories are personal stories
told with fire, or longing in the eyes.

A STORY

Early in my consulting career as "Improvisation Incorporated", I was seeking participants for a program called "Team
Building with Improvisation." The idea was quite new, and more
than a little radical. It was my great good fortune to come upon
Dr. Ed Metcalf, then of IBM Corporation. Dr. Ed, as everyone
calls him, is an innovator and trainer who continues to captivate
people around the world as a speaker, writer, and consultant.

I pitched my pitch with deep belief that Improvisation
works. I barely touched on the virtues of Improvisation and its
wonders in the field of team building and asked Dr. Ed if he
would attend my workshop. He immediately said he would send
two people.

I had lots more to say before he was supposed to say "yes". I
caught my breath, put on the brakes, gave him time and place,
and said thanks.

Before I could hang up, he said, "Do you know why I agreed
so quickly to send people to your program?"

"Uh, no. No, um, not really."

Dr. Ed said, "Do you know the etymology of the word 'enthusiasm'?"

No sir, I don't."

"It's from the French", he said. "It is formed by *en*, meaning
within, and *Theos*, meaning God. Nicely translated it means the

expression of the God within. I don't know anything about you or your program except that you have enthusiasm, and I want my people to get it."

If your stories are told with enthusiasm, they will be well received, and they can be valuable in creating connections as well as in advancing the practices of improvisational communication. Indeed, if your Improvisation is presented with enthusiasm, in the current moment, while striving for the "Impro" state of consciousness there will be value added all around.

Stories by an Individual

An element of creating a space of safety requires sharing our own experiences. Charlie Rose, the National Public Radio interview host, says, "We are all always telling our stories". Sharing is a vital part of a leadership process that encourages people to move toward this openness. A story that is personal and relevant and well told will do extraordinary things to open the doors between the Improvisation Manager, the project at hand, and the people gathered.

Personal Benefits of Storytelling

Sharing stories from our own lives is a practice that gives depth and clarity to our own experience. The effort of reaching into our own lives and seeking the things that teach us about our truths, and about truth itself, is its own rich discipline.

Sharing our stories forces our perceptions into the public light. This is also the embodiment of the fourth Improv idea. Sharing is extraordinarily important to our participants, our families, and our children. As we practice finding and sharing our own stories, we become more aware of the most important events that shape our thinking and that lead us to who we are in the present moment.

Developing Your Own Stories

You can begin with the creation of a list of important times in your life. At first this should be a simple effort of the mind and memory, not a research project. Then begin to build a short list of people who have been important to you and your life. Make other lists of places you have been, and another list of things you have seen, another of places you have imagined, or from times of your childhood fantasy. Make another list of something else. Review the lists and, over time, begin to imagine possible "titles" that could describe the items or people on your lists.

Keep the lists handy so you can add to them as remembered things, and as new experiences occur. Find a time when you can work without disruption, pick one of the items on the list, and tell a little story that is suggested by the title. You may speak out loud using a recorder. If you write the story to begin with, it will be important for you to read it out loud to yourself. When you are finished you may find a helpful person to listen as you speak. It is not necessary to complete the first story the first time around. It is good to work on different stories over time. Allow the titles to guide you. Capture the essence of the stories with notes or outlines. Imagine that you are telling or reading the story out loud to different audiences: To a group of 12 year olds, to a group of moms/dads, strangers, elders, etc.

As you build on the details of the stories and add more of your own, you can begin to understand how the best ones relate to your sense of yourself and your needs, and ultimately how they relate to the needs of your participants.

Once you have a set of your own stories, you may wish to collect more of them from a variety of other sources. A basic collection of old, simple stories that provide quick points will serve your development: allegories, parables, and fables work well. Always give credit to the sources.

Telling Your Stories Well

Learn to tell your stories well. Practice telling them at the highest level your time and ability will allow. Find a storytelling class. Join a storytelling club. Listen to storytellers. Listen for the stories others are telling, especially in general conversation. Read about storytelling in Keith Johnstone's book, and in Kat Koppet's book. Read any book about storytelling. Volunteer to read stories to children or elders. Tell a story to your family twice a week. Better to do that three times a week. That's right! Three times a week. Tell the same story three times, each a different way. Tell yourself a story twice a week. Keep working on your list of events with their titles. Tell a stranger a story once a month. OK, once every three months. OK, once this year. OK. So you are really serious? Go and button-hole strangers and tell each of them every day at lunch time. Do whatever is fun and new to integrate storytelling into your presentation style.

Guidelines for Telling Stories Applied Improvisation Settings

- Always have a clear and relevant point, even if you are not sure of precisely what that is.
- Use the "rule of the sandwich", taught by my friend, the humor teacher, Jeff Justice. Introduce the point you wish to offer, tell the story that illustrates the point, and then offer your point again.
- Practice telling your stories. Practice out loud. Do this more than once.

Do this more than twice.

- Keep a story as short and clear as possible. Cut out all unneeded words. Add details only when absolutely necessary.
- Develop a simple and inviting opening to the story.
- The conclusion works best when it is simple and easy. Do not add new information once you start the conclusion of your story.
- If you are telling a story from another source, tell it in your own words and give credit to the source.
- If using the story of another, practice it often so that it sounds as seamless as your own experience.
- Remember that the point of your story is not really the point of the story. You are the reason the story is being told. The audience is the point of the story. The relationships in the gathering are the point of the story. Communication is the point of the story. Becoming an Improvisational Thinker is the story.

Telling Funny Stories

A funny story, or one told just for laughs is a very different instrument than that which we have discussed above. Telling funny stories should be approached as its own specialized form. If we do not study and practice some of the skills needed when seeking laughter for its own sake, we can encounter serious problems. If we attempt a humorous story and do it well by accident, we may risk being typecast as a humorist or entertainer, and it can be a very hard act to re-create.

Improvisation and Storytelling

It takes a great deal of preparation to create an environment where Improvisation techniques work well, especially when we are telling memorized stories. The best guidance is to do everything you can to learn the most you can about the people for whom you will be telling the story.

Invest your greatest possible effort into understanding your organization and its participants. (This is an intentional repetition.) This organizing idea works whether the gathering is in a huge corporation, a small business, an academic department, a non-profit group, volunteer group, study group, a family, an association, leadership training group, continuing adult education class, business education class, a professional development group, or an individual. Then engage in your activities as completely in the present moment as possible.

The more completely you understand the people with whom you will be working, the more relevant will be your stories. The more relevant your stories, the more they will connect you to the people who are there. The more connected you are, the more people will learn, and change, and remember. This is the point of storytelling.

Know also that when you have done everything you can, and you have learned everything that is available to you, in reality you know very little of the whole picture, and it is good to begin your co-exploration with a beginner's mind, with a child-like mind, with clapping hands and glee.

The best, and most fun tool you can use to learn about your audience can be found in the field of Applied Improvisation.

Improvisational Storytelling Forms

Group Storytelling

Group storytelling is simply having the whole gathering tell little bits of a story. We can go around a circle, or invite random people to continue the story suddenly by pointing or tapping until everyone has been engaged. It can generate a great deal of energy and insight. As a training and learning program, it can help participants become more adept at telling their own stories. More people will come forward with small bits who would not or could not contribute if they were required to speak at length by themselves. Listening and memory skills are encouraged and sharpened.

This exercise can be used to help executive level participants to a more accessible level in the eyes of others. With care it is not embarrassing. The process reveals the players as "normal" people. Group storytelling can also enhance the stature of people who are not regularly included in decision making and planning by giving them the limelight for a moment.

As with all Improvisation Exercises, early practicing with light topics should be followed by stories of greater substance and consequence. It can be very interesting to have storytellers relate a "history" of the company, or agency, the larger organization, the industry, or some event they have all experienced. It is possible to personify issues or conflicts. The history of a particular individual, department, product, or organizational initiative is a little more risky, yet often quite revealing and good fun. As with all events, creating a space of safety will facilitate positive results.

The story may be focused on the future. Have the group tell the story of the expected outcome of the current meeting. Another good future focus can be elements of strategic planning. A group tale of the future history of the organization can be very powerful as a starting place for team building, as can large scale change initiatives. Group storytelling can also serve as a brainstorming mechanism.

Group Story Writing

This is a simple exercise that begins with the facilitator announcing a story title, or eliciting one from the group, that is written at the top of a page of lined paper on a pad or clip board or a solid pad. The story title may be functional or fanciful. An interesting way to come up with a story title is by using *Word for Word*.

Each participant is to write a single line of the story. With a small group, the story may come around more than once. Designated "teams" may be each assigned to a story or a story pad may be sent around one group and then traded with another group.

As part of the Improvisation discipline ask the participants to read a few lines before their own entry, enough to get a sense of the flow. Then they need to write only enough to keep the flow of a sentence, not to force the "sense" of the larger story. Let the story form itself.

Be sure to let the gathering know that the story or selected stories, will be read out loud at the end of the process. The pad can be passed around the room over any length of time. It may take the length of a meeting, a work week, a business quarter, a workshop, a seminar, or a conference. Reading the group's story to the general session can be an excellent closing or transition activity. For teachers and trainers conducting courses of a monthly, quarterly, trimester, or semester basis, a rather long story can be developed.

This exercise is great for changing the energy of any group. Writing calls on a different set of senses and mental processes than does oral story-telling. The form is more private and personal than most group activities. The exercise can be very effective in developing community. At the least, group story writing can provide a fun closing activity. At its best it can bring the group together as they gain interesting or powerful insights. This is mostly because everyone knows the story will be read out loud at some point, or points.

This activity can be an excellent precursor for training and learning sessions. Use titles such as, "The future of...", or "When the change was made, we...." Start the story a few days before the event and read some stories as an opening to the actual exercise.

Story, Story

A great form of group Improvisation Storytelling is more risky for participants. It is also more energetic. It can be done in front of an audience by a brave group, or by sets of participants arranged in circles. Volunteers are needed to facilitate the telling of the story.

A facilitator points to a person who must speak continuously until the facilitator suddenly stops pointing and begins pointing at another participant who must pick up the story where it just left off. It is possible to catch people in mid-sentence and mid-word, so the next person learns to begin from a place completely outside his or her own mind.

If there are individuals who are not yet comfortable in the group, or if group unity is not sufficiently developed, the process will be slow and perhaps labored. A goal of the game is to help it to go quickly, though there is nothing wrong in it being slow or labored if people are learning, and enjoying the path.

Story, Story for a Show Game

This game can be used as a performance event at the end of a meeting to demonstrate the power of the Improv, and to have fun with failing in a safe environment.

Using a line of storytellers facing an audience, it is best to elicit a story "title" or theme from the audience. You may present this presentation as a competition by giving the audience a way to judge its merits. You could have them watch for errors, for example, "the pause". If you point to someone and she takes a long pause before speaking, the audience can remove that participant from the game by yelling out, "Gone", or "No! No! No!", or "You're outta here!" It is a good idea to practice with the audience yelling as a group a few times. Urge them to yell loudly and enthusiastically. The observing participant's responses can add delightful energy to the playfulness.

Traditional Improv Theatre usually coaches the audience to shout out "die!" I recommend against this in most Applied Improvisation settings.

The types of mistakes that can take a player out are not really important, though you may wish to give the audience some guidelines. For example, "errors" may be grammatical errors, errors in the logic of the story, or lack of enthusiasm. Pausing may be called an error; so can repeating the words of a previous player. Three or four possible errors are enough for the audience to look for at one time.

When a player stumbles into an error, he or she must quit playing immediately. It is important for players who are "gone" leave playfully. The process continues until there is one player left to finish the story. Sometimes it is good to have the last remaining player provide a moral or conclusion to the story.

As the facilitator, you may point to more than one person at a time. You may point at each person for as long as you wish, or move among the group as quickly as you wish. The pointing becomes like conducting an ensemble. The more playful you are, the more playful the game. The more playful the game, the more powerful it will be.

A further challenge has them choose the style. The styles may be such things as "headline news", "mystery story", "wildlife documentary", "adventure story", "sportscast", or travel show.

As with all Improvisational Exercises, you can eventually have the group move up to more relevant and serious stories. At that level you can elicit interesting insights.

The Metaphor

Almost all stories are either based on a metaphor, or can function as one. We naturally search for comparisons to give meaning to objects and events. We say things such as, "This is like my...", or "That is like the time I...", or "This is like the problem with...." The metaphor is a simile if the word "like" is used to compare the original object with something else. Each person we know can provide a simile. We say things such as, "This person is like me!" We may say, "This person is like the person I wish to be." Perhaps we say, "This person is not like me; I don't want to be like this person".

We tend to compare like and unlike things in order to search for connections and understanding. The case can be made that every action or interaction in which we are engaged is a metaphor of some sort. The metaphor is a way to learn about life and the universe in which we live.

We are exploring the storytelling quality of *The Simile*, described in more detail in Chapter Seventeen, "Advanced Exercises".

The Simile for Improv Storytelling

Ask the participants to write down a number of short similes. It is good to prompt about fourteen of these. Begin with basic statements such as: "My work is like (fill in the blank) because...", "The world is like ( ) because...", "Life is like ( ) because...", "Love is like ( ) because...", "Fear is like ( ) because...." The participant should fill in the blank with the first thing that comes to mind and then let the creativity answer the "because" statement.

NOTE

It is important that the blank be filled with the first thought that comes to mind. This structure is not about logic, or about being correct. It is about connections.

Then ask a player to select one completed simile and to begin telling a story about how this "truth" came to be. Depending on the group, it may work for the individual to complete the story, or it may work best to use a group Improv storytelling technique.

Archetypal Stories

It is possible to invoke deep human thought in the process of telling stories. This can be done by having a story start with an ancient or historical reference using forms such as these:

- "The year 2017 is like the time of the Ancient Egyptians because...."
- "Our reorganization is like the time the Cherokee people first became a nation because there was a wise woman   who...."
- "Political structure is like the story of Paul Bunyan because . . . ."
- "The new client program is like humans emerging from the African Continent because...."

Combine a simile for the basic premise, an invocation of a deeper idea, and the use of group Improv storytelling and you can produce a wonderful story and a delightful effect, and you may gain valuable insight into the deeper nature of your organization or your client.

Feed a Story

For this technique, a storyteller is given a story title. As she is telling the story, the storyteller pauses at key places and points directly at another participant. The person indicated speaks up with a noun or an adjective that does not relate to the story. The more creative the word, the better, as this example shows. "The agency director had..." (The storyteller pauses and points to another who says, "The Great Pyramid at Giza.").

The storyteller continues, "Yes, uh, the agency director had The Great Pyramid at Giza on his desk as he contemplated. . .", (pauses and points to another person who says, "Pizza receipts").

The storyteller integrates each new word into the story. The teller must use the story to justify each new word or idea. It is good to have four or more people feeding the storyteller.

Variations include using words that are on slips of paper pulled from a hat. This process can be done starting with pairs of a storyteller and a word giver and adding people until four or five word providers are working with one storyteller. You may also work in a circle with the added option of rotating the role of storyteller.

A nice variation is to focus the story title to fit specific training or educational goals and subject matter, the subject matter of your presentation, your training course, or real matters at hand. Using titles that are descriptive of actual world events and problems provides a broad platform from which to create applications. These types of focus may be added to any of the Improv storytelling forms. Here are some possible story starters:

Tell the Stories

- "The Day PC Met Apple."

- "The Subatomic Particle That Would Not Stay Put."
- "The Retreat of the Butterfly from Singapore."

Go Deeper

- Tell a story about yourself.

- Tell about your own developmental path.
- Tell about the paths of others.

Beyond its value as an interpersonal communication tool, the telling of our stories enhances the quality of our communication at all levels by giving us insight into the paths of people and our processes.

These games are useful for focus on specific business matters, for problem solving, for thinking on your feet, for team building, for competition, for public speaking, and for language skills at all levels.

Summing Up

Just plain storytelling by the facilitator is a peripheral Improvisation activity. Effective use of single person stories requires practice, rehearsal, and research into the stories as well as into the group with whom you are working. Storytelling is a valuable skill for executives, managers, presenters, and teachers. Work with storytelling will enhance your work with Improvisation as well.

Storytelling with Improvisation is a doorway to a wonderful world all its own. A lifetime can be spent understanding that it is our stories that define our humanity. If we can tell stories, our leadership can take us and our organization wherever our imagination can go. We can explain our vision and goals in plain, understandable, human, realizable terms.

CHAPTER SEVENTEEN

Advanced Exercises

In formal situations you might wish to call Improvisation games by a more formal name such as "overt, intentional, interactive, intra/inter-human, interpersonal, introspective, co-developmental, programmable, analog, analytic, virtual, communication matrices for future needs fulfillment."

Effective use of advanced Improvisation Exercises requires good understanding of at least three or four basic forms. The structures of *Word for Word*, *Babble*, and *Four Square Matrix* are easy to master. You will fare better when you have worked with these basic formats before using advanced

Improvisation exercises in public. It is possible to use any set of Improvisation structures to teach Improvisation ideas, yet I recommend that you use the suggested basic forms before trying any of the advanced exercises presented here, as they are complex and often more daunting.

My personal list of Improv performance games includes over 350 forms and growing. Some games are better suited for creativity development, some for the purpose of teaching Improvisation basics. Some are better for developing interpersonal communication and for the creation of workplace unity. Most of the forms help with public and professional speaking skills. Edward Haig at Nagoya Women's University in Japan is a primary example.[34] Many are excellent for teaching and testing specific topic material.[35] Some are better for creating a sense of safety by addressing planning practices and training and learning needs. Some games help us approach our groups, networks, and other individuals with a spirit of cooperation and exploration. Some help us define and develop "community."

Some formats help us to practice spontaneity among ourselves, help us to release creative impulses, allow us to develop our personal voices and our organizations. Most of the games give us clear and consistent feedback that gives us better than "pretty good" measurement ability and analysis tools that allow us to develop the quality of our communication and thereby the quality of our working. All the structures can be focused on Improv ideas for performance. All of them work best in the spirit of playfulness. All the games have not been invented.

About fifty classic games are known and have been played either in shows or in workshops by virtually every experienced Improvisation player in the world. Probably another one hundred games are well known and have been played at one time or another by most serious performance players.

Virtually every Improvisation team, teacher, and director has a few specialty games or variations that are their signature or trademark pieces. All Improv games have variations in form or structure, which could bring the total named Improv games to somewhere around a thousand. There are only about seventeen exercises described in this chapter, depending on how we count them.

The number of available forms expands enormously when we consider the elements of theme, focus, purpose, specific topics, explorations, research, and creative playfulness. The games noted here, and the applications

---

[34] Andrew Haig, "Rehearsing the Revolution: Language Teaching and the Theatre of the Oppressed", Journal of Nagoya Women's University, No. 42, March 1996, and "Sudden Speaking: TheatreSports for Language Learners", No 43 March 1997.
[35] Dr. Leonard Teel of Georgia State University was presented with an outstanding teaching innovation award in 1997 for use of Improvisation as a final examination format wherein students demonstrated their knowledge base in Journalism using Improv formats.

discussed are not intended to be exhaustive. Many of the games detailed in this chapter have suggestions for various applications.

These are meant only as suggestions to prompt your own thoughts on how to use them. The bibliography will also lead you to a host of other games, sources of exercises, and sources of playful thinking. Your own exploration and inventiveness will lead you to still more. The serious playfulness of your participants will lead you to ideas no one has yet seen.

All the Improvisation games may be used to teach and reinforce the skills of Improvisation, spontaneity, creativity, and playfulness, as well as offering the gift of laughter and human connectedness.

A to Z

This is a great game for playing with information and ideas. If we are able to play with information we can remember it more efficiently. When we can play with information it becomes our own when it is our own, it can change our behavior.

Basics

A to Z is played with two people. A situation is established. The first player starts a conversation that must begin with a word beginning with the letter "A." The second player responds continuing the dialogue with a statement beginning with a word that starts with the letter "B", then on through the alphabet. The players converse back and forth in this fashion until they have gone through the entire alphabet.

Competition in *A to Z*

A to Z can generate a very positive competition level, with other participants replacing those who may falter. The replacement can be done in a "tag-team" fashion. If a player falters, uses the wrong letter, or pauses too long, he or she is replaced by a new player who must pick up at the point of the error and continue. One way to handle the transition is to have someone who caught the error call out, "Freeze!" stop the action, and replace the player who has faltered. It is important that the person who is "frozen out" not dispute the freeze. The game can be made increasingly complex by starting in the middle of the alphabet, by going backward through the alphabet, or by assigning one player to progress forward two letters while the other goes in the opposite direction. Switch to other language alphabets or mix them. This works particularly well in multilingual settings.

By assigning a topic, we can focus the players on specific organizational concerns. With a given topic as the focus, we begin to see the power of Improvisation as a learning tool. As we use *A to Z* in a conversation with co-workers about material being learned, we can gain great insight into what has been earned and retained.

Advertisement

This game can produce a lot of fun and energy. Any focused topic can support its usefulness. The players spontaneously create a commercial of fifteen to sixty seconds in length. An extended project may be created by improvising a fifteen to thirty-minute infomercial focused on the matter at hand. This form can be used by creative presentation teams to polish skills. In order to improvise advertisements for a departmental change or OSHA regulation, participants will have to have a very good basic understanding of the information. If they cannot create such advertisements, they may not have that understanding.

If this is the case, you can use it as a teaching opportunity with the most knowledgeable participants demonstrating.

During, Before, After

This game can be used to review historical patterns and explorations of cause and effect. The basic form can be played by three sets of two players each.

Set up a business problem. It may be imagined or real. It may be a real or possible historical event. Another good scenario could be a story of what might have happened the day of the invention of your most important tool, or your most important product. Another possibility is to use the invention, or discovery, of such things as electricity, the right angle, algebra, or the wheel.

The first set of players speak out, or maybe even act out, the story of the event as though it is happening in current time. The players may pretend to be participants in the story or observers of the event. It is good for the players to give each presentation of the story a beginning, a middle, and an end.

The next players accept the premise and play out or talk out the "before" that led to the "during". The last team brings the whole thing together by presenting what must have happened "after" the "during" event.

With imagination and cooperation, the possibilities are endless.

Directed Symphony

This is a fine exercise for exploring cooperation, expressing emotions, learning listening skills, and committing to a process. It provides a good feedback device for discovering the level of participation that has been achieved. It's also a good for ending a program or workshop event.

Seven or more participants stand next to one another in a line facing the larger group. Each player selects an emotion and a noise that could possibly sound like the emotion selected. (The sound does not really have to make sense.) We may learn a lot about our group if they become stuck in the effort to find a match between the emotion and the sound.

Once the players have selected their emotions and the sounds, tell them, in these exact words, "Say the name of the emotion, loudly, and then create a sound that might go with it". This step will allow you to see how closely your participants are following instructions. Often people will produce a sound while saying the name of the emotion. This is not according to the instructions and is an indication that the participant is not with you completely, and may be lost in personal thoughts. It is not a problem as the game will absorb it. Just note it.

If more than one of the participants is not following directions, you may need to go over the process again using the exact words, "Say the name of the emotion, loudly, and then make a sound that might go with it". Gently repeat the process until the environment begins to support the level of participation you feel is needed to proceed. Perfect cooperation is not required. *Perfect* is never required.

If you are doing this to generate energy and have fun, then the rules are not awfully important. If you are trying to develop listening skills or a sense of community, the ways in which the participants respond becomes more important, and this exercise can be used as a demonstration.

Once the group is in synchronization and has established the sounds, you will conduct the group like an orchestra. As you point to a player he or she must sound his or her sound and continue until you point to another player. You may also point to more than one player at a time.

If you lift your hand the player or players you are indicating should become louder. Lowering your hand directs the players to become quieter. Watch a symphony director in action, to gain information about how to direct an Emotion Symphony.

Levels of participation can be analyzed by watching how attentive people are to the needs of the process or how self-concerned they are in their discomfort. The participants' clearly audible sounds, and to increase and decrease the intensity of the sounds, is an indication of their ability to engage in behavior modification and to express emotions.

Interesting realities may be used in place of the emotions. You may try "board meeting symphony", "historical symphony", "training meeting symphony", "client meeting symphony", or "Windows 10 symphony". "Pinterest symphony".

Emotional Blow Up

This form is a fine workshop exercise, originally called "It's Tuesday"

216

after the first line used when it was discovered. It is best to introduce the process and play the first segment for an example. Stand before the group or gathering and offer a simple remark that has little emotional content such as, "The sky is blue". Begin to say the phrase over and over while slowly increasing emotional energy as you speak. It is best to select a particular emotion on which to build. It is particularly powerful if you can let the *Impro*, that state of consciousness created by being totally in the present moment, release the emotion as energy, confidence, and commitment grows to a grand crescendo.

As you do this, continue to build on the emotional content by talking about the initial statement and finding more and more reasons to become emotionally involved. Take the event to as high a level of the emotional content as possible. Demonstrate a slow build. The tempo of the emotional build is important; many people will rush through this process in order to avoid dealing with the feelings that may come up.

Once you have reached the highest possible levels of emotional expression, you abruptly bring yourself to neutral, and then offer a neutral statement such as, "Dinner is ready". The next player starts with the phrase "Dinner is ready" and then builds the emotional content with a new emotion in the same fashion you demonstrated. In smaller groups all the participants play, one after the other in a "roll through" style.

This exercise will help people learn to engage in emotional content in their play, their work, and their communication. By requesting that the neutral statement focus on a particular business matter, we can use this structure to encourage emotional involvement with real time information. If there is emotional involvement in real time information, personal development, and life surroundings, there tends to be a good chance of behavioral change.

This exercise is also very helpful for developing creativity, professional and public speaking, interpersonal communication, and quality of communication in general.

First Line, Last Line

This exercise can be very effective in a general exploration of presentation information, course materials, or particular business matters at hand.

With two players a situation is established by you or the participants in the gathering. Select a phrase that must be used as a "first line" to start a conversation between the people working with the process, then select a phrase that must be used to end the scene, a "last line".

To begin the game, lines, from the general culture work well, such as "Stop, look, and listen", or "Frankly, my dear, I don't give a damn." As the players become more skilled and confident, lines may come from a specific culture, as in "What's the bottom line?", "Publish or perish", or "An actor's first job is to be seen and heard". As the game progresses, a line from a current organizational or work matter will serve, such as "The ideal pressure is 150 PSI", "Always back up your work", or "Seek to understand and then to be understood". The purpose of the exercise is for the participants to logically move the scene to the point at which the second player is compelled to speak the "last line".

To make the exercise more complex, it is possible to insert a third person who must bring in another line somewhere in the middle of the exercise. People may be given their "lines" with instructions to use them whenever possible in the general conversation or the "conversation" may be carried on over the length of the workshop or conference.

Applications of this game include study, analysis, and understanding specific topics, progressions, and relationships. Improved goal setting and enhanced achievement are benefits of using this structure.

Freeze Tag

This is a classic Improv form used to warm up observers and participants. Two people come to the playing area and begin moving freely about, swinging arms, twisting, turning, bending at the waist, touching their heads and shoulders, knees and toes until you yell, "Freeze!"

The participants literally freeze immediately, holding the complete position. The players then construct a conversation based on the frozen positions in which they find themselves. It is important that they attempt to justify or explore the positions as they talk. They can describe directly or suggest more subtly why they are in such positions and doing what they are doing. It is important that they continue moving their whole bodies as they conduct the conversation. When a conclusion or a high point to the conversation is reached, you yell "freeze" again and new players take the places of one or more of the "frozen" players *while taking the exact physical position in which they were frozen.*

Notice whether the players freeze their entire bodies exactly at the moment you call out, or whether there is random following movement. Note whether the replacement players take the exact positions of the persons they replace. If the participants are not doing this, consider it as feedback and think of the possible need to alter your pace, or to reconsider your next steps, instructions, or goals.

You may increase the level of seriousness if you direct the participants to base the scenes on the real matters of the day. They can associate with and focus their conversation on the matter suggested while paying attention to making unusual movements and functioning in an unusual relationship. You may encourage participation and develop ownership of the material being explored and the process itself by guiding the players who are

218

watching, to take responsibility for the freezing of the scenes.

This process can help people use new mind connections while dealing with serious material. It can help in the development of groups, networks, and individuals. It can be used for community development, as well as for training and learning needs.

Headlines

The use of *Headlines* apparently came from the Viennese physician, Jacob Moreno, who formulated the field of psychodrama. His group performed the very first Improvisation for entertainment in the U.S. as "Theatre of Spontaneity", using newspaper headlines as suggestions, in New York, sometime after 1925.

This is an excellent mechanism for familiarizing participants with subject matter in business or popular periodicals. Among the things you can use are policy manuals, in-house newsletters, product brochures, newspapers, magazines, annual reports, or instruction manuals. You may use management training books, or computer instruction manuals.

Simply read a headline from a selected periodical and have the participants act out a representation of the main idea. The players may create a "thought storm" or a visual image. The representation may be done by any number of people or by the whole set of people working together. The representations, at first, do not need to be accurate to obtain good results. End one scene by saying "black out", clapping your hands loudly, and yelling "freeze", or by dimming or flashing the lights and then reading another headline. The first attempts may only last a few seconds. This exercise primarily requires commitment and energy.

As the participants develop and become more confidant, they will move from simple conversation to more elaborate presentations. If you play this game often over a period of time, you will be able to chart the progress of the group's creativity and cooperation.

Who, What, and Where

I learned what was called *Who, What, and Where* from my first Improv teacher, Don Victor. Then I learned more about the idea from the work of Viola Spolin in *Improvisation for the Theatre: A Handbook of Teaching and Directing Techniques*.

For many years I mistakenly called the form a "Harold". After publishing the first edition of this book I discovered that "The Harold" is a much more complex scene structure format created by Del Close, and developed further with Charna Halpern, and Kim "Howard" Johnson, *Truth in Comedy, The Manual of Improvisation*

In a humor setting *Who, What, and Where*, and its variations are generally sub-structures of advanced Improv exploration and "Long Form" Improv, forms that have two or more people playing together with a simple "setup", usually provided by the participants in a training session, lasting as long as the purposes of the meeting dictate. Fifteen to 25 minutes makes it long form.

The Set-up

You may provide a predetermined setup to help the people become comfortable and get started with the game, or you may call for the elements from other participants in the gathering. If the setups are provided by the non-playing participants, it engages them more deeply. It is best not to call them "audience" in non-theater settings.

The elements are **Who** are the characters playing? **What** are these characters doing? **Where** is the action taking place? The participants interact with one another as directed by these suggestions and the activity is developed within the scope of these elements.

The situations created by the Improv process can lead you and your organization into a wide variety of creative activities. The emphasis of these games should be on problem-solving efforts, rather than on "playing a part." If the participants are trying to "act" correctly, they will have entered into the realm of theatre engendering its fears and special requirements.

Variations

As comfort and skills develop, it becomes possible to use any one of the setup elements (who, what, or where) to generate purposeful exercises. The setup may be designed to facilitate any goal. You may take one of the parts yourself in order to develop or teach the process. Participants may play in a tag-team format if anyone gets stuck; he or she may call on another team member to take his or her place and to continue the scene. You may signal a change to include others in the process. The following variations can add useful levels of complexity, and real world explorations to the design.

Emotional Spot

To change *Who, What, and Where* into Emotional Spot, simply call out "Freeze! Continue in (   )" and name an emotion. The players continue to work with the problem using the emotions as directed. The simple form is to name one emotion that both players must use. More complex will be to give each one a different and contrasting emotion. It is a good idea to be very well prepared with a long list of emotions and to speak very clearly and crisply. To develop such a list, see A Survey of Feelings, in Chapter Eight.

It is often best for you to be prepared to provide the emotions. It is also a good idea to encourage others who may become engaged in this exercise to call out the names of various emotions as a warmup for getting into the spirit of the exercise.

Emotional Spot can be very effective in discharging stressful or tense situations in an organization or gathering. This can be accomplished by calling for odd and unexpected emotions in familiar situations. This structure is particularly effective in helping to overcome emotional resistance to the very act of learning and change, in connecting emotions to the human development process, and in conflict resolution.

Style Spot

Who, What, and Where becomes *Style Spot* when we call our, "Freeze! Continue in the style of (   )" and fill in the blank. The participants then can immediately do their best to continue playing in the next style as directed, Both players can be given the same style, or each can be given a different style. Creative contrasts of style can lead to some very interesting events.

Styles describe different types of organizational settings: (corporate headquarters, sales and promotion, accounting, engineering, annual reports), scientific disciplines (civil engineering, biochemistry, mathematics), academia (history, business communication, English literature), theatre (Shakespeare, musical comedy, avant-garde), movies (action, comedy, film noir), literature (Steinbeck, Rowling, Stephen King), as well as cartoons, computer programs, architecture, paintings, and TV shows. You may name styles from any source you can think of.

Another group of styles can come from situations that are typical to your organization stockholder meetings, volunteer meetings, board meetings, customer service encounters, job interviews, or team meetings.

Style Spot may be used to explore organizational and operational contrasts. "Continue in the style of: Windows 10, UNIX, County Council meetings, the 19th Century, the 24th Century, management, or labor; "Continue in the style of: one who refuses to learn, one who learns with ease, one who knows, one who does not know, one who does not know he does not know, one who learns visually, one who learns by sound. This form has been used to examine business style contrasts, as well as regional, national, or historical contrasts. The variations turn out to be endless.

Playbook

Playbook is great for familiarizing participants with new materials in written form. It also works well in building the individual skill of scanning printed material while speaking in public.

This exercise starts with two players and a *Who, What, and Where* setup. One player engages in a conversation in which he or she can say anything, while the other player is limited to a book for all his or her lines, and must scan the book looking for short phrases with which to respond. The responses selected from the book need not be whole sentences.

Recently Improv Troupes have been asking for a cell phone from the audience so a player can be limited to what is found in the messages. Be careful about using this in a tightly wound business setting, or where sharing private information could create problems.

The book may be a new training text or product or regulations manual. To learn the game and build confidence, a work of popular literature or fiction works well. Children's books provide for wonderful expansions in perspective. Consider a setup with a marketing vice president and a chief financial officer, or an agency director, and chairman of the board of directors encouraged to discuss a real problem of development versus costs with one of them limited to responses from *The Little Prince.*

When working with larger groups it is easy to organize many sets of two, each with its own book. Working with sets of two within a group of six to twelve provides a good forum for this exploration. This structure is also a nice way to introduce your organization's new written material. Applications including: text familiarization and analysis, perspective training, eye and speech

Further work in text development can be accomplished having two people engaged in conversation with both of them limited to the same book or manual.

Using Poetry Structures

You, or the general gathering, provides topics to be explored in the forms of poetry. You may prompt for a particular focus, depending on your overall organizational focus or purpose.

The form of poetry often brings resistance merely by the use of its name. Take care to move slowly and to bring fears and resistance to open discussion.

This begins with having people speak lines in a form that sounds like a poem. Each person's line needs to be short and about the same length. Rhyming and rhythm are not required to begin with. When rhyming and rhythm become desired, they will add levels of difficulty, fun, and wonder.

Simple rhymes can be created using the form of A A' B B' where player A says a line and player A' tries to match the length or rhythm and must rhyme with the line made up by player A. (Fun – sun, tree-bee) then players B and B' try to keep the length or rhythm the same yet they use a differ ent rhyme. A little simpler is to have all four use the same rhyme You may also ramp the work up by rearranging the players so that every other player must rhyme a sequence such as A B A' B'.

This can be a risky game. For the sake of pure fun, failure at making a poem work is fine and acceptable. It is also good for helping people begin to lose their fear of failure. In order to create a fully satisfying poem with Improvisation, the players need an understanding rhythm, which is a matter of cadence, scansion, and various forms of poetry. Use this form cautiously, remembering that "small, successful incremental steps" foster development. A fun-filled failure can be a success. Also note that this form can be a very effective tool for teaching the subject of poetry itself.

Variations

Variations include having sets of people write single lines of a poem on a single sheet of paper passed around the group to be rhymed or not as is appropriate, or feels correct. A single group of four or five may work on a poem in a circle.

Placing mundane events and concerns into poetry form can change the emotional foundation of the organization or business matter being explored. The poem may serve to diffuse tensions, to alter perspective, and to generate laughter and joyfulness. It can also reinforce the learning of any subject of interest to your gathering.

Applications may include team building, linguistic development, broadening of a reference base, the interrelationships of topics, and just plain fun.

Prop Montage

Beside its obvious power for developing creativity and imagination, Prop Montage can be an effective form to use in helping trainees become familiar with tools and equipment.

It was originally a line game that can also be done in a circle or with sets of two with an audience or observers. Keep numerical dynamics in mind. Players turn a simple item into many things. The term prop is from the traditional theatre term "property", being any item used by actors on the stage. The twist to the exercise is that the item cannot be used or identified for what it is in reality. This can be done with actions and words yet mostly imagination.

In a circle, each person either describes or pantomimes the prop as something it is not. Encourage the use of words and actions. It may be named as something that is suggested by its shape or other physical attributes, yet any response is acceptable. The object is to practice offering whatever comes up, and sometimes the only thing that comes to mind has noth ing to do with the object at hand. Holding a feather it works to say "This sewing machine is quite unique".

A second time around the circle with the same object can create interesting new results. A third time around can open new channels of the creative spirit. It may be necessary to go around more times than is comfortable for the participants in order to elevate the group to the next higher level of creativity.

You can prompt the participants by having each player fill in the blank after using the words, "I see this as (   )".

An entire exercise may last up to half an hour, depending on the number of people involved. The structure can be developed by going through each of the senses, one at a time: "I hear this as (   )", "I smell this as (   )", "I taste this as (   )", "I feel this as (   ). You may wish to attempt another level by having your folks say, "In my heart of hearts I know this to be (   )".

A complete exercise can be developed by taking any item and asking the gathering to pass it around a circle until the participants tire and break through to new peaks of imagination and creativity.

My favorite group doing this exercise was a set of five-year-olds in a Montessori school. We spent more than half an hour taking a stick around the circle and never ran out of new things for it to be.

If you wish to truly enter the world of human creativity, spend a long time working with the same prop. We once spent three hours during a 24 hour Improv marathon with a set of exhausted players. Our prop was a blank piece of paper. We calculated that it became over a thousand different things.

Prop Montage Exercise

Look around the room for something you can touch it and call it something it is not. Speak out loud and say, "I am touching a (   )." If you are touching a doorknob. Fill in the blank by calling it a book, or a light bulb, or anything it is not. Do not use a synonym or anything similar. Do the same thing with another object, then another, and yet another. Keep doing this until it becomes difficult and then keep doing it until it becomes easy again.

Do this exercise with a group at the beginning of any process in which you need an open and clear mind. Work and play at this until you can do it many times, even in the same room without repeating yourself. The more you do it the easier it gets, the more creative you will become.

There is nothing wrong with having trouble with this exercise at first. It is only an indication that your mind is not clear at the moment. Your mind is stuck on the names of things as they are supposed to be, the names we have agreed on in our cultures and languages. If we will spend time do ing this practice until it becomes easy, our minds will open to many wonders.

Radio Talk Show

One participant plays the host of an imaginary radio talk show. The remaining players, standing behind or out of sight, "call in" to speak on a topic designated by the "host". "Callers" may ask questions or express opinions. Variations include working in a circle. In that case the "host" may play with eyes closed or backs turned to the group. Subject matter can be general or broad, or focused on a real issue.

Beyond simple focus on such topics, applications can include things like exploration of detailed topics, problem solving, developing the ability to think on one's feet, learning to be spontaneous, and resolving conflict.

Simile

This form can be used to explore any topic or concern you may wish. As noted above, the use of the simile is a powerful tool in all human communication. For telling stories and creating understanding, few tools are as effective for opening a person to new viewpoints.

A simile is a metaphor created by the language format with which we say, "A is like B because (   )." Understanding that one thing can be "like" another can build bridges of understanding and perspective. Making the connection with a simile is a deep value in the use of Improvisation.

The Set-up

One person takes the focus. Other participants provide the two elements of the simile. You can prompt this by asking first for a noun or verb. If the first word selected is a noun, you can say, "OK, an orange is like what?" If a verb."
Then say, "OK, flying is like doing what?"

"Someone give me another noun". This needs to happen very quickly or people will tend to give words that they have already thought through.

You then say, "A pear is like running because (   ) and the player must repeat the simile and fill in the blank with different answers very quickly three times. "A pear is like running because it goes around and around"; "A pear is like running because it is in shape"; "A pear is like running because it is goofy".

The next player starts with the same line and gives three new responses. The responses do not need to make any sense or need to be correct in any way: "A pear is like running because it is blue, it has spots, and it is named George". The next player uses the same word and gives three new responses. Eventually, if the form is played with honesty, and enthusiasm, an amazing amount of sense will develop. After a few rounds, change the base word.

To expand the form begin using different parts of speech, pronouns, adjectives, prepositions, articles, and then begin mixing them up, noun to preposition, article to verb, adverb to adjective.

There are deep archetypal processes involved when the human mind creates similes, and uses grammatical construction.

The use of this form can develop creativity, enhance professional and public speaking skills, bring insight to interpersonal communication, and help develop the overall quality of communication. The more serious and specific your topics, the deeper will be the effects.

Space Jump

This exercise can be used to explore particular organizational problems and various progressions of events in business and organizational development. *Space Jump* helps build the skills of listening and memory. It can also be used to enhance awareness of the perspectives of others.

A player takes the center of the circle and starts a story based on a word or idea suggested by you or the group. Once the opening has been established, you "freeze" the player with a loud clap and the words "Space Jump!" The participant must freeze in the physical position in which she is at that moment. She must remember this exact position. A new player then joins her on the stage. As soon as the new person enters, the first one relaxes from the "freeze" and the two people begin an entirely new conversation, not connected to the first scene.

Once the second conversation is going well, you "freeze" the two players, clapping and saying "Space Jump!" The two must freeze and remember their positions and what they were doing. A third player enters to start an entirely new conversation with three people. The process is repeated until there is a conversation or scene with up to five people playing together.

When the fifth scene reaches a completion or high point you will call, "Freeze! Space Jump! Backward!" The fifth participant leaves the game and the remaining four must return immediately to the positions, activity, and conversation in which they were engaged when the four-person scene was frozen. This process continues back through the numbers, three, two, and one. Each time the players must recreate, as closely as they can, the physical position from the earlier freeze, and they must continue and complete the conversation they left behind. This activity can be used with a large group, up to 200 if you have the PA system to support it, gathered in sets of up to 10 people engaging in scenes you can keep count of for calling back, up to about 10. It can be made wonderful by calling scene numbers out of sequence. If your group is adventurous and playing well you can even call for scene numbers that have not been played yet to see how well they are allowing the fun and creativity to proceed.

By focusing the conversations to specific business or organizational concerns or subject matter, this game can be used to review or explore any topic in depth.

In my favorite use of the *Space Jump* exercise, in a workshop with a large and magical group at Georgia Tech, we created 19 scenes early in the event and periodically through the rest of the workshop I would call out a random number. The players had to jump to the scene as it had been last frozen.

Telephone Tag, Answering Machine, Text Talk, Chat Line

Originally called, simply, Telephone Tag, this conversation exercise has been extended by technology. The participants stand so that they cannot see one another. The topic may be assigned by you, or the participants may decide the role they will play when they "answer" the ringing phone. This is a valuable game for teaching interpersonal communication skills and for enhancing listening skills.

The first player pretends to start a conversation by saying "Ring, ring" or mimes texting, or typing on a computer. If the conversation is in text or chat she can say something like, "I hope Tom is there" to signal the communication medium.

The person "answering" says, "Hello", and the "caller" can identify the recipient and the purpose of the call if he wishes. ("Tom, I have been waiting for my copy of the annual report. What is the problem?" or "Hi Sheila we have been expecting you in the B conference room. Are you coming over?") The person answering the call responds in the spirit of "Yes, and . . . ."

The recipient may also answer as he or she wishes ("Hello, this is John's whimsical house of cards"). In either case, the "caller" will have the best results by accepting whatever is offered. One should not say things such as, "I'm not Sheila" or "I don't have anything to do with the annual reports" or "Sorry, wrong number." It is more fun to go along.

For complexity and variety, the answering player may choose to be an answering machine, immediately coming up with a "recording" that ends with "beep." Then the caller must leave a message. If one is using the answering machine the message must not be planned. People will know and it will not be as fun and effective.

You, as the leader or facilitator can end the scene by freezing it. Following a freeze, the one who answered becomes the next caller and a new player answers the phone.

This format can be applied to any organizational or business topic or by incorporating real people or real areas of concern into the calls.

Other applications include training in telephone skills, including listening, clear and articulate speaking, customer service responsiveness, and thinking on your feet. It is very useful for teaching sales skills needed in fund raising, prospecting, and closing.

Television Interview

This fun and challenging structure was originally patterned after "The Johnny Carson Show". The first person plays a host and describes the nature of the program. She then identifies and introduces a guest. ("Welcome to 'Tomorrow Comes to Soon' with Loretta Farsee as your host. Please welcome the wizard Merlin who has been living his life backward for the past fifteen hundred years"). Start simple and even silly and progress to real and relevant as the people in the gathering gain confidence.

However you develop the form, it is most effective to end each interview at a high point with applause and cheering. You may also indicate the end of each segment by saying, "Blackout", or by dimming lights. When each interview ends the host leaves the scene and the guest becomes the next host and introduces a new show and a new guest. The players continue to roll through until all who wish have until all who wish have played.

A practical focus can be achieved by having the players introduce specific business or organizational development topics of their choice: a new product, training program, manual or event, and then identifying the next participant as the author or developer. It is best not to use real people or real people's names. The shift from guest to host advances the Improv and helps to develop and change management skills.

Word Montage

This exercise is the same as *Prop Montage* except that a word is used rather than a physical object. It works best with words with multiple syllables. This variation also takes the process out of the physical, and into the mental realm.

Exercise

Say something like, "A perfect day at the beach would include (   )" and insert something entirely ridiculous such as "a thumb tack". Then say "A great meal should have (   )" inserting another absurdity such as, "The king of hearts". Then begin to create your own opening lines, "A birthday really needs (   )", "A fine movie must have (   )" and fill in the blanks with things that simply do not make sense. The elements of this exercise need to be done at a very quick pace in order to overcome pondering, which

228

defeats the purpose.

This exercise will help develop open creativity and will help in advancing skills needed in professional and public communication, as well as in interpersonal communication.

Overview

This short list of advanced exercises represents a grab bag full of opportunities for you, as an Applied Improvisational teacher, trainer, and leader. Each exercise can be used to deepen the tenants of Improvisation, and each of them can be used to focus on, explore, or teach almost any specific topic. Grounding in the basic games of *Babble*, *Word for Word*, and *Four-Square Matrix* will serve in making the leap to advanced Improvisational exercises.

The Bibliography will refer you to sources of many more structures. Applications of these forms, and inventions of new forms will be your responsibility. In order to use the exercises explained here, in order to develop the ability to invent and discover new structures, and in order to receive the most value from this work, you will have to accept Improvisation as your own. In doing this you will begin creating your own creativity.

PART SIX

Making Improvisation Your Own

CHAPTER EIGHTEEN

Create Your Own Creativity

Whoopi Goldberg was apparently once asked if she would rather have a starship, or a holodeck. Her answer was that she would rather have a big box of crayons, for with them she could create a holodeck, a starship, or anything else she could imagine.

The most wonderful thing about Improvisation is that it is a multi-functional tool chest. As with a box of crayons, we may do with it whatever we wish. We are not limited to coloring with the correct colors, coloring inside the lines, or even coloring within the framework of your own ideas. With Improvisational Thinking we can Create Our Own Creativity.

The first thing we must do is to play the games and use the exercises. As long as we attend to the basic ideas and practices, Improvisation works, and it works every time. So long as we stay true to its spirit, the processes and values will reveal themselves with more and more interesting applications. So long as we approach Improvisation as "ones who learn", Improvisation will continue to teach ever increasing depths of creativity.

With creative Improvisation we can address issues of professional and public communication, interpersonal communication, the quality of any communication, many processes and levels of organizational development, as well as developmental and interdependency needs of groups, networks, and individuals. Improvisation, when applied to specific subject matter and organizational concerns, will enhance community development, planning practices, training and learning needs, measuring procedures, and the analysis of people and programs. Improvisation, practiced as a discipline, will enhance the quality of work and bring out the need for playfulness in the world of real concerns and real business problems.

Every Improvisation game and exercise embodies all of Improvisation. Each game begins as a source of learning, human interaction, laughter, and fun and extends infinitely into learning, analysis, and changes in behavior. The process itself will lead to new combinations, permutations, applications, and depth of insight. Each structure can reward its players with all the pleasures of the creative mind. In order to receive the most from Improvisation we must own it for ourselves.

Beyond the Present Moment

Primitive humans and most animals live only in the present moment, with both positive and negative effect. Living only in the present moment without studied effort can create problems. When facing the future, we most often do some essential planning, or it can be very difficult to deal with whims, crises, and the unexpected.

When we do not learn from our mistakes, we are likely to repeat them. Without a sense of the past and a plan for the future, it may also be very difficult for us to accomplish a large, or complex, or detailed, or long term goal. Yet, even when we're working on large, long-term, complex, detailed matters, the actual work must be done in the present moment, day by day, moment by moment.

Mixed Time and Present Time Consciousness

One of the ways in which we learn to develop personal ownership of Improvisation is to learn to use the consciousness of present time to deal discretely with the past, present, and the future.

Without training, we tend to do almost everything in mixed time. Reflections about the past are usually conducted in the midst of the day's activities, with interruptions from the present moment as well as hopes and fears of the future. Evaluations often are conducted in the context of future hopes and expectations, mixed with impressions of other past experiences. We tend to review our experiences and lessons in mixed time as well. Even when managers and executives are doing excellent work in review, adjustment, reinvention, and reinforcement, such events done in mixed time can produce less than the best possible results.

Using the Present to Capture the Past and Future

This theory suggests that we identify a time frame from the past, and then review it in a period dedicated to being in the present, so we can do nothing beside review the chosen time frame. Focus your attention with the same dedication and passion with which Margaret Mead focused herself while listening to a stranger. Use your present time focus to recreate the event with your mind, your heart, your spirit, and your emotions.

We can handle evaluations in the same fashion. Set time aside for doing nothing except comparing predicted results with actual results. Use your Improv discipline to keep yourself in the present moment as you conduct the evaluation. What was really done and what was actually produced? If you spend your time comparing factual results with imagined possible results, you will take yourself out of present time and muddle your conclusions. If you wish to experience the most from a comparison of actual results with possible results, do this as an analysis exercise of its own in present time consciousness.

Previews are very often conducted in mixed time, clouded by comparisons with past successes or failures, and future hopes and fears, and the successes and failures of others at other times and places. Again, you will gain the most clear results if you set aside time just to look at the future, and then to conduct the preview in present time consciousness when nothing else is going on.

It is a good idea to set aside the time for planning and conducting the act of planning in present time consciousness. If we must evaluate the plan while we are making the plan, we can use the general Improvisation skills and ideas to help us be the most effective.

We may plan in the present for a while, then shift gears to evaluate for a while, and then go back to the plan again. If you do not have disciplined and explicit transitions and time parameters, your time consciousness will mix and probably dilute your results.

As you learn the use of Improvisation, you will gain skills in the use of current time, both to learn from your efforts, and to develop yourself as a leader who is operating in the present moment, an Applied Improvisation Executive who is creating your own creativity.

Taking Delight in the Present

Another step in creating your own creativity, and making the Improvisation your own requires special disciplines. With focused effort, Improvisation disciplines become a daily delight as you seek the ability to find and to stay in the present moment. If we spend our days in the "busy-ness" of being busy, without this discipline, it can be difficult to operate in the present moment.

Creativity in Daily Disciplines

A number of games are helpful for creating your own personal discipline. My son, Jonathan Michael Mawle Lowe, helped to develop the disciplines described below.

"Let's See what We have Never Seen Before."

Jonathan was nine, and our favorite ice cream parlor had lots of windows looking out over a shopping center parking lot. While we sat with our double scoops in sugar cones, we played "Let's see what we have never seen before".

We began to gaze through the windows at the large and familiar shopping center parking lot. Our game required that one of us had to find something in the panorama that we had never noticed before. It could not be a living, or temporary thing like a bird or a person, or a car or a leaf. We had to find something that clearly had been there a long time, yet neither of us had noticed until that moment. It took a great honesty to do this fairly.

The rules required that should my son find two things, then I had to do the same. If he found three, it fell to me to follow. We did this once a week, on average, for five years. For the entire time, until the ice cream shop closed, every time, there was always some new detail that revealed itself. Some days we both found three or four new things. Some days were lean and we could see only one or two. Some days were a real challenge and we had to look, and look, and look, and look; then a breakthrough occurred. We could see everything differently and previously unseen things appeared as if by magic.

On some miraculous days I actually accomplished positive changes in my real behavior based on the effects of the game. Most days, he breezed through massive changes in his behavior, laughing, and growing as he played with this discipline.

No matter what else was going on, the game enabled us to relax into the reality of a perfect, real feedback event. We had the gift, over and over again, of a perfect moment that had never existed before and would never exist again except in the influence on how we think, and how we act.

As we play he clears his mind. He knows that he has searched this horizon time and time again. Delight surrounds him and his knowledge of play takes over. When people are working with Improvisation as a vision generator, I look for these same things signs.

Jonathan becomes so excited that his speech is quick; he becomes rushed to share the moment. He seeks challenge. Now I am on the spot. I must ready for the sport. When using Improvisation as a personal development tool or an organizational development tool, I am seeking this same excitement in the participants.

We delighted in the game and in the presence of one another. Jonathan is 28 now and I still take my clues from him. He has taught me to watch the people with whom I work and live very carefully, very gently, very openly, very honestly, and very playfully. I watch his face and eyes relax. I look for this kind of relaxation in the eyes and faces of the people who are engaged in Improvisation as an exercise. In the early days, as Jonathan lost his need to "do things right", his excitement increased and his mind and body showed that he knew there is always something new to see, even in an old familiar place.

Wherever you are at this moment is not just any old familiar place. Your spot on our small planet, spinning through the universe, is really thousands of miles away from where it was even a few moments ago.

I recommend the use of this exercise as a fun discipline. Better yet would be to invent an exercise like this of your own. I suggest that you do this exercise with someone who is important to you. If you are a young executive, I recommend that you find one person who is much younger than you, and another person much older, find a place where you may share a cup of coffee or a snack. A meal is probably too complicated.

NOTE

You may use Improvisation as a way to generate excitement, general playfulness, playfulness with focus, relaxation, honesty, hunger for the new, discipline of change, and a rush to share and be challenged.

"Let's See what there is to See"

Another game I played with my son we called "Let's see what there is to see". This exercise begins with an adventure such as a walk around a lake or around a building. Creating a model airplane is a good adventure, or exploring a creek, going out to dinner, or exploring a new store. Keeping it simple is important, best to avoid a mall. A zoo or circus would be too complex.

Whatever you choose, change it into an exercise for your creative mind. As you engage in your task, take time to name new things that you see. At the lake it may be a bird, or around a building it may be the pattern of the windows. In the office you could institute a "Let's see what there is to see" moment at some fun length and interval. Interesting things or the strange juxtaposition of objects can seem to appear out of nowhere. You may become aware of patterns and shapes, smells and sounds that can allow the familiar to appear bright and new. I suggest that you do this game in important places.

Sounds and Rhythms

There are many ways to exercise your creativity in a daily practice. In the movie, "Tap", Gregory Hines plays the son of an old-time tap dancer. His father was famous for finding new beats and tempos in the sounds of the city, the clatter of the people and machines, and their daily tasks. The cacophony became drum phrases for him, producing foot-tapping harmonies in a surreal swirl of creativity. This was his daily creativity discipline. The intent of this exercise is to overcome noise and distraction and to practice being in the current moment by listening to it very carefully.

There are stories of an Improvisation player who became expert at making sounds for the stage: doors opening, people walking, phones ringing. He apparently worked on a factory assembly line. As he made each movement of the assembly, he practiced making a noise until he is able to create the sound perfectly. These he brought to Improvisation.

Whether you focus on sight or sound, or any other sense, begin to develop the exercise of creativity as a daily practice. A conscious effort to see and know new things is part of the path to owning Improvisation and developing the leadership necessary to bring it to others.

New Names for Old Things

A different way to stretch our creative muscles is to give new names to the familiar things we handle each day. A basic form of this process has been discussed. This game can help your people discover unexpected mental connections that help free your Improvisation process.

Whether or not you notice it, each time you interact with physical things your mind names them and names the action. "My 'hand' 'reaches' into my 'pocket' to find my 'keys'". "I 'grab' the 'doorknob' to 'open' the 'door.'"

Try replacing a single word at first. "My 'windmill' reaches into my pocket to grasp my keys." Then replace various words at once, "My 'giraffe' reaches into my 'battleship.'" Then switch verbs, "My 'horse' 'guffaws' into my 'painting' to 'glorify' my 'petunias.'"

Try, "I mangle the doorknob". Then, "Tom the Tango instructor depletes the writhing doorknob". You may take this exercise to the ridiculous with such as, "Fine Frank cobbles crystals to flatten the baboon". If you take this exercise to the ridiculous with a person who is young, or old (you define these terms), you can create great laughter.

Use the same sentence again, inserting different replacement words, until you become proficient. Eventually you will be able to replace words randomly as you begin to notice the acts of unconscious naming that goes on in your brain.

This game is interesting to play with another person. It is good to play with a number of different people over time. If you play this game alone, you are likely to find yourself laughing out loud for no apparent reason as the game carries you into the creative states of mind.

Discovering New Games

Improvisation is a system in much the same way that architecture, building construction and engineering are systems. Not only can we build houses with these systems, the number and variety of houses we can build are infinite. We can also use them to build skyscrapers, bird houses, churches or temples, as well opera halls, theaters, business buildings, hotels, gazebos, tree houses, boats, green houses, tunnels, bridges, automobiles, airplanes, towers, highway interchanges, space ships, satellites, and integrated circuits. The list goes on.

You can teach yourself to generate an amazing number of Improv games and applications of Improvisation games. Improvisation process itself can be used to generate new games and new application ideas.

Creating New Formats

The designation "new game" does not require total uniqueness. A method for bringing your own style and personality to an Improvisation process is to select an exercise and "grow" a variation. At Improvisation conferences you will hear people describe new games. A common response to most new game descriptions is, "Oh, we call that . . .", or "we do that this way. . . ."

There are truly "new" Improvisation games invented daily. Variations are made up whenever Improvisers play and Applied Improvisers are at work. Time spent considering the structure of games and encouraging yourself, and others with whom you work, to create new ones is a good exercise in developing understanding of the whole process.

Inventing New Forms

You can invent a form by selecting a game type to study very carefully in order to figure out how it works. I will use the term "game" for ease of communication. The basic game structures include: line games, roll-through games, two person games, circle games, three to seven person games, and larger crowd games. After you understand your new exercise, then focus on finding applications for the game type that go beyond performance and fun. Applications in learning, pedagogy, and epistemology are especially rewarding to develop. Change the set design or seek other structural or logistical changes to the type you have selected. By playing with a game type using this discipline, you may develop whole new forms, which seem to surface as though by magic.

Final Thoughts

Daily disciplines are vital in creating your own creativity. You may use the ones I have suggested and you will find disciplines of your own. I recommend that you find playful substitutes.

Creating new games and inventing new games will keep your Improvisation discipline alive and supple. Doing this will also enhance your use of the art.

A Breath of Fresh Air

Breathing energizes many disciplines. When breathing is well-regulated and working as it should, it feeds the brain, and enhances our ability to stay in the current moment. It energizes our activity, and it helps us discover the best uses of Applied Improvisation. Good breathing is a key element in creating our own creativity.

When breathing we must both give (exhale) and receive (inhale) in equal measure. Sometimes we find ourselves always giving of ourselves: giving time, energy, emotional support, money, and more. You may have noticed that unless you receive some measure of return, you can become burned out, exhausted, even bitter. On the other hand, there are times when we can seem only to take and take and not to give back. Eventually, this also isolates us; we can become bloated, yet never full. Imbalance in either direction can keep us from working at our best, and in current time. It can turn our efforts into struggle rather than joy.

The longer we hold our breath, the more carbon dioxide we produce and maintain in our bodies. As the carbon dioxide builds, we begin to experience toxic responses. As we approach toxic shock, we panic. Actually, the instant we start to hold our breath, our cells begin to shut down activities not related to the search for oxygen. Our thinking slows, metabolism fluctuates, our heartbeat increases, blood vessels begin to constrict from the extremities inward, blood pressure fluctuates, adrenaline flows, and attendant endocrine responses ensue. Panic sets in and eventually we will pass out.

When breathing stops, even for an instant, your body does not care whether it is by decision, or the result of an accident. It takes steps in a prescribed and ancient order that leads to unconsciousness, and death.

Beyond the power to hold one's breath, it has been calculated that the average human breathes only 80 percent of the time. Furthermore, we tend to use only about 60 percent of our lung capacity. This is not a conscious act. Even on a very bad day, we do not say, "I don't like the world today. I am going to withhold my precious carbon dioxide." On a given day we may say, "I am unworthy". However, we do not say, "I refuse myself the gift of oxygen. I shall not breathe in today".

What we tend to do instead is to hold our breath for short periods of time as part of bad breathing habits. We tend to breathe in and hold our breath for a while. Or we breathe out and hold it, perhaps as a sigh, depending on our own particular habits. Unless you are trained in a breath awareness disciplines, this process is usually unconscious. Part of the process of making Improvisation your own is to begin to notice your own breathing habits.

A Short Breathing Exercise

Take a breath and don't let it out. Take in another breath. Then another, without letting your breath out. Try taking still another breath, and then another. At some point you can't do it anymore. Now, let your breath out and breathe normally for a while.

Try doing this in the other direction. Exhale. Don't take in another breath. Exhale again, and again. Can you exhale once more? Maybe not. Now breathe normally for a while. Ultimately we must breathe in and out in approximately equal measure.

Our body will fight imbalance. It will rob us of energy and clarity. Imbalance in breathing will disturb the synchronization of our bodies, minds, and spirits. If we are not in sync with our breathing, we will otherwise be out of time.

In order to assimilate Improvisation as truly your own, and to create your own creativity, you will do well to attend to your breathing. Learn to breathe fully and continuously. Learn to use your breath as a tool to keep yourself completely in the moment. There is a great deal of information available on breathing practices. Depending on our interests, we may try looking to the fields of sports, music, dance, meditation, yoga, and the martial arts for more guidance.

A Balance between Giving and Receiving

In order to achieve the ability to create our own creativity, we do best to strive for an essential balance. At the same time, in many areas of our lives we must separate giving from receiving. Often we give emotional support to our family and friends, their times of need, and then must wait for our time of need to receive support in return. We must give young children emotional support, and cannot expect emotional support from them while they are young.

Often we work for our money in one endeavor, and gain our personal satisfaction elsewhere. When we work for ourselves or in new jobs, we often must give for rather a long time before the rewards are returned. This is equally true of education and training.

Most jobs have both positive and negative aspects; satisfaction may be had by focusing on the positive. Often in our employment there must be a separation between give and take. Yet, if balance is not eventually achieved, the results can be harmful.

If we take joy in the process of work, we can gain the most from it and do the most with it. Joy can maintain the best general balance in our lives. Joy and satisfaction in the process of living create a sense of balance and ultimately a sense of well-being. In using Improvisation for any of its purposes, it is a very good idea for us to receive joy and satisfaction from the process itself. Part of our job is also to help others find joy and satisfaction to achieve balance in the process as well.

If joy and satisfaction are not present during the process of learning and change, the events themselves can become a negative experience and participants may lose the will to be open to new things. Without joy and positive feedback, the probability that information will be retained or real behavior will be changed is reduced dramatically. Without involvement and interaction in the process itself, the probability of future application, doing something real with the information is reduced.

As Improvisation Professionals, we can lead the way by our action. We must walk the talk, stride the ride, live the lesson, face the facts, vibrate with the vision, swing with the steps, wallow in the wonder, gallop with the goals, triumph with the truth, breathe the breath..., well, you come to the idea.

The Applied Improvisation Network[36]

In 1910 I was introduced to The Applied Improvisation Network and was blessed to attend the 10th World conference in Baltimore, MD, USA, in 2011. The network is composed of more than 5,000 people with members in Asia, Europe, America, Canada, and Australia. There are members also in India, South Africa, Brazil, and New Zeeland. All who are engaged in exploration of Improvisation beyond the theatre.

The most recent world conferences have been held in Oxford, UK,

---

[36] http://appliedimprovisation.network.

Montreal, Canada, Austin, TX, Berlin, and San Francisco, drawing people from all over the world. The level of work and play being achieved by these groups is wonderful to see. We have people working with disaster victims in the Philippines, with abused children crossing the Mexican border into the U.S., with hospitals and conflict resolution, and with a wide variety of other uses.

About "Joe"

Early in my Improv comedy career, a young man showed up at our workshop. I shall call him "Joe". He was apparently in his late twenties. Some years before he had been in a serious accident that had left him with the mental and emotional age of a bright twelve-year-old. He was a delightful and happy spirit. He lived in the back of a store, and supported himself by keeping the store clean.

Joe had seen an Improv show and decided that he wanted to learn how to do it. Before he came by, he bought a new suit made of brown and beige plaid polyester.

By the standards of the young people playing at that time, Joe was slow and had a limited frame of reference. To some of the youngest people in the troupe he seemed more than a little bit strange. Many were uncomfortable in his presence, and others did not enjoy playing with him on the stage. Every time Joe came to a workshop or show he wore the same plaid suit. Every time he also came with the same open heart, the same friendly smile, the same conviction that he could do the work. He always arrived with a smile, patience, willingness to laugh, and a quiet tolerance of those who shunned him.

Before long Joe settled in and everyone found ways Joe could be on the stage without inhibiting performances. Some used him somewhat selfishly, almost as a stage prop, in order to get laughs. Being on the stage when people were laughing was ambrosia on which Joe feasted. He had a bigger heart than the rest of us, and the source of the laughter did not matter to him. The limelight was itself an elixir that produced a dawn of new feelings, and he simply basked in it.

After a while everyone became more tolerant, more adult, kinder, and eventually protective of Joe. Cruelties and arrogance soon came to an end as he became a full member of our "family". Joe found his niche. He was a natural "straight man". He had all the freshness and enthusiasm of a bright and interested twelve-year-old with the wisdom of one whose life had been turned into a challenge beyond the average. He grew. His strengths became stronger, his weaknesses diminished. He was a joy and pleasure to play and work with. Joe became an inspiration to us all. He was there simply to be there.

The Improvisation Plateau

All who improvise must face plateaus. Wit and intelligence, natural funniness, and even raw talent will all run out after a while. Eventually our public face gives way to our deeper self. I have had the pleasure of knowing some extraordinary "wits" and talents who have come to Improvisation ready to float through it. However, when people are working two, or three, or more workshops and two or more shows every week, even extraordinary wit and talent runs out after a few months or a year or two at the most. Each time the wit, and brain, and intelligence, and talent, and luck, and pattern adherence run out, there is an "Improvisation Plateau" the player must reach inside for more resources, for deeper understanding of staying in the present moment, more wonder in the skill of listening, and the profound embodiment of "Yes, and . . . .", as a way of life. It is here that the creativity has its source. It is here that we can learn the value of Improvisation as our own point of view.

Improvisation Crisis

Usually between a month and six months into the process, everyone goes through the "Improvisation Crisis". This is a crisis that requires releasing all resistance and entering into the unknown world of pure Improvisation creativity. This development can be pushed by a trained and practiced Improvisation facilitator so an early Improvisation crisis, the crisis of achieving freedom can occur at a significant level within a few hours.

The Improvisation crisis looks similar each time and with each person, regardless of and when it is achieved. It looks a bit like fear and panic. The eyes may lose their focus, palms become sweaty, the heart beats faster, breathing speeds up, and dizziness may occur. The crisis often shows itself as resistance, confusion, or hostility. The person in the transition talks later of disorientation, loss of time sense, heightened sensory perception, and a feeling of breakthrough and relaxation.

With enlightened facilitation, with a participant-centered approach, including personal involvement and leadership, and with adherence to the rules, theories, practices, purposes, forms and spirit, the Applied Improvisation Professional can guide the participants through these crises directly to personal and social creativity, and into a joyous, more functional view of life.

Joe Again

The real miracle of Joe, and of the spirit of Improvisation, was demonstrated to us at the beginning of his second year of play. Some new, very talented, and exceptionally bright young people joined the Improvisation workshop group. One new player came to her "Improv crisis." Her wit, her intelligence, her extraordinary depth of reference, her talent, her innocence, her control, and her patterned responses all failed her and she was lost, perhaps for the first time in her life. She felt herself frozen in time.

That evening Joe took the stage with another experienced player and he brought down the house. All he did was to follow some of the suggested guidelines, and to walk the path with his big open heart. He relaxed into the moment, and played whole heartedly. Jonathan playing "Let's see what we have never seen before?" reminds me of the way Joe flew through his Improvisation.

The young woman in the crisis whispered out loud to herself, "If HE can do this, I can do this".

A bond was created, not just between Joe and the young woman. It was also between the young woman and the spirit of Improvisation, the spirit of creativity, the spirit of life. The simultaneous simplicity and complexity swept her off her feet. When she next took the stage, the glaze in her eyes turned to a sparkle, her hesitancy turned to commitment, and her mind released its control and gave power to her whole being. Down came the house once again. In order to use Improvisation effectively as an organizational development and executive business tool, you will have to go through your own Improvisation crises. There may be many of them. Each time you go through the crisis you will find yourself on the other side of something that has been a personal or professional limitation or barrier.

Activate the creativity of Improvisation by spending time with it over the years. Improvisation, whether for leading, teaching, playing, or for developing a profession, is a lifetime study. It begins with your breath and goes through the disciplined practice of its elements, in small, successful, incremental steps toward the ancient human vision of progress. Proceed with joy and with a playful spirit.

Epilogue

As the Improvisation movement is spreading around the globe, I see in the progression, the lowly dandelion. *Tarasacum Officinalis*, which comes from the Greek words for "disorder" and "remedy".

In her appearance she seems to be little more than a flat weed in the grass. On closer inspection it is discovered that her roots are nutritious and health giving, and her leaves a fine tea, and even wine do make.

Then up she sends a spindly stalk to a sort of funny looking, simple yellow flower; able to light up the chin of a child, creating laughter again and again.

Suddenly a breathtaking ball of faerie stuff appears, for just a moment, before a puff of life sends flying its seeds of "Yes, and, I AM listening to

YOU", floating, disbursing to seed again wherever there is enough love, light, laughter, and joy to encourage bliss.

In 1979 it was my wonderful pleasure to meet the great architect, inventor, writer, and philosopher R. Buckminster Fuller. I had read pretty much all that "Bucky" had published and loved his ideas and his thinking. His speaking was as eloquent as his writing, as inspired as his geodesic dome, and his Dymaxion car. At the end of the meeting there was a reception line.

I waited for my turn, and when I finally met him I shook his hand and gushed about his work. I must have acted like a rock-and-roll groupie. He listened kindly, nodding and smiling. Then, with a gentle and sincere voice he said, "That's very nice. Thank you. Now, forget about me and go do something".

It is my suggestion that you the same thing. Now, go do something.

Bibliography
and
Suggested Reading
for the Applied Improvisation Professional

Must Read Recommendations

Viola Spolin. *Improvisation for the Theater*. Evanston, IL: Northwestern University Press, 1963.

Viola Spolin. *Theater Games for Rehearsal*, Evanston, IL: Northwestern University Press, 1985.

Keith Johnstone. *Impro, Improvisation and the Theatre*. New York, NY: Theatre Arts Books, 1979.

Augusto Boal. *Theatre of the Oppressed: Translators. McBride & McBride.* New York, NY: Theatre Communications Group, 1985.

Stephen Nachmanovitch. *Free Play: Improvisation in Life and Art.* New York, NY: Jeremy P. Tarcher/Putnam, 1990.

Charna Halpern, Del Close, and Kim "Howard" Johnson. *Truth in Comedy: The Manual of Improvisation.* Colorado Springs, CO: Meriweather Publishing, Ltd. 1994.

Daniel Belgrad. *The Culture of Spontaneity: Improvisation and the Arts in Postwar America.* Chicago & London: The University of Chicago Press, 1998.

Paul Z, Jackson. *The Inspirational Trainer: Making Your Training Flexible and Spontaneous & Creative.* London, UK: Kogan Page Ltd., Sterling, VA, USA, 1998. (First published as *Impro Learning, How to Make Your Training Creative, Flexible and Spontaneous.* Aldershot England and Vermont, USA: Gower Publishing Limited, 1998.

Robert Lowe. *Improvisation, Inc.: Harnessing Spontaneity to Engage People and Groups.* San Francisco, CA: Jossey-Bass/Pfeiffer, 2000.

Kat Koppett. *Training to Imagine: Practical Improvisational Theatre Techniques for Trainers and Managers to Enhance Creativity, Teamwork, Leadership, and Learning,* 2nd Ed. (First Edition 2001). Sterling, VA: Stylus *Publishing, 2013.*

Patricia Ryan Madson. *Improv Wisdom: Don't Prepare, Just Show Up.* New York, NY: Bell Tower, imprint of the Crown Publishing Group, division of Random House, 2005.

Adam Blatner, Ed. With Daniel J. *Interactive and Improvisational Drama: Varieties of Applied Theatre and Performance.* (Hannah Fox, et al). New York, Lincoln, NE: Shanghai: iUniverse, Inc., 2007.

Steven Johnson. *Wonderland: How Play Made the Modern World.* New York, NY: Riverhead Books, an Imprint of Penguin Random House LLC, 2016.

Historical Perspectives

Boyd, Neva L. and Pederson, Dagney. *Folk Games and Gymnastic Play: For Kinderrgarten Primary and Playground,* Chicago, IL: Saul Brothers Publishers, 1914. (Ms. Pederson was the first author. Their names are reversed here.)

Boyd, Neva L. and Pederson, Dagney. *Folk Games of Denmark and Sweden.* Chicago, IL: H.T. FitzSimmons Company, 1915.

Boyd, Neva L. *Handbook of Recreational Games.* New York, NY: Dover Publications, 1945, and 1975.

Bridge, William H. *Actor in the Making: A Handbook on Improvisation and Other Techniques of Development.* Boston, MA: Expression Company, 1936.

Coleman, Janet. *The Compass.* New York, NY: Alfred Knopf, 1990.

Dudeck, Theresa Robbins, *Keith Johnstone: A Critical Biography*, London, New Delhi, New York, NY, Sydney, AUS: Bloomsbury, 2013.

Duchartre, Pierre Louis. *The Italian Comedy: The improvisation Scenarios Lives, Attributes, Portraits and Masks of the Illustrious Characters of the Comedia dell'Arte*. London, UK: George G. Harrap & Co., Ltd., 1929.

Hartnoll, Phyllis. *The Theatre: A Concise History*. London, UK: Thames & Hudson, 1968.

McCrohan, Donna. *The Second City*. New York, NY: Putnam, 1987.

Newton, Robert G. *Acting Improvised*. London, Edinburgh, Paris, FR, Melbourne, CAN, Toronto, CAN, and New York, NY: Thomas Nelson & Sons, Ltd., 1937.

Patinkin, Sheldon. *The Second City*. Naperville, IL: Sourcebooks, Inc., 2000.

Partch, Harry. *Genesis of a Music, an account of creative work, its roots, and its fulfillments*. New York, NY: DaCapo Press, 1974.

Pohler, Amy. *Yes Please*. New York, NY: Dey Street, an Imprint of William Morrow Publishers, 2014.

Quinn, Susan. *Furious Improvisation: How the WPA and a Cast of Thousands Made High Art out of Desperate Times*. New York, NY: Walker Publishing Company, Inc., 2008.

David Shepherd: "A Lifetime in Improvisational Theatre" (Video). Michael Golding, Director, Mike Fleischaker, with Andrew Duncan, Mark Gordon, Charna Halpern, and Howard Jerome. Produced by Canadian Improv Games, 2006. https://www.youtube.com/watch?v=t5wgtkgCH3A

Sweet, Jeffrey. *Something Wonderful Right Away: An Oral History of the Second City and Compass Players*. Toronto, CAN: New Books, 1978.

Suggested Additional Reading

Arch, Dave. *Showmanship for Presenters: 49 Proven Training Techniques from Professional Performers*. San Francisco: CA: Jossey-Bass/Pfeiffer, 1995.

Beaudoin, Marie Nathalie, and Sue Walden. *Working with Groups to Enhance Relationships*. Duluth, MN: Whole Person Associates, Inc., 1998.

Bonifer, Mike. *Game Changers: Improvisation for Business in the Networked World*. Los Angeles, CA: McKava Press, 2007.

Bonifer, Mike, and Shternshus. *CTRL, Shift: 50 Gamed for 50 ****ing Days like Today*. Atlanta, GA: BDI Publishers, 2015.

Gesell, Izzy. *Playing Along: 37 Group Learning Activities Borrowed from Improvisational Theater*. Duluth, MN: Whole Person Associates, 1997.

De Koven, Bernard Louis. *The Well-Played Game: A Player's Philosophy*. Garden City, NY: Anchor Books, 1978.

De Koven, Bernard Louis. *A Playful Path.* Pittsburg, PA: Carnegie Mellon University, ETC Press, 2014.

Darnell, G. Brent. *Stress Management, Time Management and Life Balance for Tough Guys.* Atlanta, GA: G. Brent Darnell, 2008.

Darnell, G. Brent. *The People-Profit Connection: How Emotional Intelligence Can Maximize People Skills and Maximize Your Profits.* Atlanta, GA: BDI Publishers, 2011.

Epstein, Robert. *The Big Book of Creativity Games: Quick, Fun Activities for Jumpstarting Innovation.* New York, NY: McGraw-Hill, 2000.

Frost, Anthony, and Ralph Yarrow. *Improvisation in Drama.* Houndsmill, Basingstoke, Hampshire, and London, UK: The Macmillan Press, Ltd., 1990.

Jackson, Paul Z. *58 ½ Ways to Improvise in Training.* Carmarthan, Wales, UK: Crown House Publishing, Ltd. 2003.

Jackson, Paul Z. *Easy: Your Lifepass to Creativity and Confidence,* London, UK: The Solution Focus, 2015.

Meyer, Pamela. *From Workplace to Playspace: Innovating Learning, and Changing Trough Dynamic Engagement.* San Francisco, CA: Jossey-Bass, an imprint of Wiley, 2010.

Meisner, Sanford, and Dennis Longwell. *Sanford Meisner on Acting.* New York, NY: Vintage Books, A division of Random House, 1987.

Safran, Lisa. *Using Improvisation to Build Literacy.* Lexington, KY: Princess Ellen Publishing, 2010.

Stanislavski, Constantin. *An Actor Prepares.* Trans. Elizabeth Reynolds Hapgood. New York, NY: Routledge/Theatre Arts Books, 1936.

Weinstein, Matt, and Joel Goodman. *Playfair: Everybody's Guide to Noncompetitive Play.* San Luis Obispo, CA: Impact Publishers, 1980.

Weinstein, Matt, and Luke Barber. *Work Like Your Dog: Fifty Ways to Work Less, Play More, and Earn More.* New York, NY: Villard Books, a division of Random House, 1999.

Wiener, Daniel J. *Rehearsals for Growth: Theater Improvisation for Psychotherapists.* New York, NY and London, UK: W.W. Norton Company, 1994.

Zaporah, Ruth. *Action Theater: The Improvisation of Presence.* Berkeley, CA: North Atlantic Books, 1995.

Additional Improvisational Comedy Theatre Reading

Barton, Robert. *Acting, Onstage and Off, 2nd Ed.,* New York, NY: Harcourt Brace College Publishers, 1993.

Besser, Matt, Ian Roberts, and Matt Walsh. *The Upright Citizens Brigade Comedy Improvisation Manual.* New York, NY: Comedy Council of Nicea, LLC, 2013.

Belt, Lynda and Rebecca Stockley. *Improvisation through Theatre Sports*. Seattle, WA: Thespis Productions, 1989.

Bernard, Jill. *Jill Bernard's Small Cute Book of Improv*, 3rd Edition. Minneapolis, MN: YESand.com Publishing, 2007.

Barker, Clive. *Theatre Games: A New Approach to Drama Training*. London, UK: Eyre Methune, 1977.

Fey, Tina. *Bossypants*. New York, NY: A Reagan Arthur Company – Little Brown and Company, 2011.

Halpern, Charna. *Art by Committee: a Guide to Advanced Improvisation*. Colorado Springs, CO: Meriweather Publishing, Ltd., 2005.

Johnstone: Keith. *Impro for Storytellers: Theatresports and the Art of Making things Happen*. London, UK: Faber and Faber, 1994.

Leonard, Kelly, and Tom Yorton. *Lessons from the Second City: Yes, And*. New York, NY: Harper Business, an Imprint of HarperCollins Publishers, 2015.

Philosophical Foundations

Bandler, Richard. *Using Your Brain for a Change*. Moab, UT: Real People Press, 1985.

Campbell, Don. *The Mozart Effect*. New York, NY: Avon Books, 1997.

Cook, H. Caldwell. *The Play Way: An Essay in Educational Method*. London: William Heinemann, 1917.

De Chardin, Pierre Teilhard. *The Phenomenon of Man*. New York, NY: Harper & Row, 1955.

Hayakawa, Samuel I. *Language in Thought and Action*. New York, NY: Harcourt, Brace & World, 1964.

Heckler, Richard Strozzi, Ed. *Aikido and the New Warrior*. Berkeley, CA: North Atlantic Books, 1985.

Isaac, Manson. "Aïkido" (Demonstration video), Paris, FR: Vivendi, http://www.dailymotion.com/video/x2ik3n, 2007.

Korzybsky, Alfred. *Science and Sanity: an Introduction to Non-Aristotelian Systems and General Semantics*. Lancaster, PA: Science Press Printing Co., 1933.

Lowe, Robert. *Happy Vernday Birthcox: Revolution, Evolution, and an Uncommon Commune – 1970*. Atlanta, GA: RLJ Publications, 2015.

Pearce, Joseph Chilton. *The Magical Child Matures*. New York: Bantam, 1985.

Ravich, Lenny. *A Funny Thing Happened on the Way to Enlightenment*, New Orleans, LA: Gestalt Institute Press of New Orleans/Metairi, 2002.

Ray, Sondra. *Loving Relationships: The Secrets of a Great Relationship*, Berkeley, CA: Celestial Arts, 1980.

Ray, Sondra. *Ideal Birth*. Berkeley, CA: Celestial Arts, 1985.

Stevens, John. *Invincible Warrior: A Pictorial Biography of Morihei Ueshiba, The Founder of Aikido.* Boston, MA: Shambhala, 1997.

Ueshiba, Kisshomaru. Trans. Taitetsu Unno. *The Spirit of Aikido.* Tokyo, JAP, New York, NY, and San Francisco, CA: Kodansha International, 1984.

von Oech, Roger. *A Whack on the Side of the Head.* New York, NY: Warner Books, 1983.

Wilhelm, Richard. *The I Ching, or Book of Changes.* Trans. Cary F. Baynes. Forward by C.G. Jung. Princeton, NJ: Princeton University Press, 1950.

Management and Human Interaction

Hsieh, Tony. *Delivering Happiness: A Path to Profits, Passions, and Purpose.* New York, NY and Boston, MA: Business Plus, 2010.

Mitchell, Donald, Carol Coles, and Robert Metz. *The 2,000Percent Solution: Free your Organization from "Stalled" Thinking to Achieve Exponential Success.* New York, NY: American Management Association, 1999.

Mitchell, Donald, and Carol Coles. *The Irresistible Growth Enterprise: Breakthrough Gains from Unstoppable Change.* Sterling, VA: Stylus Publishing, LLC, 2000.

Pike, Bob. *The Creative Training Technologies Handbook.* Minneapolis, MN: Lakewood Press, 1994.

Whitelaw, Ginny and Betsy Wetzig. *Move to Greatness: Focusing the Four Essential Energies of a Whole and Balanced Leader.* Boston, MA: Nicholas Brealy Publishing, 2008.

Whitelaw, Ginny. *Body Learning.* New York, NY: Penguin Putnam, Inc. 1998.

Whitelaw, Ginny. *The Zen Leader: Ways to go From Barely Managing to Leading Fearlessly.* Pompton Plains, NJ: The Career Press, Inc. 2012.

Additional Resources

The Spolin Center, **www.Spolincenter.com.**

Bay Area Theatre Sports (BATS), www.improv.org

Sivasailam Thiagarajan, The Thiagi Group, **Designing** leadership, soft skills, and technical training for corporate clients, www.thiagi.com.

Then there are the hundreds more resources that are increasing every day where you will find on your own, or hopefully, become one yourself.

A Work-in-progress Improvisation Timeline:
Including Personal, and Atlanta Influences
(A work in progress. Seeking Additions.)
Rlowe46@outlook.com

Pre-human – The first Improvisation was most likely accomplished by a primate who fell from a tree at the feet of a predator, and got out of the jam by the use of wits alone.

Pre-history - Primitive tribal dance and religious rituals appear. Mime appeared with proof that places outside temples, and people other than priests apparently were using dramatic gesture, and speech to provide drama to special occasions.

3100 BCE - Egyptian Coronation Festival plays were performed.

2750 BCE – In there were Egypt ritual dramas.

2500 BCE – Shaman elders were practicing mysterious arts.

2400 BCE – The first clowns were jesters documented in Egyptian hieroglyphs.

2000 BCE – There was evidence of Marionette puppets, which probably led to   the first instances of Improvisation recorded among humans.

1994-1781 BCE - The earliest depiction of toss juggling appeared in Egypt.

1887 BCE - Passion plays were presented at Abydos, Egypt.

800 BCE – There were dramatic dance performances.

800 BCE - Susarion formed a band of comedians in Icaria, and wandered

through Greece. They were the predecessor of the Comedia dell' Arte.

5th Century BCE - Mountbanks of Athens and Sparta improvised to sell wares, and to separate money from the crowds.

600 BCE – Saw the origin of Greek theatre.

534 BCE - Thespis invented the theatre of tragedy.

500 BCE - Comedy competitions appear in Greece.

3d Century BCE - Parodists, songsters, story tellers, and clowns dressed in white plied their trade in Greece.

356 BCE – There were the first Roman theatrical performances.

300 BCE - Imperial Chinese Jester, Yu Sze influenced the court.

200 c. BCE - Etruscans performed "The Atellanæ", Improvisations in Roman streets before and after the theater.

100 ACE - In East India, Viduska clowns interpreted the Mahabharata for the lower classes.

200 ACE - Classical Sanskrit theatre appeared.

618 ACE - Theatre appears in China.

800 - Traveling circuses appear.

925 –There was the beginning of medieval theatre.

1200 - Professional bards (story tellers) appeared in Ireland.

1250 – There was the beginning of German drama.

1325 - Noh plays developed in Japan.

253

1375 – The first English plays were presented.

1300's – There were Tarot cards, with clown pictures based on Egyptian Hieroglyphs.

1490 - Spanish drama appeared.

1520 - Jesters served in Montezuma's court.

1575 - Clowning developed a theatrical art form.

16th - 17th Century - Comedia dell' Arte appeared in Italy and France developing Harlequin (Arlecchino), Pantalone, Scaramouche, and others.

1680 - Comédie Français becomes the first national theatre.

1716 - First American theatre formed in Williamsburg, Virginia.

1750 – There was the first playhouse in New York.

1768 - Phillip Astley created the first Circus and Clown act.

1790 – There was slave dancing in Congo Square, New Orleans, Louisiana.

1700s to 1876 – Saw the beginning and development of Yiddish theater from East and East Central Europe, to Berlin, London, Paris, Buenos Aires, and New York City, probably evolving from Purim and scripture presentations.

1835 – We celebrated the birth of Mark Twain.

1868 – The births of musicians Scott Joplin, and Buddy Bolden heralds of the birth of Jazz.

1879 - November 4 was the Birth of Will Rogers.

1897 - Konstantine Stanislavski co-founded the Moscow Art Theatre beginning the revolution of acting, and including elements of Improvisation.

1897 - Tom Turpin's "Harlem Rag" was the first published piano Rag.

1899 - Scott Joplin sold 100,000 copies of "The Maple Leaf Rag".

1890 - 1917 - Jazz was born with Buddy Bolden. A majority of the original Jazz greats were born as the art of improvised music developed from African American rhythms and spirituals, minstrel music, European folk melodies, Dixieland, marching band instruments, and music, symphonic music, rag   time, and the blues.

1902 - Isadora Duncan opened the door to revolution in dance.

1908 - Chicago Parks Commission hired Neva Boyd to use Improvisation, and games to teach language skills, social skills, self-confidence, and problem solving at Hull House in Chicago.

1909 - Neva L. Boyd founded the Chicago School for Playground Workers.

1914 - Dagney Pederson, and Neva L. Boyd publish *Folk Games and Gymnastic Play: for Kindergarten, Primary, and Playground.*

1915 - Dagney Pederson, and Neva L. Boyd published *Folk Games of Denmark and Sweden: for School, Playground, and Social Center.*

1915 - Charlie Chaplin created "The Little Tramp" for world cinema.

1917 - February 26 -The history of recorded Jazz began with "Livery Stable Blues" by "The Original Jass (later Jazz) Band." An all-white group led by James "Nick" LaRocca, selling 250,000 copies. Most records sold to date.

1920 – Five Marx Brothers improvised their way into the laughter and hearts of the world.

1924 – Winifred Ward founded The Children's Theatre of Evanston, IL.

1925 – Jacob Moreno brought *Stegreiftheater*, the Theater of Spontaneity, to the New York stage.

1925 - Martha Graham freed formal dance for Improvisation.

1927-1941 - Neva Leona Boyd was on the faculty of Northwestern University.

1929 - Pierre Louis Duchartre published *The Italian Comedy: The Improvisation Scenarios Lives Attributes Portraits and Masks of the Illustrious Characters of the Comedia dell' Arte.*

1931-1959 - Robert M. Hutchins created the "Chicago College Plan" at the University of Chicago and opened the doors to the greatest explosion of creativity since the Renaissance.

1935 - Beginning of the Federal Theatre Project – See *Furious Improvisation: How the WPA and a Cast of Thousands Made High Art out of Desperate Times.* 2008.

1935 - Sanford Meisner joins the faculty of The Neighborhood Playhouse.

1936 - William H. Bridge publishes *Actor in the Making: A Handbook on Improvisation and Other Techniques of Development.*

1937 - Robert Newton publishes *Acting Improvised.*

1939 - 1941 -Viola Spolin was employed by the Recreation Project of the Works Project Administration in Chicago, IL.

1940's - Neva Boyd's work was introduced to every military hospital in the U.S.

1945 - Neva L. Boyd published *Handbook of Recreational Games*.

1945 - The works of Berthold Brecht influenced future founders of "The Compass."

1945 - Joan Littlewood founded The Theatre Workshop Company in East London. At one point she was arrested for doing public Improvisation.

1946 - Viola Spolin founded "The Young Actor's Company" in Los Angeles. Alan Arkin was among the players.

1946 - August 29 - Robert Lowe begins his exploration of the universe.

1946 - 1960's - Improvisation and spontaneity developed on a foundation of early 20th century Existentialism, Jungian psychology, Dada art, relativity and quantum physics, the chaos of WWII, and the arrival of Buddhism, Taoism, and Hinduism in the west. These and other elements continued to develop new cultures in America with Critical writing (William Carlos Williams, Charles Olson); Spontaneous painting (Joan Miro, Jackson Pollock); Spontaneous writing (Jack Kerouac, Neal Cassady); Modern Dance (Martha Graham, Merce Cunningham); Creative Ceramics (Bernard Leach, Shoji Hamada, Soetsu Yanagi); Beat and Improvised poetry (Alan Ginsberg, Lawrence Ferlinghetti); Bebop Jazz (LeRoi Jones, Charlie Parker); computer scientific and medical technologies and the advent of Improvisational Comedy Theatre in Chicago.

1948 - Paul Sills, the son of Viola Spolin, arrived at the University of Chicago.

1950-1953 - "Tonight at 8:30" gathered the first, second half of the 20th Century Improvisers, including Paul Sills, David Shepherd, Mike Nichols, Elaine May, Sheldon Patinkin, Eugene Troobnick, Zora Lampert, and others see *The Compass* below.

1953 - June 23 - David Shepherd founded "The Playwrights Theatre Club" with Paul Sills, Mike Nichols, Elaine May, Sheldon Patinkin, Tony Lampert, Tony Holland, Ed Asner, and later Barbara Harris, Bernard Sahlins, Omar Shapli, and others. –See *The Compass*.

1954 - Viola Spolin taught and directed at "The Playwrights Theatre Club".

1955 - July 5 – The first Improvisation Performance of "The Compass" in Chicago.

1955 - Jim Hanson's Muppets premier on television.

1956 - Albert Grossman opened "The Gate of Horn" in Chicago, featuring Bob Dylan, Peter, Paul & Mary, Odetta, Bob Gibson, and other folk legends. Paul Sills was an early manager.

1956-1966 - Keith Johnstone, at England's "Royal Court Theatre", became Associate Director, exploring spontaneity in acting.

1959 - December 16 - Paul Sills, Howard Alk, and Bernie Sahlins opened The Second City in Chicago.

1960 - May 3 - "The Fantastiks" brought "The Comedia" to offstage New York, for a run of 42 years.

1963 - The last "Compass" in New York performed at "The Upstairs at the Downstairs".

1963 - Viola Spolin published *Improvisation for the Theater.*

1963 - April 10 – "The Committee" formed in San Francisco – It included Gary Austin – Founder of "The Groundlings." (With David Ogden Stiers, Rob Reiner, Del Close, Roger Bowan, and more.)

1972 - Howard Jerome, and David Shepherd co-founded the Improv Olympics, premiering at the "Space for Innovative Development" in New York City.

1972 - Contact Improvisational dance was inspired by Steve Paxton at Oberlin College, Ohio.

1973 - Second City Toronto Opened,

1974 - "The Groundlings" was founded by Gary Austin; named for poor Shakespearian audience members who stood on the ground – (Loraine Newman, Peewee Herman, Will Farrell, Maya Rudlph, and others).

1976 - SCTV began filming to debut in the U.S. in 1977.

1977 - Willie Wiley and David Shepherd co-created the Canadian Improv Games.

1977 - Theatre Sports and "Loose Moose Theatre" were pioneered by Keith Johnstone.

1978 - Jeffrey Sweet publishes *Something Wonderful Right Away: An Oral History of The Second City & the Compass Players.*

1979 - Keith Johnstone publishes *Impro: Improvisation and the Theatre.*

1979 - The Groundlings School of Improvisation opened with 17 students.

1970s - Improvisational dance was founded in San Diego with "Dance Jam" and the Movement Choir" directed by Judith Greer Essex, a movement therapist originally trained in Improvisational dance by Merce Cunningham.

1980 - "The Interval Foundation", exploring Improvisational, microtonal music was formed by Jonathan Glazier, a student and friend of Ivor Darreg, and Harry Partch.

1981 - David Shepherd developed Improv Olympic with "The Player's Workshop".

1981 - Charna Halpern and Del Close founded "iO Chicago", Formerly Improv Olympic, (Mike Myers, Chris Farley, Tina Fey and more) and development of the "Harold", and long form Improvisation.

1981 - International Blend, Robert Lowe's 1st Improv Troupe, is directed by Don Victor.

1982 - Improv Boston was founded by Ellen Holbrook – Prompted by "The Proposition"

1983 – "Unexpected Productions" became the first Theatre Sports Company; Seattle, Washington.

1983 - Jackie Lowell conducted Creativity Workshop in San Diego.

1984 - January – Robert Lowe's first Improv Workshop in Atlanta, GA, with   Andrew Einspruch, Alison Mawle and two others.

1984 - September 20 – First open Atlanta Improv workshop at the Nexus theatre, now in another location, as The Atlanta Contemporary Arts Center.

1984 - December 13 – First Atlanta public Improv show, "Just for Laffs", appeared as "The Open City Players".

1984 - Cirque du Soleil updates the Circus with ancient methods.

1985 - Augusto Boal published *Theatre of the Oppressed*, using Improvisation as   guerilla theatre.

1985 - March – "The Lightside City Players"; ("Open City Players" for one show), and Atlanta's first Improv Comedy Troupe included: O'Clare Alexander, Rich Bailey, Andrew Einspruch, Marc Farley, Tommy Futch, Keith Hooker, Alison Dukes Gilmore, Joel Gilmore, Stuart Hill, Eileen Kimble, Shari Kottcamp, Robert Lowe, Maggie McClaney, John O'Hagan Ward, Emelio Perey, and Phil Tardiff.

1985 - October - "A New Attitude" video is produced by AT&T – It may have been the first documented use of Applied Improvisation at a major industrial level in the U.S.

1985 - December - "Laughing Matters" broke off from "The Lightside City Players", and is now the longest running Improv Troupe in the South eastern U.S.

1985 – Comedy Store Players began in London.

1987 - Rebecca Stockley conducted the first Theatre Sports workshop in San Francisco for "Fretelli Bologna", which became "BATS".

1987 - Donna McCrohan published *The Second City: A Backstage History of Comedy's Hottest Troupe.*

1987 – The Annoyance Theatre (Originally Metra Form) Opened in Brooklyn, NY.

1988 - January 6 – "The Next City Comedy Theatre" opened as the first Improvisational Comedy theatre in the Southeastern U.S.

1989 - "The Let's Try This Players", now "LTT! Improv Comedy program at the Georgia Institute of Technology, was founded to become the longest playing college or university team in the Southeastern U.S.

1989 - Second City opened in Los Angeles.

1989-Lynda Belt & Rebecca Stockley publish *Improvisation through Theatre Sports.*

1989 - November 22 - "Transformation by Laughter" was presented in London by Robert Lowe.

1990 - Janet Coleman published *The Compass: The Story of the Improvisational Theatre that revolutionized the Art of Comedy in America.*

1990 - Stephen Nachmanovitch published *Free Play: Improvisation in Life and Art.*

1990s – Atlanta Improvisers begin to show up on IMDB (Internet Movie Database) with Nick Jameson, Gary Anthony Williams, and Mitch Rouse.

1991 - Patricia Ryan Madson founded "Simps", the Stanford Improvisers in Palo Alto, California.

1991 - October 25 – Robert Lowe opened Improvisation, Inc., presenting "Team Building with Improvisation" at Georgia State University, with 26 attendees from 22 companies.

1993 - Second City Detroit is opened.

1994 - Del Close, Charna Halpern, and Kim "Howard" Johnson published *Truth in Comedy: The Manual of Improvisation.*

1994 - Daniel Wiener published *Rehearsals for Growth: Theater Improvisation for Psychotherapists.*

1997 - "iO West" Opened in Los Angeles.

1998 - Daniel Belgrad published a massive history, *The Culture of Spontaneity: Improvisation and the Arts in Postwar America.*

1998 - Paul Z. Jackson published *Impro Learning: How to Make Your Training Creative, Flexible, and Spontaneous.*

1998 - BATS in San Francisco began "Laughing Stock", free Improvisation classes in support of people with chronic, and life threatening diseases.

1999 - February 4 - Upright Citizen's Brigade (UCB) opens in NYC with Matt Beser, Amy Pohler, Ian Roberts, Matt Walsh.

2000 - Robert Lowe published *Improvisation, Inc.: Harnessing Spontaneity to En gage People and Groups.*

2000 - *The Second City: Backstage at the World's Greatest Comedy Theater* was published by Improvisers Sheldon Patinkin, Robert Klein, Alan Arkin, Dan Aykroyd, George Wendt, James Belushi, and Harold Ramis.

2000- Robert Lowe taught and produced an Improv Comedy show with Arbor Montessori Middle School 8th and 9th grade students. Brian McElhaney later to become a writer for "Saturday Night Live".

2001 - Ken Burns Directed the documentary, "Jazz".

2001 - Kat Koppett published her first book, *Training to Imagine: Practical Improvisational Theatre Techniques to Enhance Creativity, Teamwork, Leader ship, and Learning.*

2001 - February 1 - Interview with Robert Lowe, 'Improvisation in the Workplace' was published by "Harvard Management Communication Letter".

2002 - Paul Z. Jackson, Michael Rosenburg, and Alain Rostain Founded the Applied Improvisation Network, AIN. There as of 2017 there were 5,800 Facebook group members.

2002 – Silly People Improv Theatre (SPIT) with Gabe Mercado in Manilla.

2005 - July 1 – UCB opened in Hollywood, CA.

2005 - Patricia Ryan Madson published *Improv Wisdom: Don't Prepare, Just Show Up.*

2006 - Charna Halpern Published *Art by Committee: A Guide to Advanced Improvisation.*

2006 – Chicago Improv Productions produced the first College Improv Tournament with regional and national competition.

2007 - Adam Blatner and Daniel J. Wiener, edited and published *Interactive and Improvisational Drama: Varieties of Applied Theatre and Performance.*

2009 - Sandy Bruce founded "Autism Improvised" (Originally Shenanigans), in Atlanta, GA; Applied arts and theatre for Autism".

2010 - Lisa Safran published *Using Improvisation to Build Literacy.*

2010 – The feature length documentary, "David Shepherd: A Lifetime of Improvisational Theatre", with Andrew Duncan, Mark Gordon, Charna Halpern, Howard Jerome, Bernie Sahlins, and Suzanne Shepherd, was produced by Mike Fleischaker, Michael Golding. Executive Producer – James "Willie" Wyllie. https://www.youtube.com/watch?v=t5wgtkgCH3A

2013 - Farnaz Tabayee received her DEd with the thesis, "Effects of Improvisation Techniques in Leadership Development".

2013 - The Use of Applied Improvisation for disaster relief and prepared ness was developed in the Philippines, spearheaded by members of SPIT, the Manilla based Improv Team, and Gabe Mercado.

2015 – Belina Raffy completes a world tour "Using Improvisation to Save the World – and Me".

2016 - J-Star assists in the founding of "8848 Improv Nepal" in Kathmandu, Nepal - The height of Mount Everest in meters.

2016 - Charna Halpern was featured in "The New York Times".

2016 - UCB founders were interviewed on PBS by Charlie Rose.

2016 - "Don't Think Twice", became a nationally distributed independent film by Mike Birbiglia, making famous a confabulated Improv Troupe in New York City.

2016- Saturday Night Live hired comedy team BriTANicK (Atlanta's Brian McElhaney and Nick Kocher) for 42nd season writing team.

2016 – The Improvisational Wonder continued to explode around the world.

2016 – Oglethorpe University, Atlanta, GA, formed a new Improv Team, mOUthing Off.

2017 – Georgia Tech's Improvisational Comedy Team, *LTT!* won the College Improv Tournament Southeastern regional competition to compete in the 10th national competition in Chicago, with Lucas Isbill,

Miranda Frye, James Nugent, Caleigh Derreberry, and Thompson Berton.

The Future – Children born into, and raised by Improvisational families ushers in the "Collaborative Age of Humanity", which may not bring Utopia, yet it sure will be fun.

Good Words from 2000 and 2017

Dr. Ginny Whitelaw

The creativity and playfulness of improvisation opens up vast possibilities for business, and Robert Lowe shows the way second to none.

Author of *BodyLearning: How the Mind Learns from the Body: A Practical Approach.* (2000 Edition)

A big "yes, and" to Robert Lowe's revised edition, showing us how we can bring the creativity, playfulness and presence of improv into working at our best and bringing the best out of others.

Founder, Institute for Zen Leadership,
Author of, *The Zen Leader* (2017)

Emory Mulling

Not only very enjoyable to read, but a necessary training tool. Lowe's 'Improvisational' method of thinking is how the new generation of business people will deal with one another. This book is worth reading.

The Mulling Group. (2000 Edition)

On the cover of the first edition, seventeen years ago, I said, 'Lowe's Improvisational method of thinking is how the new generation of business people will deal with one another.' The Revised Edition, *An Applied Improvisation Handbook*, is for this generation of business and community leaders who are doing just that today, all over the globe.

Chairman, Mulling Corporation (2017)

Dave Arch

I admire the skills of someone good at improvisational theatre. Now, thanks to Robert Lowe and this new book, I can go behind the scenes and learn how to further develop those desirable skills of quick thinking and spontaneity in myself as well as those I train. Thank you Robert.

Dave Arch, author, senior training consultant, Creative Training Techniques International (2000 Edition)

Being able to 'think on one's feet' has consistently proven itself a valuable skill. Robert Lowe is the undisputed guru in bringing the disciplines of Improv to the strengthening of an individual's ability to think and react in the moment.

Internal Sales and Management Consultant, Tenaska, Inc. (2017)

From Friends of Improvisation

Improvisation is not only an art form, it is a survival skill. Because things like work and family and community are unscripted. And those of us who are most skillful at responding to the exigencies of any of the spheres of social existence are those who are skilled in improvising, adapting, thinking flexibly. Theatre is a great training ground for this art, and so are things like jazz, and dance, and raising children.

Bernard Louis De Koven
Author of, *A Playful Path*

Improvisation is a tool to open one up to the world, and its multiple possibilities. As a student of the Georgia Institute of Technology Improv Comedy Troupe, I have learned invaluable skills that have helped me with acceptance, and spontaneity in an engineering workplace.

Neeta Thawani
Former Leader of *Let's Try This!*
Georgia Institute of Technology Alumna, 2017

Improvisation, is not a way to give one an edge in the business world by improving one's ability to innovate. And it's not an easy path to creation, or the lazy man's approach to composition. While it is true that improvisation can be those things, and for many people this is enough, I would argue that we should hold out for improvisation's greater possibility(s). We should adopt Jacques Derrida's pronouncement (1982) that improvisation is an impossibility. His reasoning isn't meant to sound defeatist. Instead, Derrida is opposed to the possibility of improvisation because by accepting it as part of the possible, one *limits* its achievements; one reduces improvisation to just another tool to use in the pursuit of a pre-determined goal, one reduces improvisation to just another tool to use in the pursuit of a pre-determined goal. When this happens any chance at a dialogical encounter suggested by William Pinar (1994) is removed, and the rupture of something new being created, whether it be the justice Derrida sought in the law, or the democracy to come; a new form of art, like cubism, a new scientific theory, like relativity, or a new way of shaking up the academic canon will be lost.

Dr. Barry Krakovsky
Teacher

Learning about improvisation from Robert Lowe has been an invaluable source of inspiration for my teaching about conflict resolution in law school, where I teach negotiation and mediation. The skills of a good negotiator or mediator are remarkably similar to those of a good Improv performer: listening well, being present, making the other person look good, making good offers, accepting new ideas, being open-minded, and above all, saying "Yes, and . . ."

The hilarious fun and laughter (in a law school class, no less!) that my students have during our Improv games help to deepen their understanding about many core lessons for resolving conflict and helping clients solve hard problems. Thank you, Robert, for all the amazing and wonderful doors that you have opened for me and my students!

Charity Scott, JD, MSCM
Catherine C. Henson Professor of Law
Georgia State University College of Law

Improvisation is woven throughout my work as a trial attorney. People will always surprise you. If listening skills aren't developed then the surprises become obstacles instead of gifts. My love and respect for Improv grounds me as a professional and inspires me as a person.

Elizabeth Grofic, Esq.

As a young person, working my first job in the world of corporate America, around the mid-seventies it was very different than it is today. Having conversations with many professionals required constantly adjusting my thinking. I had to create outcomes to fit the moment very quickly and often.

When I was introduced to Improvisation in the mid-nineties, it was very new to me. It opened other aspects of opportunities to share my learned skills as a professional salesman, which made things "click" much easier and more quickly. Now, in reflection, that was the time my life changed! I began to feel like my blood was flowing as never before. Thank you, Improvisation for opening new way of dealing with all aspects of human endeavor!

Gaston Armour
Known as "The Gusto"

The essence of applied improvisation is integrating the improvisational 'way of being' with an improvisational 'way of doing' in public view. As Robert Lowe so eloquently says, it is, "Being together and moving together into the truly new." I have used applied improvisation for over twenty years- to help people in healthcare organizations improve their ability to work as a team and provide safe care; in the legal community to help mediators better respond to those in conflict; and in the high tech industry to foster innovation and openness to the truly new. I am consistently surprised and delighted when I see Robert's insightful words come to life as groups consistently become more present, and more honest with themselves and one another. Robert's book is a gift to all of us who aspire to bring the magic of improvisation into the workplace to create connection and inspire the best in every human.

Debra Gerardi
RN, MPH, JD- Chief Creative Officer, EHCCO, LLC

Acknowledgments

My first acknowledgement is to all the Improvisers throughout time who have loved the creative spirit. There is little in this book that I have invented and much that has been given to me by the great predecessors noted in the time line. There has also been a great deal that has come from the thousands who have played with me, some of whom I have named below.

Some of what you have read here you will read in work that has come after me, very little of which has come directly from my writing. If others have presented it as their own, some of it may have arrived by word of mouth, yet it will most likely have come from their own discoveries because Improvisation is a force of nature, much like the wind and waves, that carry life with them wherever they go.

Regarding the people who must be thanked, I must start with the notion that contradiction is a funny thing. They say that talk is cheap, yet the best advertising is word of mouth. If you ever sit down to write a book you may discover that you are there, all alone. There is no one to cheer you on or hold your hand into the long nights, and deep parts of your soul. Writing really is a lonely thing.

However, if you sit down to thank the people who made it possible for you to write a book, you will find yourself surrounded by too many to name, and by a sea of love and encouragement. Here are most of the names of the people without whom I could not say, "Here is my book!"

First is my son, Jonathan Michael Mawle Lowe. Next are my mother, *Emily Lowe*,[37] who taught me love and toughness, and my father, *Robert Lowe*, who taught me the most about love and focus. He also taught me to write, and more importantly, how to work with an editor. My grandfather, *A. C. Warner*, carried the genes of delight and playfulness, and passed them on to us all. My grandmother *Louvisa Warner* gave me keys to the doors of the spirit.

The people who gave me guidance when I was young include Vernon S. Cox who showed me how to live with love, light, and strength in the real world[38] my aunt Francis Warner, who has shared my love of life and laughter forever; my aunt, *Edith Warner*, who had faith in me from the beginning, my cousin Anne Kuoppamaki, who laughed with me through tempest, storm, and gale, and the brothers of Beta Omega Sigma, who continue to give me a continuity. *T. J. Mullins* and *Joe Stanovich* gave me direction. A thousand others just gave of themselves.

Where would I be without the work of *Viola Spolin*, God rest her creative soul, and the wonderful improvisational life and explorations of Keith Johnstone? On the path of Improvisation, I owe a great deal to Judith Greer Essex, who taught me Improvisational dance, and *Jon Glasier*, and Jonathan Glasier, who opened the doors to microtonal Improvisational music. Deep blessings to my first Improvisation teacher, Don Victor, and to my first creativity teacher, Jacquie Lowell. In my own improvisational explorations, I would never have made it without the love and help of Alan Freedman, Andrew Einspruch, Billie Dean, Chris Kauffman, Alison Clare Mawle, Jerry Farber, *Gene Dale*, and the late, great *Jim Sligh*.

I learned an immense amount about Improvisation from all who played with "The Lightside City Players" with special thanks to Jay Russell, Bruce York, Leslie Truman, Mike Scarbro, Tommy Futch, Emilio Perey, Keith

---

[37] The names of dear ones who have graduated from this plane of existence are in italics.
[38] *Happy Vernday Birthcox: Revolution, Evolution, and an Uncommon Commune – 1970*, Atlanta, GA: USA, RLJ Publications, 2015.

Hooker, Joel Gilmore, Allison Dukes Gilmore, Marc Farley, O'Clair Alexander, Stephanie Astalos Jones, Eileen Kimball, Irv Wardlow, Donna Holland Veach, Phil Tardif, Rich Bailey, Leila L'Abate, Bill Troschek, Judith Young, Pac McKibben, Tommy Chappelle, Carol Haynes, Anna Collins, and John O'Hagan Ward.

There are additional thanks to many who came later to my Improvisation, including Deb Calabria, Gil Puffer, Bruce Hansen, Ian Cook, Nick Jameson, Mitch Rouse, Clark Taylor, Georgia Dial Davidson, *Vince Tortorici*, Janet Wells, and Susan Andrews. *Charles McGivern*, and *Chris Passante* both left us too soon yet deep thanks are offered to them as well. Then there are the hundreds of Improvisation players from venues that included The Next City Comedy Theatre to The Let's Try This Players of Georgia Tech, and the thousands of business and community participants who have played with me over the years.

Special thanks for special reasons are due to Jeff Justice, Frank Hamilton, (who studied as a child with Viola Spolin among "The Young Actors"), *Mary Hamilton, Sacha Dzuba, John Vitek*, John Bolton, Dick Leitgeb, Mark Weiss, *Clabe Hangan, Bagavhan Sri Sathya Sai Baba*, Baba Gi, *Rob Bigalki*, Pauline Temple, *Mary King*, Sondra Ray, Ken and Jane Stanbridge, *Rodney Grantham*, Janet Grantham, *Greg Abbott*, Scott Hawkins, Don Mitchell, Diirga Brough, Jean Houston, Edward Haig, Sr. Miriam McGillis, Terry O'Keefe, Dr. Carol Winkler, Emory Mulling, and Dr. Ed Metcalf.

The Applied Improvisation Network was founded in the U.K. shortly after the original publication of *Improvisation, Inc.* Much of the revision of this book is due to meeting the people in this wonderful organization. Many are listed in the bibliography with their own published work in the field. A partial list must include Paul Z. Jackson, Belina Raffy, Matt Weinstein, Zohar Adner, Caitlin McClure, Rich Cox, Diane Rachel, Alan Montegue, Gary Schwartz, Patrick Short, Patricia Ryan Madson, Ted DeMaisons, Kay Ross, Teresa Norton, Deb Girardi, Charity Scott, Gabe Mercado, Amy Angelli, Gema Bulos, Mike Bonifer, Rebecca Stockley, Hal Peller, Pablo Suarez, Eric Nepom, Simo Routarine, Marvin Stottlemeire, Adam Blatner, Sue Walden, Diego Caro, Farnaz Tabaee, Christian Lang, Eric Farone, Burgert Kirsten, Jessie Sternshus, Denise Jacobs, Bernie De Koven, Helene Brown, Amelia Isabel, Asaf Ronen, Henk van der Steen, Alieke van der Wijk, Raymond van Driel, David Razowsky, Theresa Dudeck, and Genie Joseph, Apologies to those whose names don't come to me just now. Everyone I have met in AIN has had an influence.

Grand bridges between Improv Comedy and Applied Improvisation have been advanced by Kat Koppett with The Mopco Improv Theatre in Schenectady, NY, and Amy Angelli's growing Improv Community in St. Augustine, Florida.

During the revision of *Improvisation, Inc.* there have been a large number of Atlanta Improvisers and organizations who have influenced my life and my work, beginning with Matthew Mammola, Valerie Jane Thoma, and Lex Lewis – documentary crew for "Laughter is a Global Event", The Atlanta Improv Documentary - work in progress.

In Atlanta, Improvisational Theatres have included: The Basement Theatre – J Star, Whole World Theatre Company – Chip Powell, The Village Theatre – Blair Holden, Dad's Garage Theatre Company – Kevin Gillese, Highwire Comedy Company – Ian Clavelle, and Relapse Theatre – Bob Wood. Applied Improvisation organizations include: Dumoreimprov – Allison Dukes Gilmore, The Brink Improv – Kristy West, and Brent Darnell International – Brent Darnell.

Among the many Atlanta area Improv Troupes there are: Laughing Matters, BANSHEE, Automatic Improv, OTC Comedy Troupe, Perfect Strangers, Chalk Outline, Rufio, and Botox or Bangs, Salon du Shoguns, Shark Party, Witless Protection, Babies Mit Bearden, and Diversionary Tactics.

The development of Improvisation in Atlanta area Colleges and Universities has been magnificent, beginning with *LTT!* at Georgia Tech, and growing to include *Rathskeller* at Emory University, *KISS* at Kennesaw State University, and *mOUthing Off* at Oglethorpe University, and harkening to place-names of the ancient beginnings of Improvisation with Improv at Barry College in Rome, GA, and *Improv Athens* at The University of Georgia in Athens, GA.

A special thanks goes to René Dellefont, of Dad's Garage Theatre, for his creation, and long running production of the "Dottie", show which has had a powerful crossover effect using single a person sketch form that has influenced creativity at its foundation in Atlanta.

For *Aikido*, which is so much a part of my Improvisation, I must give personal thanks to my teachers in the order they came to me: Steven Samuels, *Fumio Toyoda*, Dick Kedlubowski, Kazuo Chiba, *Rodney Grantham*, Yoshimitsu Yamada, George Kennedy, Daryl Tangman, and Ginny Whitelaw. There are another thirty or more *Aikido* teachers who have helped me along the way and another thousand or so *Aikidoka* with whom I have shared time on the mat.

The original book would not have been started without conversations between the wonderful teachers and magicians Max Howard, and Dave Arch; this followed by action on the part of Bob Pike of Creative Training Technologies, Inc.

With apologies to any I have overlooked, and to the others, too numerous to name, who have helped and encouraged us all in our work. I offer special thanks to all who are playing, teaching, exploring, and leading the way toward creativity, spontaneity, purposeful collaboration, and love, light, laughter, and joy in our world.

271

About the Author

Robert Lowe is a retired Improvisation elder. He was the founder, and chief executive of Improvisation Incorporated, a pioneering educational consulting firm specializing in the use of Improvisation Theater techniques for organizational development, and for business, professional, and interpersonal communication. His work included such early clients as AT&T, Georgia Pacific Corporation, The Southern Company, Medtronics, Inc., the Government Services Administration, Metro Atlanta Rapid Transit Authority, the Southeastern Regional Association of Girl Scout Executives, Centers for Disease Control and Prevention, Georgia Baptist Medical Center, the Fulton County Staff Development Council, and the Center for Puppetry Arts, among many others.

In his thirty-seven-year exploration of Improvisation, Lowe has been a dancer, a player, a teacher, a director, and a mentor in the uses of Improvisation for purposes beyond performance.

In Atlanta, Georgia he is known as "The Godfather" of Improvisation, having founded and directed the first Improv Comedy Theatre Troupe in Georgia – "The Lightside City Players", and The Next City Comedy Theatre, the first Improvisational Comedy Theatre in the Southeastern U.S. Robert was a co-founding mentor and teacher of The Let's Try This Players (Now LTT!) the resident Improvisation Troupe at Georgia Institute of Technology in 1989.

He has taught Improvisation and stand-up comedy, public speaking and presentation, and community and personal advocacy in a variety of venues.

Robert's Improvisation Comedy Workshop™ with graduation performances placed hundreds of "just plain folks" on Improvisation stages facing live audiences. His work in Improvisation is known in many countries.

Robert Lowe has been a management consultant, a public speaker, an adjunct university professor, a corporate vice president, a national sales representative, a program analyst, a project director, a welfare supervisor in the San Quentin district of Northern California, a customer service manager in South Central Los Angeles, a U.S. Navy officer, a legal services paralegal and community educator, and a legal secretary. He has been a Boy Scout executive, a corporate collector, a carpenter, an electrician, a political activist, a community activist, an advocate for handicapped accessibility, an actor, a dancer, a meditator, a poet, an historian, and a philosopher. He is also an Eagle Scout, which pleased his mother and father to no end.

Robert was a teacher with the Department of Communication at Georgia State University for twelve years, specializing in "Human "Communication", "Public Speaking", "Business and Professional Communication", Voice and Articulation", "Acting I", and "Special Studies in Improvisation" during which time he received the honor of being named an Outstanding Part-Time Instructor.

Lowe holds the rank of *Nidan* (second degree black belt), and the status of *Fuku Shidoin* (teacher) in *Aikido*, with over twenty-two years on the mat, including more than seven years specializing in teaching children. His articles have been published in "Aikido Today Magazine" and "The Journal of Asian Martial Arts".

He is the father of a fine boy who is now 28, and the delight of his father's life. Robert spends some time each day playing some music, writing, reading voraciously, delighting in the beauty and abundance of this life, and in grateful thanks to God for all that is.

More than anything else, Robert Lowe is a man who one day nearly 40 years ago found the power of focus on the current instant, and has been unwilling, and unable to let go of its pursuit for even a moment since. When he talks about Improvisation, and about creativity, and about the human spirit, and about the power of spontaneity, and the salvation of human collaboration, his eyes light up, the air crackles, and his feet only barely touch the ground.

He truly sees the explosive development of Improvisational Thinking as the next, and most vital, step in the evolution of human culture.

Robert grew up in a neighborhood which had one of the highest juvenile crime rates in America between 1950 and 1970. There were youth gangs in the schools before it was the fashion, and motorcycle gangs on the streets where he learned to walk in awareness and hope. He worked in poverty communities in South Central Los Angeles during the "first" Watts Riots. Through an era of revolution and evolution, he has seen the world come abruptly against itself only to find the desperate need of some real personal, internal, and creative human work in human cooperation.

Robert spent 10 years in an extraordinary community of communes, social services, and politics during the time of radical change between 1970 and 1980, just before discovering Improvisational Dance in San Diego, California. His second book, *Happy Vernday Birthcox: Revolution, Evolution, and an Uncommon Commune – 1970*, a true story, was published in 2015 and tells of the extraordinary people and times that prepared him for a life engaged in Improvisation.

www.ingramcontent.com/pod-product-compliance
Lightning Source LLC
Chambersburg PA
CBHW061630220326
41598CB00026BA/3942